STUDYING IMPLEMENTATION

CHATHAM HOUSE SERIES ON CHANGE IN AMERICAN POLITICS

edited by Aaron Wildavsky, *University of California, Berkeley*

STUDYING IMPLEMENTATION

Methodological and Administrative Issues

WALTER WILLIAMS

AND

RICHARD F. ELMORE

JOHN STUART HALL

RICHARD JUNG

MICHAEL KIRST

SUSAN A. MacMANUS

BETTY JANE NARVER

RICHARD P. NATHAN

ROBERT K. YIN

CHATHAM HOUSE PUBLISHERS, INC.
Chatham, New Jersey

STUDYING IMPLEMENTATION
Methodological and Administrative Issues

CHATHAM HOUSE PUBLISHERS, INC.
Post Office Box One
Chatham, New Jersey 07928

PUBLISHER: Edward Artinian
COVER DESIGN: Robert Sabol
COMPOSITION: Chatham Composer
PRINTING AND BINDING: Hamilton Printing Company

LIBRARY OF CONGRESS CATALOGING IN PUBLICATION DATA

Main entry under title:
Studying implementation.

      (Chatham House series on change in American
politics)
      Includes bibliographical references and index.
      1. Policy sciences--Addresses, essays, lectures.
2. Evaluation research (Social action programs)--
Addresses, essays, lectures. I. Williams, Walter.
II. Series.
H97.S85   350'.007   81-21734
ISBN 0-934540-12-8   AACR2

MANUFACTURED IN THE UNITED STATES OF AMERICA

10 9 8 7 6 5 4 3 2 1

Contents

About the Authors

WALTER WILLIAMS is the director, Institute for Public Policy and Management and professor of public affairs, Graduate School of Public Affairs, University of Washington.

RICHARD F. ELMORE is the associate director, Institute for Public Policy and Management and associate professor of public affairs, Graduate School of Public Affairs, University of Washington.

ROBERT K. YIN is president of The Case Study Institute in Washington, D.C. and a visiting associate professor in the Department of Urban Studies and Planning, Massachusetts Institute of Technology.

RICHARD P. NATHAN is professor of public and international affairs at the Woodrow Wilson School of Public and International Affairs at Princeton University, director of the Urban and Regional Research Center, and a member of the associated staff of the Brookings Institution.

JOHN STUART HALL is director, Center for Urban Studies and associate professor of public affairs at Arizona State University.

SUSAN A. MACMANUS is an associate professor of political science at the University of Houston.

RICHARD JUNG is a senior research analyst for Advanced Technology, Inc. and at the time this chapter was written he was a doctoral student in the Educational Administration and Policy Analysis Program at Stanford University.

MICHAEL KIRST is a professor of education and business administration at Stanford University.

BETTY JANE NARVER is a research consultant in the Institute for Public Policy and Management at the University of Washington.

Preface

In 1971, based on my years at the Office of Economic Opportunity, where I had had a ringside seat at the War on Poverty (at least as viewed from Washington, D.C.), I argued that "implementation was the Achilles heel of the Johnson Administration's social policy." Since my Great Society days, I have moved my observation point three thousand miles to the other Washington and followed the New Federalism and Carter administration programs from the vantage point of the field. Implementation still is the bane of federally funded social service programs, and, I suspect, of almost all federal grants-in-aid programs, although I have not studied domestic policy outside the social areas. Nor have I seen any signs that programs supported solely by subnational government funds escape the curse of implementation. So, figuring out how to do implementation better is a critical policy need across all levels of government.

A key question is what the systematic analysis of implementation can contribute. For roughly a decade now, the rapidly expanding cottage industry studying implementation has been producing numerous investigations of efforts to put new policies in place. A growing bookshelf of studies reports on the implementation experience in most of the major social programs started in the last decade or so. Some of these studies yield rich information about the implementation process and support a number of useful insights.

I am convinced, however, that the really important work on implementation remains to be done. A basic issue is the degree to which studies individually or collectively can support the development of policies that are more sensitive both to implementation problems *and* to improvements in the management of field implementation efforts. Whether implementation studies fade away as just another fad, or worse yet, become an academic specialty divorced from policy reality, depends on how researchers proceed over the next several years.

As the interest in implementation has grown, a gap has developed in the implementation literature: There is a dearth of material on strategies for studying implementation; and what is available thus far is often difficult to obtain. Some implementation studies provide thoughtful discussions of methodology. A few authors have explicitly devoted articles to conceptual, methodological, and administrative issues in investigating implementation. But what is available is scattered and often so difficult to find that certainly newcomers to the study of implementation, and sometimes even veterans, have a difficult time drawing on past experience to guide them in the design and execution of implementation study strategies.

The book is a beginning effort at filling that gap. Its essays are based on papers presented at two panels on implementation. The Nathan and Elmore essays come from a September 1979 American Political Science Association panel; the others from a March 1980 Western Political Science Association panel devoted exclusively to the questions of studying implementation.

All of the papers presented at the panels have been extensively rewritten and my introductory essay was prepared especially for this volume. The following appeared elsewhere and we are grateful for permission to reprint them here: Richard F. Elmore, "Backward Mapping: Implementation Research and Policy Decisions," *Political Science Quarterly* 94, no. 4 (Winter 1979-80): 601-16; Robert K. Yin, "Studying the Implementation of Public Programs," Solar Energy Research Institute, SERI/TR-352-577, January 1980; Michael Kirst and Richard Jung, "The Utility of a Longitudinal Approach in Assessing Implementation: A Thirteen-Year View of Title I, ESEA," *Education Evaluation and Policy Analysis* 2, no. 5 (September 1980): 17-34, copyright 1980, American Educational Research Association, Washington, D.C.

I wish to thank Ms. Lucille Fuller of the Institute for Public Policy and Management for her help in preparing the index and checking the galleys and page proofs for the entire manuscript.

I see these essays as both a progress report on implementation research efforts to date and as an indicator of possible future directions in a research area that is likely to see much change over time. Clearly, we are not at a point where an author can specify tried-and-true approaches based on years of research experience and on extensive conceptual and methodological critiques of research strategies. At the same time, there seems to be no reason for people to reinvent the wheel or to use outmoded strategies because they lack a reasonable critique of current research options.

Walter Williams

1

The Study of Implementation: An Overview

WALTER WILLIAMS

A policy perspective dominates the essays in this volume. The primary criterion for the worth of implementation studies is policy relevance. At basic issue is the extent to which implementation studies can yield "pertinent, sound, timely" information to aid those who formulate and execute public policies.[1] Even if others see the potential of implementation studies in more traditional scholarly dimensions, I am convinced a real academic payoff will come only if researchers face up to the issue of policy relevance. If not, the study of implementation will be a kind of poor country cousin to the more established work on organizational theory and management. Only if implementation researchers are able to make their product more useful to policymakers are they likely to extend our notions about organization and management. And this could reshape important segments of the social sciences.

THE ESSAYS

The six essays in this volume stress overall conceptual design and field strategy issues far more than details of protocol development, field staffing and training, and interviewing techniques because so much material already is available on the details. For example, once a decision is made to use open-ended interviews rather than structured ones, there is a vast literature to guide those who would execute implementation studies.

Backward Mapping and Implementation Analysis
Policymakers are admonished to analyze implementation issues when consider-

ing new policies—in fact, they are made to feel guilty for not doing it. But as Elmore's paper underscores, little is available to guide them in such analyses. Elmore provides a conceptual pivot point for considering the implementation feasibility of proposed policy by comparing the notions of *forward mapping* and *backward mapping.*

"Forward mapping" is the traditional top-down view of the implementation process. The approach is based on the strong assumption of power at the top: The highest-level (in hierarchical terms) policymakers have a significant degree of control over the political, organizational, and technical factors that influence implementation. The "backward mapping" analytic strategy turns things upside down by centering on the point of service delivery. The orienting point of analysis is where the street-level bureaucrats meet the clients. Backward mapping works from there sequentially through the various organizational actors until the traditional top of the policy process is reached. It concentrates on both the resources available and those needed for taking a new policy direction from the perspective of those delivering and receiving services. Elmore argues that this implementation perspective provides a more powerful base than forward mapping for judging implementation feasibility. He explores how one might do an implementation analysis for social service delivery programs using the backward mapping notion through a discussion based on his recent work for the Carter administration Vice-President's Task Force on Youth Employment.

A Review of Exemplary Studies

Robert Yin uses eleven exemplary studies as a basis both for surveying current research strategies and for indicating preferred practices. From it we can see how implementation studies grew in number and complexity during the 1970s, moving from single-site studies to far more complex multiple-site designs.[2] Yin's essay is the most thorough critique to date of the tools, techniques, and administrative approaches practitioners are now using and of the field strategies that offer promise in the future.

Yin points out that exemplary studies used multiple sources of information including interviews, internal documents, news reports, other published reports, and extended observation including that by participant observers. Highly structured questionnaires and sample surveying may be part of exemplary studies and can complement other techniques. Nevertheless, Yin finds that unstructured interviews with respondents picked because of their status or their reputed knowledge, and not by random methods, represent the main vehicle for information in the exemplary studies to date. He argues that the open-ended approach is the preferred technique and observes pointedly, "structured interviews are notoriously inefficient devices in substituting for the strength of unstructured discussions — i.e., the acquisition of 'explanations' for an event or complex description of a situation."

The Field Network Evaluation Approach

The Nathan and Hall and MacManus papers are complementary. Both treat the same research approach from different perspectives — Nathan from the top of major projects involving a relatively large number of field researchers and Hall and MacManus as individual field researchers where "our view is from the bottom up." The major field network evaluation studies conducted by the Brookings Institution, the National Academy of Sciences, and Princeton University may be characterized as follows: (1) The focus is on large-scale federal programs such as the Comprehensive Employment and Training Act or the Community Development Block Grant program, which are nationwide in scope and cover hundreds of communities; (2) the studies have a central unit responsible for designing the implementation research project, choosing research sites and researchers (hereinafter referred to as *research associates*), coordinating the research efforts over time, and finally writing the research report; (3) a relatively large number of sites are chosen for the project (in the four projects from which these characteristics were drawn, the number of field sites ranged from 28 to 65); (4) the sites studied by the individual research associates generally are relatively large political jurisdictions such as cities and counties so that observation is of a broad institutional process; (5) research associates generally are experienced individuals (the typical one is a university faculty member) who are likely to have a considerable knowledge of the community setting including the political/bureaucratic process in which the project operates and who may see the project as an opportunity to pursue their own research interests;[3] (6) research associates, once in the field, have a goodly amount of freedom to develop information on the evolving implementation process; (7) the studies run several (at least three) years, often with the same research associates; and (8) the central unit prepares a report or reports drawing on the results from all sites that is intended to aid in developing future policy.[4]

Nathan's focus is the total research effort looking at issues involved in deriving information useful for national-level policymaking from the summations of individual projects. Hall and MacManus are looking up from the field concerned about the problems confronting the research associates as individuals operating in their own localities and as a group in their interaction with the central staff of the research organization. As to the latter, they consider such problems as the "we-they" splits between central staff and research associates and the competition among research associates. Also of crucial interest are the problems research associates have in exercising their discretion during the field studies when a central staff is trying to keep them from exerting too much independence and from not providing information that can be summed across the projects. Thus, the field network evaluation approach raises serious administrative issues both for the central staff, which must hold together a research team and keep it working within the framework of the overall design, and for the individual research associates, who may be trying to pursue their own research interests in the course of the larger study.

A Longitudinal Approach

Kirst and Jung argue that following a major program over a long period, where the effects of important social, economic, and programmatic changes have time to have worked themselves through, provides an important means of understanding the implementation process. By looking at Title I of the Elementary and Secondary Education Act of 1965 over thirteen years, the authors are able to draw on many sources of information including major studies of Title I performed at different times in its history.

Over the period of observation the basic legislative provisions of Title I were virtually unchanged, and there were no marked shifts in funding, only a slow, steady rise. In terms of legislative provisions and funding, Title I was remarkably stable, and at the same time it spanned a period of great change in other areas. In 1965 the act was the first attempt by the federal government to provide funds to state and local governments for supporting elementary and secondary education. With the long-held views that states and localities reigned supreme in this area, the federal government entered it with great trepidation, and the early years of ESEA showed almost no effort to enforce compliance. Studies based on the early ESEA years (1965-70) indicated the laxity of federal compliance and no classroom performance gains, leading critics to label the program a failure in administrative and program terms. Kirst and Jung are able to show that changing circumstances including (1) the shifting power of pressure groups, (2) the emergence of a vertical network of specialists with careers depending on the program, and (3) broad-based social movements have contributed to incremental changes that, when aggregated over time, have resulted in a program in 1979 that is substantially closer to realizing the categorical intent of the legislation than was evident in the earlier years of Title I.

The Consultant/Researcher Role

Narver and Williams consider the methodological and administrative issues raised by their consultant/researcher role in working with the Office of Nursing

Home Affairs (ONHA), a component of Washington State's consolidated social and health agency, to devise a management strategy and carry out an initial assessment of that strategy. What led the authors to take on this role was their belief that ex post facto case studies, and probably even studies where researchers follow an ongoing implementation at a distance but are cut off from key action points, do not establish a strong operational base for generating and testing organizational hypotheses. The work for ONHA was an opportunity to participate in a dynamic setting where specific organizational guidelines could be developed and tried out.

In their consultant/researcher role the authors saw helping their clients with their specific organizational problems as the primary task. At the same time the authors believed both that previous implementation research offered organizational propositions that would guide their consulting effort and that the consulting arrangement would yield insights useful in their continuing study of implementation. In particular the consulting effort pivoted off two organizational propositions:

1. Capacity at the point of service delivery should center organizational inquiry including the analysis of high-level management issues.

2. The professional staff of the organization is a main source of ideas about needed changes in organizational structure and management. This staff must be convinced of the feasibility of proposed organizational changes through their participation in developing these changes and through negotiations with them about the changes if organizational changes are to be found that have a reasonable likelihood of successful implementation.

The consultant/researcher team wrote a report indicating organizational problems and remedies that became the basis both for extended discussion on organizational strategy and for a series of organizational changes initiated by management. In addition, they carried out an assessment showing that ONHA was beginning to implement such changes. Of particular interest, the major changes centered on delivery capacity and involved professional staff in developing major changes. While recognizing the limited nature of their evidence (one case), Narver and Williams believe the results suggest the consultant/researcher role has real potential as a future research strategy in providing a base for testing the extent to which current notions about implementation are sufficiently well thought through to provide specific guidance for directing organizational changes.

THE POLICY PAYOFF OF IMPLEMENTATION STUDIES

This section indicates a policy perspective from which to consider the essays. Drawing whenever possible for illustration on the six essays, I raise several key questions that are important in assessing how much implementation studies can aid in policy formulation and execution. The first question concerns whether implementation studies provide a useful analytic framework for public officials who either develop new policies and determine their feasibility or manage the implementation of these policies. Next is the broad question of how pertinent, timely, and sound is the evidence from the preferred research strategy that relies heavily on extended, open-ended interviews. Two related questions focus on the potential usefulness of implementation-type information for national-level programs and for individual projects or changes in organizational structure. How much can current techniques aid policymakers responsible for large-scale programs, including those operating at the national level, in judging how well new programs or major program changes are being carried out and in deciding on field corrections of future distributional or programmatic changes? What means are available for getting information that is relevant to the development and management of new individual projects or efforts to determine and implement structural changes in an existing organization? Finally, there is the question of the extent to which implementation study techniques may be used beneficially by internal staffs of public organizations, perhaps working in concert with outside organizations, in managing the implementation of new policies or the modification of existing ones.

An Analytic Framework
Two concepts are emerging as central to the study of implementation. First is the usefulness of capacity at the point of service delivery as the organizing concept guiding implementation inquiry; second is the importance of organizations as devices for working through complex public problems. In their essays Elmore discusses in depth how these concepts might provide a useful framework for implementation analysis; Narver and Williams use this implementation perspective in their effort to aid policymakers in devising and implementing changes in organizational structure and procedures.

This "view from the bottom" that concentrates attention on service deliverer and client and the organizational structure and process within which their interaction takes place is crucial both in studying implementation and in analyzing and developing policies. It cuts to the core of the implementation question by highlighting the *barriers* faced by the service delivery organization and the *resources* it has or can develop for serving clients. As I have observed elsewhere in discussing social service delivery programs: "The commitment and capacity of the final service delivery organization and concomitantly the individual persons who actually provide services are the central focus of the implementation perspective. Here the crucial institutional investment must be made in managerial and staff capability that allows these organizations to exercise reasonable discretion in providing needed services at the point of delivery and to cope with the implementation of program changes."[5]

Discretionary behavior by those who deliver services is characteristic of most programs and projects studied by the implementation researcher. If change is to result, it must manifest itself in the behavior of these front-line people. Ouchi observes in discussing organizational control that "real control comes about only through changing the worker's behavior."[6] It is this behavior over time—particularly whether or not service deliverers can engage in the discretionary action needed to cope with complex situations—that will determine the outcome of programs and projects.

This individual behavior, however, is shaped in part by the structure and process of the organizations providing the services. Organizational behavior and learning, then, are central to the analysis of implementation feasibility and capacity. Nelson stresses that "the core of analysis of alternatives becomes the prediction of how alternative organizational structures will behave over a not inconsiderable period of time."[7] How to use organizations effectively stands as a critical policy problem for complex programs. It will not do for analysts to see organizations mainly as barriers to performance with our only salvation being the play of market forces.[8] As Elmore points out in his essay: "*[O]rganizations can be remarkably effective devices for working out difficult public problems*" (italics added).

The Relevance, Timeliness, and Believability of Implementation Studies

The question looms large as to how much policymakers can rely on evidence from implementation studies that so often is based mainly on unstructured, nonrandom interviews. With these techniques, validation problems lie much closer to the world of historians, anthropologists, and journalists than to that of survey researchers. The former, like the implementation researcher, must work in settings in which controlled (experimental) comparisons are seldom if ever possible, encounter multiple versions of events or perceptions, and investigate complex events the understanding of which usually requires extensive search procedures, several sources of information, or extended observation over time.

A main concern of the Yin essay is to indicate means of verifying the information and insights drawn from the unstructured interviews through the use of additional validating interviews and the perusal of documents and reports. As Yin stresses, it is critical not to abandon this relatively powerful technique that yields such rich information because it seems to fly in the face of standard surveying techniques that rely so heavily upon sophisticated sample frames and highly structured interview protocols.

The Hall and MacManus essay focuses on another aspect of believability, treating the problems of researcher bias and of being coopted by the unit of observation that must be faced by the individual research associate. Associates either live in the area or near it, interview repeatedly over time, and often serve on projects for several years. The problem of bias grows larger over an extended period; research associates seem prone to become either advocates or critics. Further, they frequently get pressed by local officials either to divulge information or to provide advice. If they give extensive information or advice, they well may become part of the "establishment" protecting the project more than investigating it. But if research associates refuse requests for aid, local respondents may be angered at the lack of cooperation after all the interview time they have given the associate and refuse further participation. It is a difficult research role with a number of not necessarily reconcilable conflicts.

Implementation studies, thus, present a basic dilemma in terms of policy relevance. The need for rich and diverse data that speaks to complex processes going on over time is likely to rule out experimental studies or sample survey techniques with highly structured questions so that findings are difficult to verify and subject to a number of biases.

To what extent can these relatively "soft" implementation studies yield pertinent, sound, timely information on large-scale programs and individual projects to support policymaking and operations at various institutional levels? In elaborating on this question, some distinctions I made earlier in work on federal social program grants-in-aid are useful:

> It is helpful to divide this long federal governance process from Congress to local service project operators into three parts, labeled the "decision," "administrative and support," and "operations" domains. The decision domain includes Congress and the top decision makers in the executive branch who make the "big decisions" that others down the line are expected to execute. At the other end, the operations domain comprises the social service delivery organizations dealing directly with project participants. Here is where the big decisions become operating policy. . . . The administrative and support domain is the area in between . . . [stretching] from the middle levels of a [federal] social agency through the administrative structures of local governments.[9]

In terms of the three domains, we can think of at least five organizational or institutional levels where information demands might differ. The decision domain that includes Congress and stretches down into a social agency through assistant secretaries and major bureau heads and perhaps through the next echelon or two of the major bureaus clearly needs aggregate data from large numbers of projects. The operations domain requires project information to meet the needs of social service delivery organization managers and service deliverers (street-level bureaucrats).

The administrative and support domain is by far the most complex level with at least three different sets of organizational needs. First, the rest of the federal agency headquarters staff below the decision domain will need more detailed management information than those in the decision domain but will generally still want macro information pertinent to *all* federal regions. Second, the federal regional office staffs also use macro data but can benefit too from information about specific grantees. Third, local government bureaucracies—the prime sponsors in the Comprehensive Employment and Training Act are good examples—can use both macro (assuming there are a number of projects involved) and micro information to help them administer the funds that they have received from the federal government and have distributed to local social service organizations.

Large-scale programs. The field network evaluation studies offer a good example of addressing some organizational demands for pertinent, timely, and sound information but not others. As already discussed briefly, the field network evaluation studies to date have concentrated upon the development of macro information expected to be useful to Congress and the top of the agencies. A careful selection of projects operating under different political and socioeconomic conditions can provide the basis for showing diversity of administrative and programmatic approaches, if in fact such diversity exists. Further, the experienced research associates observing the projects over an extended period should be able to gather a rich variety of information on organizational behavior and processes. It also should be possible to get data from the research associates rather quickly and to use them as a sounding board for considering possible program adjustments and corrections.

As to the critical problem of believability, it can be expected that various difficulties of the individual research associates including personal bias may work themselves out because of the number of observers. Certainly, if most of the research associates report the same results or agree on possible changes, there would appear to be a relatively strong base for aiding agency policymakers in considering programwide changes.

At the same time we need to be clear that, thus far, the field network evaluation efforts have yielded information that is mainly useful in illuminating programwide compliance issues. The studies discussed by Nathan, for example, focused on whether CETA funds were used to employ workers who would have been hired without CETA (what is called *displacement*), whether CDBG funds actually went to low- and moderate-income areas as prescribed, and whether local grantees provided citizens a role in the CDBG decision-making process. What has not been looked at in any detail is the extent to which information derived from individual projects can be used in the federal regional offices, in the local administrative process (e.g., by prime sponsors), and in the management of local projects. Of particular interest is the question whether comparative information from a *number* of local projects would enhance the value of the information from a *specific* project for use in that specific project.

Individual projects. The critical need in the field is for specific information on organizational behavior or institutional processes that can help the staffs charged with administering (e.g., federal regional office staff) or operating projects improve local compliance or raise future performance capacity. At basic issue is how well our implementation techniques can be used to support (1) the actual diagnosis of the problems of an individual project or service organization emanating from its particular set of political, organizational, and socioeconomic circumstances; (2) the development of new organizational or programmatic approaches to cope with these problems; (3) the process of implementing the chosen alternatives.

Only the Narver and Williams essay comes close to addressing this issue when they draw on previous work on implementation to aid a client in formulating and implementing a new organizational strategy. None of the essays considers organizational or programmatic redirections in individual projects. Based on the field network evaluation studies, however, we can ask both how useful aggregate information from numerous projects might be for guiding individual projects and the extent to which individual research associates might have been able to provide specific guidance to projects if their roles had been different. Interesting questions, indeed; unfortunately, in the case of individual projects where there may be the greatest need for a contribution from implementation studies, we have little to go on in terms of proven results.

The Internal Use of Implementation Study Techniques

Implementation study techniques and work on implementation can be drawn on directly by public agencies in their development and management of new programs, program modifications, or structural reorganizations. Monitoring is the activity in public organizations where implementation study techniques and the work on implementation seems most applicable. And help clearly is needed as Waller and his colleagues at the Urban Institute have pointed out: "Government offices are full of 'monitoring reports' that have not been read by anyone except their authors. Personnel expected to use such monitoring reports frequently find them useless."[10] This is so because monitoring in the past has focused far too much on relatively low-level administrative practices, financial accountability, and the most narrow kinds of compliance questions. The opportunity to address broader organizational issues is there, and the available implementation study techniques and strategies that the essays in this volume address may offer useful guidance in that regard. Moreover, career civil servants should have a number of comparative advantages in developing information about organizational behavior and institutional processes because of their extended bureaucratic experiences.

Let me offer an example, to this point not widely discussed, that indicates the potential of implementation study techniques being employed by career civil servants to yield relevant and timely information in the decision-making process. When Joseph Califano, Jr., became secretary of the Department of Health, Education, and Welfare (now Health and Human Services), he was concerned about the the availability of policy-relevant information. In particular, he believed that major evaluation efforts in the department did not provide information until long after the question at hand had gone away, that the language of such studies was difficult to follow and translate into policy decisions, and that he did not have information from field studies that spoke directly to the problems that were concerning him. The department set up, under the general administrative jurisdiction of the Inspector General, a service delivery assessment (SDA) effort with the individual SDAs carried out mainly by personnel in the ten federal regional offices.

The typical service delivery assessment would come about because of a specific question of the secretary or undersecretary. The national project leader, chosen from one of the regional offices, would be responsible for getting the issue formulated (including meeting with the secretary to clarify points), developing a study strategy, and putting together the necessary study teams drawn from HEW staff. The studies were done in-house and had a relatively quick turnaround time ranging from two to six months. The main device used in these studies were extended, open-ended interviews. The studies were directed toward how services were delivered to clients looking at the organizational behavior of service providers and the process through which these services were administered. Particular studies well might have focused on a specific implementation effort. The study results were presented in a relatively short report, sometimes

backed up with a much longer technical paper, for the secretary and undersecretary and written in straightforward language meant to facilitate decision making. There also was likely to be an oral report with some policy decisions being
made at that time. It would appear that at least in Califano's tenure, he considered the SDAs a useful means of getting decision-making information. This
effort appears to be the most creative attempt to date within an agency to have
its own staff apply implementation study techniques.[11]

In discussing the direct usefulness of implementation study techniques by
government staffs, I do not mean to imply that there is no role for outside researchers. In fact, my view is just the opposite: If implementation study techniques get used directly by government officials, it can increase the demand for
external help. Not only is there likely to continue to be a need for large-scale
efforts such as field network evaluation studies that are probably not doable on
the inside, growing government interest should stimulate the need for work in
concert with government staffs and outside researchers. This could be by far the
most important long run payoff of implementation studies in terms of policy
relevance.

Let me offer a case in point drawn from a recent Institute for Public Policy
and Management project in which institute staff and federal agency employees
did actually work together in carrying out an implementation assessment. The
facts briefly are as follows: In the Civil Service Reform Act of 1978, which established the much publicized Senior Executive Service for civil servants in the top
three grades (so-called super grades), there also was provision for establishing
merit pay systems for the next three grades (GS-13 through GS-15). Merit pay
systems were to be implemented in the federal agencies within a year. To provide guidance for the implementation of the program throughout the federal
government, some agencies started merit pay systems in October 1980. In late
1980 the Region X (Seattle) office of the Office of Personnel Management, the
agency charged with the overall implementation of merit pay as mandated by
the Civil Service Reform Act, approached IPPM and other institutions to determine the feasibility of assessing the ongoing efforts of two federal regional
offices in Region X that were in the process of implementing merit pay systems.
The purpose of the assessment was to provide the Region X OPM office with information that would help its staff to prepare for workshops aimed at aiding the
various federal offices in the region in developing their merit pay systems and to
provide guidance in these efforts in the time remaining before these systems
were to be put in place.

IPPM was chosen for the implementation assessment and one of the authors in this volume (Betty Jane Narver) headed an institute study team that
worked directly with OPM staff. Both the study design and the actual field in-

terviews were carried out by a combined team from the institute and the Office of Personnel Management. Not only did OPM commit able staff members to the project but they freed a person with extensive study design and interview experience so that she could join Narver in the extended interview efforts.

Since there were fairly severe time constraints on the study, OPM's willingness to take an active role and assume responsibility for establishing contacts with the two Region X offices that were implementing the merit pay system was critical. OPM working alongside of us provided extensive knowledge about federal pay systems generally and merit pay specifically (knowledge the IPPM staff definitely did not have) *and* quick access to information and people. It was a happy marriage of our implementation study techniques used previously on work on organizational change efforts (IPPM had just finished the nursing home study reported in this volume) and OPM's knowledge and access to information and people. The study results corroborate and extend our earlier findings on the implementation of organizational change. I shall not try to summarize the findings but shall simply observe that the combined effort produced an extremely rich information base in a relatively short period of time, one much shorter than would have been possible if the institute had been doing the study without the direct involvement of the federal agency. Finally, I would imagine that the direct investment of OPM staff time made it more likely that the information would be taken seriously.[12] Policy relevance, after all, is not an intrinsic quality (say, as the silver content required for the designation of sterling); rather, it is what some policymaker decides based on a variety of factors is pertinent to a policy question at hand.

SOME CONCLUDING OBSERVATIONS

I considered closing this volume with a short essay to get in the "last" word on studying implementation. But I decided it would be more useful to the reader to indicate where I think we are now as my final introductory remarks before the several essays.

Elsewhere I have argued that we could characterize implementation research to date as follows: (1) The focus has been on the *detailed* investigation of what takes place in the field when people try to put a programmatic or organizational innovation into place; (2) studies generally have had a wide scope in considering the interplay of various political, bureaucratic, technical, organizational, and socioeconomic factors that impinge on implementation efforts; (3) issues rather than disciplinary concerns have guided the studies so far, and no dominant theoretical framework has emerged. Moreover, the central organizing concept of more and more studies has been the point of service delivery. I then made this summary judgment:

> What I see in these studies is a healthy eclecticism—a willingness to take bits and pieces of theories or approaches as they provide insights, but not to get locked in. Also, the researchers have started with what they perceived as the right questions and moved toward them with the techniques that seem most appropriate, rather than reformulating questions to fit dominant methodology or theory. This flexibility in blending the useful parts of earlier theories where helpful, while discarding the rest, has yielded a relatively rich knowledge base in a fairly brief period of time.[13]

The mark of the implementation studies has not been the development of radically new field instruments or methods (technique qua technique) but the adroit application of a combination of existing field interview techniques ranging from the "hard" methods of survey research to the "softer" approaches of journalism, cultural anthropology, and history. For those trying to glean implementation study techniques from the research thus far, what is most important are (1) the framework of analysis (the implementation perspective), (2) the innovative approaches to carrying out inquiry over an extended period of time, and (3) the strategies and tactics for eliciting useful information about organizational behavior.

The best past implementation studies generally have been driven by policy concerns and, in some instances, have been responding directly to a client's demand for information to support decision making. Implementation study techniques can produce a rich variety of information on organizational process and behavior relatively rapidly so that decision makers early on can consider corrections and modifications in ongoing implementation efforts. Or, the implementation perspective can guide organizational analyses aimed at improving existing programs or organizational structures. Policy relevance and timeliness are payoffs implementation researchers may promise with a reasonable expectation of acceptable delivery. Moreover, they often can claim quicker delivery for more relevant organizational information than can the "quantitative" types.

Soundness is a debatable issue. The relatively unstructured, open-ended interview techniques that have come to dominate extended implementation studies yield information that cannot be replicated and may be difficult to verify at a later date. Moreover, the demand for relevant and timely information may require a critical tradeoff in terms of soundness to obtain policy information quickly enough to support decisions. There may be another, more controversial "tradeoff": It is between organizational data that meet prevailing statistical standards and policy-relevant information, the statistical soundness of which is more suspect, where the two kinds of data cannot be substituted for each other.

It often is a "hard-soft" conflict where "rigor" in terms of statistical conventions and prevailing theoretic frameworks and "relevant" in policy terms become code words. We policy types, however, cannot walk away from statistical soundness. Indeed, much of the discussions in the upcoming essays focus on the various issues concerning how to increase the validity of implementation studies.

Let me try to sum up on policy relevance. I believe the implementation framework and techniques now available clearly can help both decision makers charged with implementing large-scale programs and managers concerned with structural reorganization. Indeed, I think policymakers err if they do not draw on these available approaches both in implementation (organizational) analyses to help in deciding how or whether to proceed with a major program change or with a structural reorganization *and* in assessments to aid in making adjustments during the implementation effort. In the case of individual projects, the supporting evidence is less strong. The more sophisticated study efforts of late have been concentrated on major programs and structural reorganizations. However, I see no reason not to think that analyses prior to undertaking a project change and assessments along the path of implementation will provide useful policy information for decision makers concerned with individual projects.

Even if implementation studies are relevant to policy, the question remains concerning the potential payoff in scholarly terms. Is such research anything more than warmed over public administration, or organizational theory revisited often by people who do not seem to have a very firm grasp of the massive work done on organizations in the past? Kai Lee in his review of Eugene Bardach's *The Implementation Game* argued that it was an improvement over "Pressman and Wildavsky's *Implementation,* the book that heralded the [implementation] fad," but chided the "Berkeley Know-Nothing School" for its failure to appreciate earlier work. He concluded that "nothing in the slender implementation literature of the 1970s so far improves noticeably upon the vast—if largely disappointing—output of students of public administration dating back six decades."[14]

I am more optimistic. Even though students of implementation are raising once again fundamental issues of organization and management that have perplexed scholars and practitioners in the past, stressing that critical part of the policy process called implementation does bring a different perspective for considering basic problems in the public management of complex organizations. Moreover, those studying implementation in recent times not only have exhibited the humility (good grace, or what have you) to recognize the contributions from past work in public administration and organizational theory but are developing a better base for utilizing these contributions in their own work.

To claim that the students of implementation are trying to look at the public management of complex organizations in a different way is not to indicate that they will be successful at it. There is no guarantee of seminal theoretical breakthroughs. Frankly, at this point, I think it best to focus mainly on the potential policy contributions of implementation studies, not the theoretical contributions. This holds even if the implementation scholar has as a main goal contributions to theory. Only through a policy perspective that keeps the researcher focused on the organizational dynamics of public programs are such theoretical breakthroughs likely.

NOTES

1. For a discussion of "pertinent, sound, timely," see Walter Williams, *Social Policy Research and Analysis* (New York: Elsevier, 1971), pp. 55-58.
2. The difference in size and scope may be seen by comparing two of Yin's exemplary studies—the study published in 1971 by Gross and others (the earliest of the exemplary studies) looking at the effects of an educational innovation in a single school and the study by Berman and McLaughlin carried out over several years that looked at 293 federally funded education projects including in-depth case studies of 29 of them. While the former study involves a rather elaborate research design, intensive interview development, and extensive observations, it is of one small school with a handful of teachers. On the other hand, the study by Berman and McLaughlin is one of the first of the really large multiple-site studies utilizing questionnaires in a stratified sample frame combined with a subset of intensive field interviews. See Neal Gross and others, *Implementing Organizational Innovations* (New York: Basic Books, 1971); and Paul Berman and Milbrey McLaughlin, *Federal Programs Supporting Educational Change,* vols. 1-8 (Santa Monica, Cal.: Rand Corporation, 1974-78).
3. The central unit clearly lacks the control of the typical project involving graduate student interviewers.
4. Hall and MacManus in their essay provide detailed reference for a number of field network evaluation studies and indicate the dimensions of each one including two much smaller one-year studies (see Hall and MacManus, table 5.1). The two papers, however, treat only the major studies by the Brookings Institution, the National Academy of Sciences, and Princeton University. Two brief comments are needed. First, the big studies are the ones that best indicate the research strategy development to date. Second, the approach itself appears relevant to much smaller programs and over a lesser period of time.
5. Walter Williams, *The Implementation Perspective* (Berkeley: University of California Press, 1980), p. 17.

6. William G. Ouchi, "The Relationship between Organizational Structure and Organizational Control," *Administrative Science Quarterly,* March 1977, p. 97.

7. Richard R. Nelson, *The Moon and the Ghetto* (New York: Norton, 1977), p. 40.

8. See Eugene Bardach, *The Implementation Game* (Cambridge, Mass.: MIT Press, 1977), pp. 282-83.

9. Walter Williams with the assistance of Betty Jane Narver, *Government by Agency: Lessons from the Social Program Grants-in-Aid Experience* (New York: Academic Press, 1980), p. 4.

10. John D. Waller and others, *Monitoring for Government Agencies,* Urban Institute Report No. 783-41, February 1976, p. 11. The Urban Institute report is one of the few works devoted to the issue of monitoring.

11. The whole SDA operation was kept out of the spotlight. Indeed, it is difficult to get the actual reports, but the ones that I have seen would be classified as implementation studies. As far as I can tell, Secretary Patricia Harris did not treat the SDAs as an important information source but had not done away with them, and there is no indication of what the Reagan administration will do.

12. An IPPM report, *Implementation of Merit Pay: Experiences in Two Federal Agencies,* by Betty Jane Narver was issued in late March 1981. Initial interest both at the regional level (the client was OPM Region X) and national level has been high.

13. Williams, *The Implementation Perspective,* p. 12.

14. Kai Lee, review of Eugene Bardach, *The Implementation Game* (Cambridge, Mass.: MIT Press, 1977), in *Policy Sciences* 10 (1978): 225-26. Jeffrey Pressman (now deceased), Aaron Wildavsky, and Bardach were all associated with the public policy program at the University of California at Berkeley.

2

Backward Mapping: Implementation Research and Policy Decisions

RICHARD F. ELMORE

Students of implementation repeatedly argue that implementation problems should be considered when policies are made. Better policies would result, we are told, if policymakers would think about whether their decisions could be implemented before they settle on a course of action. The argument is often made in an accusatory way as if policymakers were somehow deficient for not routinely and systematically thinking about implementation problems. Yet when one looks to the implementation literature for guidance, there is not much to be found.

Implementation research is long on description and short on prescription. Most implementation research is in the form of case studies. This fact, by itself, is neither good nor bad. But it does present special problems when it comes to translating research into useful guidance for policymakers. Cases, if they are well written, focus on a particular sequence of events and a specific set of causes and consequences. When drawing conclusions from their data, case writers are characteristically and honestly cautious. They are typically careful not to generalize more than a step or two beyond their data, and they do even that apologetically. Thus, when we look to the most influential implementation studies for guidance about how to anticipate implementation problems, we find advice that is desultory and strategically vague.[1]

Vague advice is better than none. But one wonders whether this is the best that implementation researchers have to offer. Wringing more out of the literature, however, requires a brand of risk taking that academics and policy analysts typically find uncomfortable. It requires offering *a logically ordered sequence of questions* that policymakers can ask, prior to making a policy decision, that will provide prescriptions for action. The problem with this approach, as opposed, for example, to cataloguing the fragmentary advice that falls out of case studies, is that one can err in a variety of ways: in interpreting the literature, in determining the logic that ties the questions together, or in choosing the questions. It is this fear of erring, I suspect, that has resulted in a failure of nerve among implementation researchers. The important issue is not whether the framework of analysis is "right" or "wrong," but whether it is sufficiently clear to be controvertible. It is less important to agree on a single framework for analyzing implementation problems than it is to be clear about the consequences of adopting one framework over another.

The essential argument of this chapter is that there are at least two clearly distinguishable approaches to implementation analysis: *forward mapping* and *backward mapping.*[2] Forward mapping is the strategy that comes most readily to mind when one thinks about how a policymaker might try to affect the implementation process. It begins at the top of the process, with as clear a statement as possible of the policymaker's intent, and proceeds through a sequence of increasingly more specific steps to define what is expected of implementers at each level. At the bottom of the process, one states, again with as much precision as possible, what a satisfactory outcome would be, measured in terms of the original statement of intent.

Forward mapping of a federal policy might begin with a statement of congressional intent. It would then outline federal agency regulations and administrative actions consistent with that intent. It would elaborate a division of responsibilities between central and regional offices of the federal government (or among federal, state, and local administrators) such that each implementing unit had a clearly defined mission. It would then state an outcome, usually in terms of an observable effect on a target population, consistent with the initial purpose of the policymakers.

Numerous variations of this approach are possible. One need not map only administrative actions and organizational arrangements. If political feasibility is a problem, one can describe the major political actors and the agreements necessary among them at each level. If the implementation of the policy depends on the adoption of some form of technology (e.g., emission controls, medical equipment, or plant construction), one can describe the state of technology necessary at each stage. The analysis may also be elaborated by describing a number of alternative streams of action under varying assumptions about organizational, political, and technological factors.

The details of forward mapping are less important for our purposes than the underlying logic. Forward mapping begins with an objective, elaborates an

increasingly specific set of steps for achieving that objective, and states an outcome against which success or failure can be measured. It is consistent with the
standard framework of policy analysis and with conventional techniques of
management science and decision analysis (program evaluation and review
technique [PERT] and critical path method [CPM]). Insofar as implementation
analysis is treated at all in textbooks on policy analysis, it is treated as forward
mapping.[3]

What the textbooks do not discuss are the weaknesses of forward mapping
and its severe limitations as an analytic technique. The most serious problem
with forward mapping is its implicit and unquestioned assumption that *policymakers control the organizational, political, and technological processes that
affect implementation.* The notion that policymakers exercise, or ought to exercise, some kind of direct and determinant control over policy implementation
might be called the "noble lie" of conventional public administration and policy
analysis. Administrators legitimate their discretionary decisions by saying that
their authority is delegated and controlled by elected and appointed policymakers. Policy analysts justify their existence by arguing that informed, rational
choices by policymakers are necessary to guide and control administrators.
Neither administrators nor policy analysts are very comfortable with the possibility that most of what happens in the implementation process cannot be explained by the intentions and directions of policymakers.

By assuming that more explicit policy directives, greater attention to administrative responsibilities, and clearer statements of intended outcomes will
improve implementation, forward mapping reinforces the myth that implementation is controlled from the top. This myth is increasingly difficult to maintain
in the face of accumulating evidence on the nature of the implementation process. Moreover, forward mapping, as an analytic strategy, treats only a narrow
range of possible explanations for implementation failures.[4] The most persua-
sive explanation for the persistence of forward mapping in the face of its obvious limitations is the lack of a suitable alternative. It is one thing to appreciate
intuitively that policymakers may not exercise decisive control over the implementation process; it is quite another to formulate an analytic strategy consistent with that intuition.

Backward mapping shares with forward mapping the notion that policymakers have a strong interest in affecting the implementation process and the
outcomes of policy decisions. But backward mapping explicitly questions the
assumption that policymakers ought to, or do, exercise the determinant influence over what happens in the implementation process. It also questions the
assumption that explicit policy directives, clear statements of administrative re-

sponsibilities, and well-defined outcomes will necessarily increase the likelihood that policies will be successfully implemented.

The logic of backward mapping is, in all important respects, the opposite of forward mapping. It begins not at the top of the implementation process but at the last possible stage, the point at which administrative actions intersect private choices. It begins, not with a statement of intent, but with a statement of the specific behavior at the lowest level of the implementation process that generates the need for a policy. Only after that behavior is described does the analysis presume to state an objective; the objective is first stated as a set of organizational operations and then as a set of effects, or outcomes, that will result from these operations. Having established a relatively precise target at the lowest level of the system, the analysis backs up through the structure of implementing agencies, asking at each level two questions: What is the ability of this unit to affect the behavior that is the target of the policy? And what resources does this unit require in order to have that effect? In the final stage of anlaysis the analyst or policymaker describes a policy that directs resources at the organizational units likely to have the greatest effect.

Although backward mapping takes the policymaker's perspective on the implementation process, it does not assume that policy is the only—or even the major—influence on the behavior of people engaged in the process. Furthermore, it does not rely on compliance with the policymaker's intent as the standard of success or failure. It offers instead a standard of success that is in all respects *conditional;* that is, one's definition of success is predicated on an estimate of the limited ability of actors at one level of the implementation process to influence the behavior of actors at other levels and on the limited ability of public organizations as a whole to influence private behavior.

Forward mapping assumes that organizational units in the implementation process are linked in essentially hierarchical relationships. This assumption has two corollaries: The closer one is to the source of the policy, the greater is one's authority and influence; and the ability of complex systems to respond to problems depends on the establishment of clear lines of authority and control. Backward mapping assumes essentially the opposite: The closer one is to the source of the problem, the greater is one's ability to influence it; and the problem-solving ability of complex systems depends not on hierarchical control but on maximizing discretion at the point where the problem is most immediate.

BACKWARD MAPPING AND IMPLEMENTATION RESEARCH

Applying forward and backward mapping to the same problem gives much different results. The analytic solution offered by forward mapping stresses factors that tend to centralize control and are easily manipulated by policymakers: funding formulas, formal organizational structures, authority relationships among administrative units, regulations, and administrative controls (budget, planning, and evaluation requirements). The analytic solution offered by backward mapping stresses the dispersal of control and concentrates on factors that can be influenced only indirectly by policymakers: knowledge and problem-solving ability of lower-level administrators, incentive structures that operate on the subjects of policy, bargaining relationships among political actors at various levels of the implementation process, and the strategic use of funds to affect discretionary choices. The crucial difference in perspective stems from whether one chooses to rely primarily on formal devices of command and control that centralize authority or on informal devices of delegation and discretion that disperse authority.

The stakes involved in choosing an analytic approach are clearer when they are put in the context of current thinking about implementation. As the literature on implementation has accumulated, certain issues have emerged that demonstrate the consequences, both intellectual and practical, of seeing implementation either as a hierarchically ordered process or as a dispersed and decentralized process.

Organizational Processes and Outputs

The emergence of implementation as a subject for policy analysis coincides closely with the discovery by policy analysts that decisions are not self-executing. Analysis of policy choices matters little if the mechanism for implementing those choices is poorly understood. In answering the question, "What percentage of the work of achieving a desired governmental action is done when the preferred analytic alternative has been identified?" Allison estimated that, in the normal case, it was about 10 percent, leaving the remaining 90 percent in the realm of implementation.[5] Hence, in Nelson's terms, "the core of analysis of alternatives becomes the prediction of how alternative organizational structures will behave over . . . time."[6] But the task of prediction is vastly complicated by the absence of a coherent body of organization theory, making it necessary to posit several alternative models of organization.[7]

Those policy analysts who are economists, impatient with the complexities of bureaucracy and the lack of precision in organizational theory, have tried to reduce implementation analysis to a simple choice between market and non-market mechanisms. Schultze states the basic argument when he says that the "collective-coercion component of intervention should be treated as a scarce resource" in the formulation of policies, and that policymakers should learn to "maximize the use of techniques that modify the structure of private incentives."[8] Wolf furthers the argument, stating that the whole enterprise of implementation analysis can be reduced to a diagnosis of the pathologies of nonmarket structures, or as he calls it, "a theory of nonmarket failures."[9] The simplicity of the argument is comforting, but its utility is suspect. It seeks to solve one kind of organizational problem, the responsiveness of large-scale bureaucracies, by substituting another kind of organizational problem, the invention and execution of quasi markets. There is little evidence to suggest that the latter problem is any more tractable than the former. One would hardly expect, though, that a detailed framework for analysis of organizational alternatives would emerge from an intellectual tradition that regards organizational structure of any kind as a second-best solution to the problem of collective action.[10]

Defining implementation analysis as a choice between market and nonmarket structures diverts attention from, and trivializes, an important problem: *how to use the structure and process of organizations to elaborate, specify, and define policies.* Most policy analysts, economists or not, are trained to regard complex organizations as *barriers* to the implementation of public policy, not as instruments to be capitalized on and modified in the pursuit of policy objectives. In fact, organizations can be remarkably effective devices for working out difficult public problems, but their use requires an understanding of the reciprocal nature of authority relations. Formal authority travels from top to bottom in organizations; the informal authority that derives from expertise, skill, and proximity to the essential tasks that an organization performs travels in the opposite direction. Delegated discretion is a way of capitalizing on this reciprocal relationship; responsibilities that require special expertise and proximity to a problem are pushed down in the organization, leaving more generalized responsibilities at the top. For purposes of implementation, this means that formal authority, in the form of policy statements, is heavily dependent on specialized problem-solving capabilities farther down the chain of authority. Except where a policy requires strict performance of a highly structured routine (e.g., airline safety inspections), strong hierarchical controls work against this principle of reciprocity. To use organizations effectively as instruments of policy, analysts and policymakers have to understand where in the complex network of organizational relationships certain tasks should be performed, what resources are necessary for their performance, and whether the performance of the task has some tangible effect on the problem that the policy is designed to solve. Analysts and policymakers do *not* need to know how to perform the task, or even whether the task is performed uniformly; in fact, diversity in the performance of the task is an important source of knowledge about how to do it better.

The notion of reciprocity lends some concreteness to the strategic calculations involved in implementation analysis. Instead of stating the central analytic
problem as a choice between competing abstractions—market and nonmarket
alternatives—it focuses on the *process* by which organized problem solving
occurs and the *output* that results from problem solving. Understanding reciprocal dependencies in organizations also simplifies the conduct of analysis considerably. One is not concerned with mapping all the formal authority relationships that could possibly bear on a policy problem but with isolating the one or
two critical points in a complex organization that have the closest proximity to
the problem and describing what needs to happen at those points to solve the
problem.

Shrewd organizational analysis does not preclude the selection of market-
like structures to implement policy. In fact, it clarifies the choice considerably.
There is nothing to prevent the analyst or policymaker from concluding that,
for purposes of a specific problem, the best strategy is to move problem-solving
responsibilities outside formal organizations and rely on individual choices. But
the decision to pursue that strategy is based on a prior understanding of the setting and the actors, rather than a presumption that marketlike structures are
more effective.

The Complexity of Joint Action

Pressman and Wildavsky were the first to observe the inverse relationship between the number of transactions required to implement a decision and the likelihood that an effect, any effect, would result. Even when the probability of a
favorable result is high at each step, the cumulative product of a large number
of transactions has an extraordinarily low probability of success.[11] This analysis is complemented by Bardach's extended discussion of the devices that administrators use to delay, divert, and dissipate the effect of policies and by the
attempts of other scholars to specify the effect of bureaucratic structure on implementation.[12] These notions have now become part of the standard repertoire of explanations for why policies fail. But they have had surprisingly little
payoff in increasing our understanding of how to prevent failure. If we accept
that the complexity of joint action is a serious problem, for both policy analysts
and policymakers, what can we do about it?

Very little can be done about the problem if analysts and policymakers persist in viewing implementation as a hierarchically ordered set of authority relationships. That is, to the extent that the implementation process is dominated
by regulation, formal organizational structure, and management control, one
would expect problems of complexity to increase. The tighter the structure of
hierarchical relationships, the greater the number of checks and decision points

required to assure compliance, the more opportunities for diversion and delay, the greater the reliance of subordinates on superiors for guidance, and the lower the reliance on individual judgment and problem-solving ability. One of the great ironies of increased attention to implementation is that the harder we try, using conventional tools of hierarchical control, the less likely we are to achieve.[13]

Forward mapping, as an analytic strategy, reinforces the pathologies of hierarchy. With a sharp pencil, a good eye for detail, and a pocket calculator, one can demonstrate without much trouble that any policy will fail, simply by counting the number of discrete clearances and decisions, assigning a probability to each, and multiplying them seriatim. The flaw in this kind of analysis lies not in its internal logic but in its failure to perceive an alternative to hierarchy. Demonstrating so simply that hierarchies increase the probability of failure should suggest the need for an alternative model of the process. A promising lead comes from Bardach's discussion of "fixing," by which he means the skillful and selective intervention of policymakers at various points in the implementation process.[14] The key element of fixing is its deliberate disregard for hierarchy; a good fixer is one who is willing to intervene wherever a breakdown occurs, with scant regard for the line of authority relationships that precedes it. The difficulty with Bardach's account of fixing is that it does not provide very clear guidance about formulating a strategy of intervention: How does one decide among a number of possible points of intervention? What does one do when a point of intervention is identified? And how does one determine whether fixing has succeeded or failed? In other words, fixing, by itself, is a kind of behavior, not an analytic strategy. Having decided to fix something, one is still left with deciding how to do it, and that requires a logic of some sort.

Street-Level Discretion

Distrust of discretion is deeply ingrained in conventional theories of administration and government. Kaufman confidently asserts, without argument:

> If leaders exert but little influence on the actions of subordinates, then one of the axioms of democratic government ceases to apply. . . . Democracy in the modern state presupposes that changing a handful of officials in high places will ultimately change the actions of thousands of employees throughout the system.[15]

Substituting "changing policy" for "changing a handful of officials in high places" yields the essential statement of implementation as a process of hierarchical control. Kaufman argues that the "major contribution" of his own work "lies in the enhancement of leaders' capacities to neutralize tendencies toward non-compliance."[16] Discretion, though inevitable in any complex administrative system, is to be carefully bounded, contained, and controlled by an assortment of devices (selection, monitoring, routinization) that strengthen the top of the system against the bottom. Even theorists of public administration who argue that policymaking and administration cannot be separated harbor a strong distrust of discretion:

> Much of the actual discretion used in administration is used at the very bottom of the hierarchy, where public servants touch the public. The assessor who walks into the home and sees the furniture and the condition of the house, the policeman who listens to the motorist's story, the health inspector who visits the dairy, the income tax auditor who sees the return and interviews the taxpayer—all these people are compelled to exercise more discretion, and more important discretion, from the point of view of the citizen than many other functionaries further up in the organization. While this is the actual situation in badly organized and poorly directed administrative units, it cannot be completely eliminated even in the best.[17]

This theme has been picked up and extended in the implementation literature by Weatherley and Lipsky in their analysis of the role of street-level bureaucrats. The heavy overload of demands and expectations resulting from new policies, they argue, means that street-level bureaucrats are essentially free to develop their own "coping devices" for simplifying, and often distorting, the aims of policymakers. The solution to this problem, they suggest, lies mainly in devising more sophisticated ways of bounding and controlling discretion.[18]

The dominant view that discretion is, at best, a necessary evil and, at worst, a threat to democratic government pushes implementation analysis toward hierarchically structured models of the process and toward increased reliance on hierarchical controls to solve implementation problems. Uniformity of implementation, or low variability in the response of street-level bureaucrats to policy directives, has a positive value, whether or not it is positively related to outcomes. Compliance with orders and procedures displaces competence, or becomes the equivalent of competence, in interactions between lower-level public servants and clients. Nowhere in this view is serious thought given to *how to capitalize on discretion as a device for improving the reliability and effectiveness of policies at the street level.* Standardized solutions, developed at great distance from the problem, are notoriously unreliable; policies that fix street-level behavior in the interest of uniformity and consistency are difficult to adapt to situations that policymakers failed to anticipate. Adaptation under these circumstances consists either of subversive, extralegal behavior or a complex procedure of hierarchical clearance. There is little or no room for the exercise of special skills or judgment, not to mention deliberate invention and experimentation.

When implementation consists essentially of controlling discretion, the effect is to reduce reliance on knowledge and skill at the delivery level and increase reliance on abstract, standardized solutions. Hence, a certain proportion of the learning required to adapt a broad policy to a specific set of circumstances is lost; adaptive behaviors by street-level bureaucrats are never well understood by policymakers because they are viewed as illicit. Variability and discretion at the delivery level can just as easily be viewed as an asset — a broad-based body of data on unanticipated, adaptive responses to highly specialized problems. To capitalize on this knowledge, however, one's view of implementation has to put a higher value on discretion than compliance.

Coalitions and the Bargaining Arena

One of the earliest and most robust findings of implementation research was that the local effect of federal policy depends, in some critical sense, on the formation of local coalitions of individuals affected by the policy. Derthick documented the helplessness of federal administrators, trying to use surplus federal land as an incentive for the development of "new towns," when local support for the projects failed to gel into a strong coalition.[19] Pressman concluded an analysis of federal programs in Oakland with the observation that their impact depended on the existence of "effective bargaining arenas," in which the competing demands of local groups could be worked out.[20] Banfield concluded his analysis of the Model Cities program with the observation:

> As perceived from Washington, a city government was an entity capable, if sufficiently prodded and when provided with a grant, of making decisions in a rational manner. . . . City officials knew, however, that only in a rather limited sense did such a thing as a city government exist; for them the reality was bits and pieces of power and authority, the focuses of which were constantly changing. Bringing the bits and pieces together long enough to carry out an undertaking was a delicate and precarious operation requiring skills and statuses that few persons possessed.[21]

Unless the initiators of a policy can galvanize the energy, attention, and skills of those affected by it, thereby bringing these resources into a loosely structured bargaining arena, the effects of a policy are unlikely to be anything but weak and diffuse. Once bargaining is recognized as a key element of implementation, certain other conditions follow. Bargaining requires real stakes. Local actors have no incentive for participation in a bargaining arrangement unless the possible payoff is tangible and valuable. The terms of the deal cannot be fixed in advance by law; sufficient flexibility must exist in the outlines of a policy to allow the local bargaining process to work. Carefully specified, hierarchically controlled policies limit incentives to form strong local bargaining coalitions.

Another consequence of local bargaining is that policy implementation has no clear, decisive end point. The outcome of one bargaining episode is the starting point of the next. Success in bargaining is completely relative in one important respect: Each participant judges success in terms of his own objectives, not in terms of an overall set of objectives that applies to all participants. The only measure of success that all participants can agree on is maintenance of the bargaining arena, since it provides them access to the goods dispensed there. To acknowledge that bargaining is essential to the process of implementation is to accept the consequence that policy outcomes will never be discrete, determinate end points that can be measured and objectified. An analytic framework that requires the comparison of a clearly specified outcome with a clearly specified intent—a comparison implicit in forward mapping—is inconsistent with a conception of implementation that includes bargaining.[22]

To summarize, the implementation literature provides strong support for an analytic framework that takes account of reciprocity in the relationship between superiors and subordinates in organizations, the connection between hierarchical control and increased complexity, discretion as an adaptive device, and bargaining as a precondition for local effects.

. Recall the logic of backward mapping outlined earlier: Begin with a concrete statement of the behavior that creates the occasion for a policy intervention, describe a set of organizational operations that can be expected to affect that behavior, describe the expected effect of those operations, and then describe for each level of the implementation process what effect one would expect that level to have on the target behavior and what resources are required for that effect to occur. The advantage of beginning with a concrete behavior and focusing on the delivery-level mechanism for affecting that behavior is that it focuses attention on reciprocity and discretion. It puts the policymakers' problem in the following form: "If we propose to affect that behavior, where is the closest point of contact we have with it?" It emphasizes, in other words, that it is not the policy or the policymaker that solves the problem, but someone with immediate proximity. Problem solving requires skill and discretion; policy can direct individuals' attention toward a problem and provide them an occasion for the application of skill and judgment, but policy cannot itself solve problems. Hence, the connection between the problem and the closest point of contact is the most critical stage of analysis. After that, analysis consists of describing the most direct means of reaching the point of contact, focusing resources on those organizational units and coalitions that have the greatest likelihood of affecting delivery-level performance. Strategically, the more direct the path for reaching the point of contact—that is, the greater the reliance on delegated discretion, and the less the reliance on hierarchical controls—the greater the likelihood of affecting the target behavior. Rather than reason from top to bottom, through successive layers, trying to discover how each layer can control the next, one begins at the point of the problem and tries to find the most parsimonious way of reaching it.

BACKWARD MAPPING ON
YOUTH EMPLOYMENT POLICY

Federal policymakers recently have been engaged in an extensive review of youth employment policy.[23] The occasion for the review was the pending expiration of the Youth Employment Demonstration and Projects Act of 1977 (YEDPA), which provided support for a variety of locally administered employment and training activities for young people. Among the topics under discussion has been whether the existing system for implementing youth employment programs is effectively addressing youth employment problems.

As in most discussions of federal policy, debate has focused on how to allocate federal money among competing administrative agencies and competing purposes within agencies. Thus, for example, one of the most pressing issues, as defined by federal policymakers, is the problem of cooperation between the Comprehensive Employment and Training Act (CETA) prime sponsors and local educational agencies (LEAs). YEDPA provides financial incentives for collaboration between local educational agencies and prime sponsors, the units of local government designated to administer the federal Comprehensive Employment and Training Act. For example, 22 percent of the funds in one category of YEDPA are set aside for jointly administered programs, but the funds go from the U.S. Department of Labor directly to local prime sponsors, where the LEA agreements are made. Federal youth employment funds do not pass through educational agencies at the federal or state level, and LEAs have no independent share of the funds at the local level. Education advocates at the federal level have argued that federal, state, and local educational agencies would be more likely to take an active interest in youth employment problems if they were given an independent source of funding. Others have argued that the important issue is local collaboration between CETA prime sponsors and LEAs and that allocating funds through federal and state education agencies would not necessarily serve that purpose.

Another issue that has surfaced is the problem of knowledge development. While the federal government has been involved in youth employment at least since the mid-1960s, employment and training specialists argue that they know very little about how to solve the unique employment problems of young people. YEDPA was intended to stimulate the development of new program ideas that could be used to improve the overall performance of youth employment programs. The interpretation of this knowledge development objective by local administrators has been diverse, and knowledge development activity has been uneven from one locale to another. Many observers question whether the federal government has a role to play in such a diffuse and ill-defined area, and if so, what that role should be.

The final major issue that has surfaced is the problem of private-sector linkages. Federal policymakers are sensitive to widespread criticism that neither adult nor youth programs administered through the CETA system are effectively connected with private-sector employers, which means that the people who exit training are not adequately prepared for unsubsidized employment. Policymakers are concerned about how federal funds can be used to increase linkages between youth employment programs and private employers.

These issues are in many ways typical of how problems are framed by federal policymakers. They are broad, abstract, and disconnected. They tend to focus on immediate problems of policy formulation rather than more distant problems of implementation. Allocation of funds among competing agencies tends to dominate, even though the consequences of allocation decisions for the delivery of services are vague and unspecified. The issues, therefore, are all framed in a manner consistent with forward mapping: They all state or imply a federal objective and then ask what the federal government can do to make people act consistently with that objective. They all suggest that it is the federal government's responsibility to make something happen at the local level, but the mechanism for making it happen is unspecified beyond the allocation of funds to agencies.

What is missing from this formulation is a clear picture of what transactions are critical to the success of youth employment programs and how the federal government can influence those transactions. Why is CETA-LEA cooperation important? What constitutes effective cooperation? For whom, precisely, is knowledge development a problem, and why? Where would we expect to see the effects of knowledge development if it were successful? What exactly constitutes a "linkage" between an employment training program and a private employer? Most importantly, though, against what concrete delivery-level behavior are we to judge federal allocation decisions? In order to address these questions, one must start from an explicit statement of the behavior that federal policy is designed to affect.

From this perspective it is clear that the major factors affecting employment of young people are outside the sphere of direct government control. *The target of public policy is the transaction between the young person and the em-*

ployer. The major determinants of this transaction are the employer's preferences for entry-level personnel, the young person's preference for a certain kind of work, and local labor market conditions, none of which is directly controlled by federal policy.

Public institutions try either to affect the attributes of the young person that might increase his or her employability or to influence the preferences of employers for entry-level personnel. Two sets of public institutions have the closest proximity to the transaction: schools and employment training programs. The two sets of institutions operate from very different legal and political bases. Schools are the creations of state government but are largely administered and governed at the local level. Employment training organizations are the creations of the federal government and are administered and governed at the local level by CETA prime sponsors. At the delivery level there is considerable variability from one locale to another in the kind of services offered, the level of resources invested by the public schools in preparing young people for job entry, and the level of cooperation between operators of employment training programs and school personnel. In the variability of local settings, however, one thing remains constant: *The point at which public policy intersects private choices is in the transactions between young people, service providers* (schools and employment training organizations), *and employers.*

At least three sets of delivery-level decisions are important in determining the effects of youth employment policy: service providers' decisions about who gets access to which services, young people's decisions to enter particular kinds of training and seek particular jobs, and employers' decisions to fill entry-level positions. These decisions cannot be standardized, managed, or controlled using conventional administrative tools. Matching young people to services is a highly discretionary task, requiring judgment, skill, and imagination. Some combination of cognitive skills, vocational skills, job-search skills, and work experience is required for labor force participation; and it is the task of the service deliverer to respond to individual differences in the need for these skills. The decisions of young people and employers are likewise highly discretionary. The central problem for policymakers is not how to make these decisions consistent with some predetermined, uniform plan of action but to maximize the likelihood that the net effect of the decisions will be to increase the employability of young people. The strategic targeting of resources on discretionary decisions is more important than attempts to control behavior according to plan.

The three-cornered relationship between service providers, young people, and employers, and the interdependent decisions among members of the triad, become the reference points against which to judge the potential effect of policy choices and implementation strategies. The closer and more direct the influence on these relationships, the more likely the choice will affect the employability of young people; the more distant, the less likely.

Viewed from this perspective, the issues raised initially by federal policy-makers now make a good deal more sense. Instead of phrasing them in terms of a federal objective disconnected from a delivery-level target (more CETA-LEA cooperation, more knowledge development, more private-sector linkages), they can be phrased in terms of their anticipated effect on delivery-level decisions. Without first stating explicitly where the delivery level is, what the critical decisions are at that level, and what the federal interest is in those relationships, one cannot formulate an intelligible policy question. In other words, the process of framing questions from the top begins with an understanding of what is important at the bottom.

What effect would we expect greater CETA-LEA cooperation to have on delivery-level decisions? From the federal level, cooperation among local administrators looks good. The federal administrator's job is simplified considerably by having a tidy, consolidated box at the local level into which federal money can be put. From the delivery level, though, its advantages are far less obvious. Does cooperation among administrators mean that school personnel and operators of employment training programs will work side by side on common problems? Not necessarily. It might, and probably does, mean only that school administrators and CETA prime sponsors have devised a peaceful way of dividing up federal funds and using them for separate activities. Even if we could have a completely consolidated delivery system at the local level, would we want it? What effect would it have on the discretionary choices of service providers, young people, and employers? A major advantage of the CETA system over the school system is that it allows small, marginal, unconventional organizations to form in competition with established providers and schools. Would tighter CETA-LEA collaboration squeeze out marginal providers and reduce the choices available to young people? On grounds of simplicity, standardization, and management control, CETA-LEA cooperation seems good. On grounds of delivery-level performance, its benefits are mixed, at best.

Viewing the knowledge development problem from the delivery level, it becomes clearer that the notion has very little meaning apart from its effect on how delivery-level personnel understand their work and share knowledge with each other. Federal and local administrators can direct that certain kinds of studies be done, evaluate the performance of program deliverers, and construct elaborate management information systems—all of which have been done in the name of knowledge development—but the net effect of these devices is to increase the knowledge and control of administrators, not delivery-level personnel. Would it not make sense to put a certain proportion of the funds dedicated to knowledge development directly in the hands of the delivery-level personnel?

The problem of private-sector linkages, viewed from the delivery level, looks something like a problem of coalition building. Employers cannot really be expected to take a serious interest in youth employment programs without a tangible stake in the outcome of those programs. One strategy for giving them a stake is to view them as part of the delivery system at the local level, rather than as consumers of a product that someone else produces. This might make them competitive providers of services. It could also bring them into a formal bargaining relationship with CETA prime sponsors and school system administrators for purposes of determining allocation of funds at the local level. Or it could require constructing something like a school-work council at the lowest level of the system, with discretionary control of a certain amount of money for program and knowledge development. In order for employers to alter their preferences toward young labor force entrants, they have to be drawn into a relationship in which they can perceive a benefit.

The critical issues in the formulation of a federal policy toward youth employment, thus, are not how the federal government should allocate its resources among competing, national objectives and how it can manipulate other levels of government to accomplish those objectives, but where, in the complex welter of relationships at the delivery level, are the individuals who have the closest proximity to the problems and what resources do they need to address it. The logic of backward mapping connects policy decisions directly with the point at which their effect occurs.

NOTES

1. Pressman and Wildavsky conclude that the "length and unpredictability" of implementation processes should lead policymakers to consider "more direct means" (Jeffrey Pressman and Aaron Wildavsky, *Implementation* [Berkeley: University of California Press, 1973], pp. 143-44). Bardach advises policymakers to base policies on explicit theories, to prefer market-like mechanisms to bureaucratic ones, to forecast problems by using scenarios, and to "fix" implementation problems with political intervention (Eugene Bardach, *The Implementation Game* [Cambridge, Mass.: MIT Press, 1977], pp. 250-83). Berman and McLaughlin suggest policymakers should pay more attention "to all stages of the local change process," provide "adaptive implementation assistance," and improve "the capacity of school districts to manage change" (Paul Berman and Milbrey McLaughlin, *Federal Programs Supporting Educational Change* [Santa Monica, Calif.: Rand Corporation, 1978], 8:35-43). Weatherley and Lipsky con-

clude that policymakers should attend more closely to the behavior of street-level bureaucrats, regarding behaviors that are consistent with policy and penalizing those that are not (Richard Weatherley and Michael Lipsky, "Street-Level Bureaucrats and Institutional Innovation: Implementing Special Education Reform," *Harvard Educational Review* 47 [May 1977]: 196).

2. I am indebted to Mark Moore of the Kennedy School of Government, Harvard University, for introducing me to the notion of "backward mapping," though he should not be held accountable for my version of it.

3. See, for example, Harry Hatry et al., *Program Analysis for State and Local Government* (Washington, D.C.: Urban Institute, 1976), p. 97; Edward Quade, *Analysis for Public Decisions* (New York: Elsevier, 1975), p. 253; Grover Starling, *The Politics and Economics of Public Policy* (Homewood, Ill.: Dorsey, 1979), p. 430.

4. For a detailed discussion of alternative explanations of implementation failures and their consequences for modeling the implementation process, see, Richard F. Elmore, "Organizational Models of Social Program Implementation," *Public Policy* 26 (Spring 1978): 185-228.

5. Graham Allison, *Essence of Decision: Explaining the Cuban Missile Crisis* (Boston, Mass.: Little, Brown, 1971), p. 267.

6. Richard Nelson, *The Moon and the Ghetto* (New York: Norton, 1977), p. 40.

7. See for example, ibid., p. 41; Elmore, "Organizational Models," pp. 187-89.

8. Charles Schultze, *The Public Use of Private Interest* (Washington, D.C.: Brookings Institution, 1977), pp. 6-7.

9. Charles Wolf, "A Theory of Non-Market Failures," *Public Interest,* Spring 1979, pp. 114-33.

10. For examples of this argument, see Kenneth Arrow, *The Limits of Organization* (New York: Norton, 1974); and Oliver Williamson, *Markets and Hierarchies* (New York: Free Press, 1975).

11. Pressman and Wildavsky, *Implementation,* pp. 87-124.

12. Bardach, *The Implementation Game,* p. 65; see also Allison, *Essence of Decision,* pp. 67-100; and Elmore, "Organizational Models," pp. 199-208.

13. Richard F. Elmore, "Complexity and Control: What Legislators and Administrators Can Do About Implementation," Policy Paper No. 11, Institute of Governmental Research, University of Washington, Seattle, Washington, April 1979.

14. Bardach, *The Implementation Game,* pp. 274-83.

15. Herbert Kaufman, *Administrative Feedback* (Washington, D.C.: Brookings Institution, 1973), p. 4.

16. Ibid., p. 5.

17. Luther Gulick, quoted by Herbert Kaufman, "Reflections on Administrative Reorganization," in *The 1978 Budget: Setting National Priorities,* ed. Joseph Pechman (Washington, D.C.: Brookings Institution, 1977), p. 400.

18. Weatherley and Lipsky, "Street-Level Bureaucrats," pp. 172 and 196.

19. Martha Derthick, *New Towns in Town* (Washington, D.C.: Urban Institute, 1972).

20. Jeffrey Pressman, *Federal Programs and City Politics* (Berkeley: University of California Press, 1975), pp. 143-44.
21. Edward Banfield, "Making a New Federal Program: Model Cities, 1964-68," in *Social Program Implementation,* ed. Walter Williams and Richard Elmore (New York: Academic Press, 1976), p. 210.
22. Elmore, "Organizational Models," pp. 217-26; Helen Ingram, "Policy Implementation through Bargaining: The Case of Federal Grants-in-Aid," *Public Policy* 25 (Fall 1977): 499-526.
23. This section summarizes a more extended analysis of the implementation of federal youth employment policy contained in Richard Elmore, "Policy Paper: The Youth Employment Delivery System" (prepared for the Vice-President's Task Force on Youth Employment, Washington, D.C., August 1979). I have drawn heavily upon extensive studies of the implementation of federal youth employment programs done by Gregory Wurzburg at the National Council on Employment Policy, Washington, D.C.

3

Studying the Implementation
of Public Programs

ROBERT K. YIN

THE INTERACTION OF METHODS AND CONCEPTS

The natural and social sciences are replete with examples in which methodological and conceptual advances have been intertwined. For instance, the development of microelectrodes in biology in the late 1950s gave researchers the ability to record signals from single nerve cells and thereby develop new insights into brain function. Similarly, the evolution of quantitative historical techniques during the last ten years has allowed social historians to construct new and more insightful portraits of life in early American cities. Finally, the continued refinement of survey research techniques, whether for the national census, for political polling, or for studies of criminal victimization, has provided fresh sources of information for theories about American social behavior.

A general proposition from these and numerous other examples is that advances in scientific knowledge depend both on purely conceptual breakthroughs and on improvements in the *craft,* or methods, available for inquiry. Moreover, this relationship between concept and craft seems to emerge most vigorously when a broad new topic of research is beginning to be explored. Typically, a new set of problems or theories leads to the need for new empirical information; the theoretical propositions may deviate from the normative science of the day, leading to the need for innovative or refined methods; and the methodological improvements and subsequent evidence often yield yet newer conceptual insights. The process is iterative, incremental, and symbiotic.

Implementation, or the installation of new policies/practices in public and private organizations, has become one such research topic. Not more than five or ten years ago, there was a truly meager amount of research on implementation (Pressman and Wildavsky 1973, Hargrove 1975, Williams 1976). This situation existed in spite of the fact that many new public programs were being implemented; for example, those initiated in the 1960s as part of the Great Society (Levitan and Taggart 1976) or of municipal reform (Yin and Yates 1975). Little knowledge was available to assist in the implementation process, and only a few observers even appreciated the need to understand why implementation failed or succeeded.

At the present time, interest in implementation has burgeoned (Berman 1978). In fact, the interest reflects a larger theme, which has to do with the study of public policymaking and organizational innovation more generally. Greenberg et al. (1977) have suggested the parameters of the overall process; whether under the guise of implementation, public policymaking, or organizational innovation, all involve

> A series of decisions that occur over a long period of time, with no clear beginning or end points
>
> Outcomes whose direct and indirect implications are too complex for single-factor theories
>
> A large number of relevant participants
>
> Situations that are rather special in terms of agency context, historical moment in time, and other key elements

Given these parameters, however, implementation and related organizational processes are likely to be difficult subjects of study.

Not surprisingly, the relationship between concept and craft has become evident in several recent works. Investigators who have attempted to clarify current issues concerning organizational innovation, for instance, have ended their discussions with suggestions for methodological improvements. One highly regarded article by George Downs and Larry Mohr (1976) is, in fact, titled "*Conceptual* Issues in the Study of Innovation," yet concludes with seven *methodological* prescriptions rather than any conceptual propositions (emphasis mine). In a similar vein, Everett Rogers has repeatedly pleaded the case for breaking away from cross-sectional analyses and one-shot surveys as the first step in appreciating the conceptual distinction between the traditional study of diffusion and the newer study of organizational innovation, which requires the ability to trace organizational processes over time (Rogers 1975, Rogers with Eveland 1975, Rogers and Agarwala-Rogers 1976). Other discussions have focused on more specialized aspects of organizational innovation but have nevertheless emphasized methodological lessons—for example, intergovernmental innovation, in which federal initiatives are used to spur state or local governments into action (Williams 1976, Bardach 1977), and innovation due to the provision of technical information to public agencies (Sabatier 1978). In the last example, Sabatier paradoxically ends his substantive discussion with a section on "implications for future research" that contains only methodological suggestions and not a hint of a substantive framework or theoretical proposition.

These examples show that concerns with craft knowledge have tended to follow only *indirectly* from substantive discussions. In contrast, the present paper deals *directly* with the interaction between concept and craft, with the purpose of improving the craft with which implementation — and organizational innovation and public policymaking processes more generally — is studied. The need for such a direct inquiry is based on the fact that many investigators are initiating new studies of implementation. For instance, the Solar Energy Research Institute has initiated a series of projects to examine the factors affecting the successful implementation of solar energy programs (Roessner et al. 1979). The investigators wisely view implementation as a key issue, noting that success will probably be influenced as much by the way the programs are implemented as by their original design. Yet, without explicit methodological guidance, such researchers will have to be careful to avoid either of two pitfalls. First, inappropriate methods of inquiry may be negligently used. Second, investigators may struggle *de novo* with methods that have already been refined by others. Overall, the methods for studying implementation are in need of better description, and the present paper is viewed as one step in this direction.

Naturally, it should also be pointed out that, because of the symbiotic relationship between concept and craft, any improvements in craft knowledge may also have implications for knowledge about substance. In part, this is reflected by the continuing problem that inquiries into method cannot be completely devoid of conceptual bias, an observation that has been carefully noted by those who have dealt with the different "conceptual lenses" imposed by different models of organizational behavior (e.g., Allison 1971, Elmore 1978). Often, the very measures that an investigator considers appropriate — on the surface, a methodological concern — may be a function of conceptual blinders and an implicit substantive model.

This report attempts to avoid some of these pitfalls by limiting itself to a few simple questions, which serve as the organizing themes for the bulk of the text:

> How is evidence *collected* in studies of implementation?
> How is evidence *analyzed*?
> What are the reasons for believing the conclusions from
> such studies?

An Exemplary Studies Approach
There are several ways of addressing these questions:

1. One could attempt to generalize about the methodological implications from one's own research (e.g., Reiss 1971, Iannacone 1975). However, such an approach fails to give the reader confidence that the methodological lessons, because they have been drawn from a narrow experimental base, are necessarily applicable to the whole range of implementation issues.
2. One could review existing studies of implementation in a strictly tabular fashion, much like previous "evaluations of evaluations" (e.g., Bernstein and Freeman 1975, Yin et al. 1976). This is an unrealistic alternative because of the small number of implementation studies.
3. One could create a catalog or inventory of research methods, systematically indicating the advantages or disadvantages of each, under different conditions (e.g., Barnes 1971, Weick 1968, Douds and Rubenstein 1975). However, these inventories also pose a problem in that they do not yield sharp insights into the methodological choices that must be made; one inventory, for instance, does not even arrive at any overall conclusions (Douds and Rubenstein 1975).
4. One could take an advocate position with regard to certain methodologies (e.g., Eckstein 1975, Stake 1978). However, the taking of such normative positions would seem to be premature at this time.

Yet a fifth approach may overcome some of the shortcomings of these four approaches, and it is one that has been pursued here. The approach is to examine the methods used in a number of exemplary studies, defined as studies that are commonly cited, in publications and conversations, by other researchers. The analysis of such studies can yield empirical information on craft knowledge, allowing the reader to judge independently the state of the art. Although there have been few exemplary studies of implementation, those that have been published include works authored by some highly esteemed investigators and cover a range of different service sectors. To this extent, the reader may gain some confidence about the validity and generalizability of the lessons to be learned.

Identification of Exemplary Studies
Exemplary studies of implementation were identified by noting those books or articles that have appeared in published form and were thus subjected to peer review. In each case the study had to deal with an actual implementation experience — that is, the initiation of a new practice within a local setting, regardless of whether the new practice was part of a federally instigated program or not. Studies and review articles containing no original empirical information were not considered.

A preliminary review revealed that the relevant works fell into two categories, the first dealing with studies of implementation experiences at single sites (*single-site studies*), and the second dealing with the lessons learned from experiences at more than one site (*multiple-site studies*). The latter category could be further divided into those studies covering only a single local service and those studies simultaneously covering a variety of services. Thus, three pools of potential studies were identified, and an attempt was made to cover a variety of service topics in each pool.

The results of a citation search and discussions with colleagues are shown in table 3.1, which identifies eleven exemplary studies. Four of these studies were single-site cases, distributed among several local services (community or economic development, education, general municipal services, and health). Another four were multiple-site studies, each limited to a single local service that partially matched the single-site studies; the last three were multiple-site studies in which each investigation itself covered a variety of services.

A few words should be said about the studies that were considered but not included in the final sample.[1] These fell into the following categories:

Single- or multiple-site studies of new service practices that mainly focused on the adoption rather than implementation process (e.g., Mytinger 1968; Feller et al. 1974, 1976; Corwin 1975; Nelson and Sieber 1976; Bingham 1976; Daft and Becker 1978)

TABLE 3.1
SAMPLE OF EXEMPLARY STUDIES OF IMPLEMENTATION

Service Sector	Type of Study	
	Single-Site	Multiple-Site
Community and economic development	1. Pressman and Wildavsky 1973	5. Derthick 1972
Education	2. Gross et al. 1971	6. Berman and McLaughlin 1974-78*
General municipal services (sanitation and fire)	3. Mechling 1974	7. Walker 1978*
Health	4. Nelkin 1973	8. Attewell and Gerstein 1979
Multiple service sectors within same study		9. Baer et al. 1976* 10. Lambright 1977* 11. Yin 1979

*This reference is to the full study, which appeared in report form; related articles, however, were published in academic journals in each case. See McLaughlin 1976, Berman and McLaughlin 1976, Berman 1978, Walker 1975, Baer et al. 1977, and Lambright and Flynn 1977.

Multiple-site studies of implementation, but which reported only aggregate findings without explicit publication of or reference to the component individual site experiences (e.g., Murphy 1971, 1973; Downs 1976)[2]

Studies that had either no published version (even in article form) or whose only available version was too skimpy to provide enough material for analysis (e.g., Banfield 1973, Eveland et al. 1977, and the various articles in Nelson and Yates 1978)

Studies whose primary concern was only with implementation at the federal level, and in which either no local agency was involved (e.g., Mazmanian and Nienaber 1979) or the inquiry was directed at the politics and bureaucracy of federal agencies (e.g., Elmore 1975 and the articles that appear in Williams and Elmore 1976)

The final sample was thus a rather exclusive collection, and it is open to challenge on the basis of nonrepresentativeness and bias. Note, however, that the goal was not to conduct an exhaustive review of works representing the field at large. Instead, the goal was to identify the best examples of implementation studies, and to determine the methodological lessons from this elite group, in hope of improving our craft knowledge.[3] Each of the eleven studies is summarized in table 3.2. In terms of external validity, the studies cover a variety of services, technological and programmatic innovations, and sites across the country.

Topics to Be Reviewed

As noted, the methodological lessons from these studies were organized according to three questions: (1) how evidence is collected, (2) how evidence is analyzed, and (3) the reasons for believing the conclusions from such studies. These questions are different from those that have been used previously in reviewing empirical studies. Most "evaluations of evaluations," for instance, examine the measures used, the research design used, and research utilization (i.e., the degree to which an evaluation study has addressed decision-making issues and has provided relevant findings in a timely manner).[4]

The different emphasis in the present paper was related to a desire *not* to impose, beforehand, a particular paradigm on implementation or related organizational research. Thus the three selected questions are legitimate concerns regardless of whether an empirical effort falls into the standard experimental and quasi-experimental paradigm, into historical or economic analysis, or even into journalistic or legal approaches. In all these situations, as long as conclusions are drawn on the basis of empirical observations, the three questions would seem applicable. In contrast, questions about the use of research measures and design are derived from a narrower orientation, that is from behavioral and biological sciences (Nachmias 1978; Yin 1977a, 1978). Although these methodological issues may be relevant to evaluation research, their imposition on the study of implementation (as well as on investigations of related organizational processes) seems premature.

TABLE 3.2
SUMMARIES OF ELEVEN EXEMPLARY STUDIES
Single-Site Studies

1. *Pressman and Wildavsky 1973.* A study of an attempt by the U.S. Economic Development Administration to implement a special project in Oakland, California. The case study covers the experiences from 1965 to 1971, describing the several public works components of the project. The study stresses the complexity of the implementation process in terms of the number of participants, decisions, and agreements involved. The study notes the disappointing results—only a couple of hundred jobs out of a promised 3000 were produced—and the reasons for this outcome.

2. *Gross et al. 1971.* A study of changes in one New England school during a school year in the late 1960s. The innovation called for teachers to follow a "catalytic role model" where they organized classroom activities according to students' interests and with emphasis on the learning process rather than content. The case was deliberately chosen because teachers were change-oriented at the outset of the innovation, but implementation failed in spite of this low "resistance to change." The case study describes the low degree of implementation and analyzes the reasons for failure.

3. *Mechling 1974.* A study of a new manpower scheduling system implemented in New York City's Department of Sanitation. The new scheduling system called for a closer match between the daily work force and the daily work load, throughout any given week. The innovation was initially conceived in 1968 and was put into full operation by 1972. The case study calls attention to the role of analysts as change agents and traces the detailed implementation process which, while successful, was nevertheless complex and extended over a long period of time.

4. *Nelkin 1973.* A study of a methadone maintenance program initiated in an upper New York State community in 1971. The case focuses on the local conditions that led to the need for such a program, on the problems of integrating the program with an existing psychiatric clinic, and on the ultimate role conflicts between the staff and clients of the program. In spite of these problems, the program was implemented, with 14 of 51 of the clients in the program being employed a year later. The study focuses, however, both on the reasons why the program has not been more successful and why large numbers of such programs have not been initiated across the country.

Multiple-Site Studies
(each study covers a single service sector)

5. *Derthick 1972.* A multiple-site study of seven projects in a federal community development program (New Towns In-Town) with the projects located in Washington, D.C., Louisville, Atlanta, an area outside Detroit, San Antonio, New Bedford, Mass., and San Francisco. The study traces the progress at each site, covering the period from 1967 to 1971, as well as the events at the federal level that led to the design of the program. The main idea was to make federal surplus lands available to cities for the development of low-income housing. Except for two sites—at which only 300 housing units were built or under construction—the projects failed to be implemented.

TABLE 3.2*(Continued)*

6. *Berman and McLaughlin 1974-78.* A study of 293 federally funded education projects, mainly initiated at the end of the 1960s. Each project was designed to change some classroom practice at the elementary or secondary level, with a focus on bilingual projects, exemplary programs, right-to-read programs, or innovation practices more generally. The study, itself reported in several separate volumes over a period of years, consisted of a survey of officials associated with the 293 projects (over 3000 respondents were interviewed in two waves) as well as 29 case studies of a subset of the projects. It was found that few of the projects were continued after the 3- to 5-year period of federal funding. More important, however, the study articulates the implementation process and identifies this process (rather than the nature of the innovation or other factors) as a prime determinant of any continuation outcome.

7. *Walker 1978.* Five case studies of the implementation of new manpower allocation policies in urban fire departments: Wilmington, Trenton, Yonkers, Jersey City, and Denver. In each case, a new allocation plan was based on a detailed analysis of existing deployment patterns and the use of mathematical models to determine various options, with increased manpower productivity the main goal. The study describes the events in each of the five sites from about 1973 to 1977, with some sites accomplishing successful implementation and others not. The study identifies several overall reasons for implementation outcomes.

8. *Attewell and Gerstein 1979.* A study of the general disappointment with methadone maintenance programs at the local level. The implementation problem is analyzed in terms of organizational theory, noting that federal regulations and other constraints forced local clinics away from therapeutic aims and created role conflicts within the operation of the clinics. As a result, organizational control was difficult to maintain, and the clinics operated less successfully than originally envisaged.

9. *Baer et al. 1976.* A study of 24 major demonstration projects, all aimed at testing new technologies for private- or public-sector use. The cases include such undertakings as Operation Breakthrough (modular housing), the nuclear ship *Savannah,* the Connecticut Yankee power reactor, a mechanized garbage collection truck, the Morgantown (W. Va.) rapid transit system, computer-assisted electrocardiogram analysis, and expressway surveillance and control project, and other projects mainly started throughout the 1960s. Some of the projects were successfully implemented, whereas others were not. Individual case studies are used to describe the implementation experiences for each project; an aggregate analysis identified the factors associated with successfully implemented demonstration projects.

10. *Lambright 1977.* A study of 20 innovations in two New York cities—Syracuse and Rochester. The innovations were mainly attempted from the mid-1960s to the mid-1970s and cover a variety of urban services (fire, police, urban development, education, and a smattering of others) as well as "hard" and "soft" technologies (e.g., a campus plan, a minipumper, a crime control team, a dial-a-bus system, cable television, a solid-waste shredding machine, and a school resources and information program). A few of the innovations were not adopted after serious initial consideration; for the others, the study examines the organizational and political changes that occurred as the innovations came into use and as some became standard practice.

11. *Yin 1979.* A study of the implementation experiences with six kinds of innovations in different local services: police computers (police); computer-assisted instruction (education); closed-circuit television (education); mobile intensive-care units (fire); breath testing for

TABLE 3.2*(Continued)*

drunken driving (police); and an explosive device for penetrating barriers (fire). The experiences are reported as individual case studies for 19 sites, and an aggregate analysis also includes 90 other sites covered through telephone interviews. The study traces the organizational events that occur as a new practice becomes "standard" practice. These events, such as the transition from "soft" to "hard" money, the establishment of internal training routines, and survival over personnel turnover, are claimed to be similar, independent of the innovation or service.

HOW EVIDENCE IS COLLECTED
IN STUDIES OF IMPLEMENTATION

The short answer here is that evidence is collected from numerous sources. Efforts are not unlike those of the historian (e.g., Barzun and Graff 1977), except that the implementation researcher, unlike the historian, also has access to contemporary informants. Thus, the implementation studies are marked by evidence from unstructured discussion, structured interviews, documents and news reports, participant observation by the research investigator, field observations, and citation of published reports written by one or more of the participants.

Unstructured Discussions
The most common source of data was based on unstructured "discussions" (the term "interview" does not seem warranted), which are found in all eleven studies and seem to play a critical role in the ultimate formulation of conclusions. Typically, field teams visited the site of the innovation and talked to an *unstructured respondent pool* in addition to using *unstructured protocols*. The results range from a quote by an unidentified respondent about the President of the United States: "[The President] did not understand," one of his aides later said, "what a mixed blessing low-income housing was for the cities" (study 5, p. 84)[5] to a quote from an informal discussion with an unidentified teacher: "Williams [the innovator] has no classroom experience so he can't think it through; his philosophy is that it's an idea that the teacher has to work out" (study 2, p. 151).

Both facts and opinions are derived from these discussions. Often the information is not directly attributed to a specific discussion or respondent, though in most studies the names of the respondents are at least acknowledged (e.g., studies 1, 7, 11). Simply put, verbal reports by participants in the implementation process, whether directly quoted or not, seem to be a major source of evidence used in the exemplary studies.

Structured Interviews
The common use of information from unstructured discussions was not accom-

panied by frequent use of *structured interviews,* represented by closed-ended questions and formal technology. An important finding is that in only one of the single-site studies (no. 2) were such interviews used and in only two of the multiple-site studies (nos. 6 and 11) were they used. (One suspects, however, that the survey method may be used more frequently in the less-than-exemplary implementation studies.) There are several potential reasons for this low frequency of use. First, structured interviews and surveys are costly to construct and conduct. Second, and more important, such interviews can lead only to verbal reports about phenomena that may really need to be assessed in other ways. For instance, Fullan and Pomfret (1977) point out that when studies rely on "reported use" as the measure of implementation, "the problem . . . is not so much that people will deliberately deceive the researcher, but that it may only reflect an attitude of acceptance." Third, structured interviews are notoriously inefficient devices in substituting for the strength of unstructured discussions (i.e., the acquisition of "explanations" for an event or complex descriptions of a situation). In such instances, the use of a structured interview is inappropriate because an unstructured description is what is being solicited.

The possible mismatch between structured interviews and the study of implementation deserves further discussion because survey research is such a popular (and legitimate) craft that it may be inappropriately used in future studies of implementation. The strength of survey research is that it enables an investigator to construct an *incidence* report about behavior or attitudes. Thus, structured interviews can be used to show the percentage of respondents who own television sets, use a particular public service, or are satisfied with a particular innovation. To the extent that items such as practitioner or client satisfaction with an innovation are important in assessing implementation, the structured interview plays a critical role.

The technique tends to be less appropriate when an implementation study is concerned with either describing or explaining the implementation process. Thus, in all three of the studies in which structured interviews were used (studies 2, 6, 11), the evidence was not the only source of evidence about implementation. On the contrary, the structured interviews were used by all studies to complement field observations and expand the number of sites or respondents covered by the study. In other words, the implementation process represents a complex interaction, over time, among a distinctive set of key actors and events at any given site; the sum of this complexity is more than the sum of the incidence reports typically created by a survey. In addition, whereas a second strength of the survey is to tap privately known behavior (e.g., attitudes or behavioral occurrences about which only the respondent knows), the key events in the implementation process may be more publicly accessible and hence better captured through other data collection procedures.

Documents and News Reports

As with unstructured discussions, each of the eleven studies took advantage of existing documents[6] and news reports as a source of evidence. The information from these external reports was not collected by following any formal research procedure, however. None of the studies, for instance, indicated the extent of the documents that were available or the reasons for selecting the ones that were cited. In fact, the reader must give the authors the benefit of the doubt in assuming that the authors selected documents in an unbiased manner and interpreted the documents correctly. As an aid, one exemplary study (no. 7) contains reproductions of numerous news articles, so the reader can reach his or her own judgment regarding the interpretive accuracy; similarly, one of the other studies (no. 3) provides a reproduction of two key documents (agency memoranda).

The exemplary studies also varied in the degree to which specific documents were cited formally. At one extreme, the text of one study contains numerous direct quotations, and the reader is made aware, in the *Acknowledgments*, that "except for a few interviews and some peripheral searches in other agencies, the HUD records are the major source for the . . . analysis" (study 5, p. xi); nevertheless, the text actually has few footnotes, and the reader cannot attribute any individual piece of evidence to any specific document. A second study (no. 4) exhibits similar problems. At the other extreme, the text of another study (no. 1) contains numerous footnotes citing specific documents and news reports. In all, there seem to be few ground rules for current citation practice, and some standardization may be worth considering.

A more pertinent question for the present paper is to ask what these documents revealed about the implementation process. First, the documents were a major source for identifying the dates, participants, and topics of key events. For example,

> On December 9, 1956 [Economic Development (EDA) officials] made their first visit to Oakland [and neglected visiting city hall]. (study 1, p. 18)

> On February 28, the Director of Public Safety formalized the decision in a memorandum to the Chief [the document is then reproduced in the text]. (study 7, p. 620)

These are the kinds of publicly knowable events that often characterize the implementation process. Second, the documents were used to provide interpretations of or reactions to key events. This interpretative function seems critical and is exemplified by the following:

> In Louisville, in contrast to Atlanta, the local reception was poor. Where the Atlanta *Constitution* had welcomed Honor Farm as a "fine opportunity," the Louisville *Journal* was skeptical and sarcastic about Watterson Model Town. (study 5, p. 58)

As indicated in the news stories reproduced in figs. 9.1 and 9.3, [the proposals] met with a cool and hostile reception. (study 7, p. 101)

In some cases, information from available documents was combined with information from unstructured discussions. Thus, "On October 5 the Oakland program suffered a severe jolt when Eugene Foley announced his resignation as head of the EDA (study 1, p. 31)." In this example, the "fact" of the resignation was announced in an internal agency document; the interpretation regarding the "severe jolt" and its implications came from the investigator's interview with Foley.

In summary, documents and news reports allow an investigator to trace both factual and interpretative information about the implementation process. The investigator can reconstruct, post hoc, the implementation experience from many different points of view — for example, public reaction (as reflected in news accounts), participant reaction (as reflected in letters and other individually authored memoranda), and official reaction (as reflected in agency guidelines and issuances). A major lesson from this review of exemplary studies thus appears to be the need to plan for the use of documents in future studies of implementation. The documents not only provide a rich source of information but also tend to capture key aspects of the implementation process: decisions, meetings, publicly stated priorities or positions, or other public actions. Where private motives or strategies are relevant, unstructured discussions may be used to complement the use of documents. *But the information from both sources of evidence must be consistent with each other.* In fact, consistency is such an important attribute that more shall be said about it later.

Participant Observation

In only one exemplary study was the author a participant in the implementation experience (study 3).[7] "Participant" must be differentiated from "observer" in that the latter takes only a passive orientation regarding the course of events. A participant, in contrast, has a real role in the implementation process and must exercise it. (In the exemplary study cited, the author was in actuality a major impetus behind the drive toward implementation.)

Although the opportunity for participant observation in an implementation experience must be considered rare, the potential advantages and disadvantages of this source of evidence should be briefly reviewed. On the positive side, the participant observer may be able to interpret key events in a manner that extends beyond the available documentary evidence. Consider the following examples:

DeLury had informally promised Elish that the union would go along with some version of the [proposed change]. A major scare came, however,

when Kretschmer forgot and broke a personal commitment with DeLury
not to publicly discuss the new system. . . . The *Times* ran the [proposal] as
a major story . . . and DeLury and Bigel were furious.

DeLury did not publicly deny his approval of the new system, however,
and his private commitment held. Eventually his irritation with Kretschmer calmed down. (study 3, p. 287)

Such a rendition of a critical event could be pieced together only by an informant who was present during the implementation experience; throughout
this exemplary study, there are similar interpretations about the motives of key
actors, the importance of external events and personnel turnover, and the strategies behind specific actions or policies.

On the negative side, the objectivity of the participant observer can always
be open to question. Even where events are not purposely being misconstrued,
the participant observer — by virtue of the participatory experience — may recall
events selectively or may arrive at an egocentric interpretation that is incorrect.
Thus, to give the reader more confidence about such evidence, there should be
ways that, at least in theory, the evidence can be confirmed. In the preceding
quotation, for instance, the people's names that are referred to are real; in principle, one could have consulted both the *Times* story and the names of persons
to check the author's interpretation.[8]

Field Observation
Most but not all of the eleven exemplary studies made some direct observations
of the implementation process in progress.[9] These observations were typically
made during "site visits" for brief periods of time to at least a subset of the sites
studied. The observations were mainly of an informal nature, in which the investigators saw the activities associated with the implementation experience
(e.g., organizational operations; the material artifacts of the innovation such as
its hardware, training manuals, or products; and the actual use of the innovation in practice).

In two studies, the investigators were actually on the scene for extended periods, and the observations were formally tabulated; the tabulations later ful-
filled an important part of the study. In the first study (no. 2) the degree of implementation of an educational innovation was claimed to be reflected only by
actual changes in practitioner roles and behavior. Thus, a key source of evidence for this study came from the use of observational protocols in individual
classrooms; the amount of time spent in different roles by the classroom teacher
was noted and tabulated (study 2, pp. 108-16). The results of these tabulations
were interpreted by using other sources of evidence (e.g., unstructured discus-

sions and formal interview data). However, the tabulations themselves stand as the major source of evidence that implementation has not occurred to any great degree. In the other study (no. 3) a major conclusion had to do with the role of analysts as "change agents." To support this conclusion the author estimated, from his own observations, the amount of time that analysts spend in performing "analytic" vs. "staff" vs. "change agent" roles. The final tabulation is presented in the text (study 3, p. 303).

If an implementation experience is in progress as a study is being conducted, the use of field observations seems to provide information that is complementary to that found in documents or derived from discussions and interviews. As with participant observation, the observations are a form of evidence that is not dependent on verbal behavior; an investigator can get underneath the labels and concepts used in either documents or discussions and observe a phenomenon directly. Naturally, there are also potential problems. Most site visits, for instance, are scheduled for brief periods of time and on a casual basis; as a result, the operations or behavior observed may not be representative of the site's normal activities. (Although it should also be pointed out that a site would have to go to considerable trouble to alter certain observable items, such as physical layouts of space and facilities, which may be important to the study.) In general, the more time spent at a site, the more confidence one can have in the observable results.

Citation of Participants' Published Reports

A final manner in which evidence was collected was through publications written by participants in the implementation experience. This kind of evidence was available and used extensively in one study (no. 1), to help explain a motive or provide information about reactions to key events. Similar evidence was also available in another study (no. 8, p. 312), but was not cited as such or used in any specific place. None of the other studies had occasion to use this kind of evidence.

The occasions on which participants' own written reports about an implementation experience have been published are, of course, likely to be rare. Moreover, as with participant observation, the potential bias of the participant must be questioned. Nevertheless, publications by participants do occur in major public policy situations (one need think only of the numerous first-person books about the Watergate coverup) and do represent another available source of evidence.

Use of Multiple Sources of Evidence

The previous subsections have noted the various ways in which evidence has been collected in the exemplary studies of implementation. Some strengths and weaknesses of these sources have been pointed out, and no single source stands alone as the best for studying implementation or organizational processes. Indeed, one of the major lessons is that two or more of these sources should be used in any given study of implementation.

The use of multiple sources of evidence was a major feature of all eleven studies. The multiple sources were used mainly to achieve two different purposes, roughly analogous to the concerns with *internal* and *external validity* in experimental research design. First, multiple sources were used within a single case study to demonstrate a certain degree of consistency and corroboration about implementation events and interpretation (internal validity). If information from an unstructured discussion is consistent with information from existing documents or field observations, for instance, the researcher's interpretation is more credible. This is not to say that implementation events necessarily have an objective truth; specific "facts of the matter" may differ, depending on the perspective of the particular actor. However, the multiple sources can and should be used to support the existence of these different perspectives, and even to explain them.

The use of multiple sources of evidence to achieve this first purpose of internal consistency and corroboration may sound somewhat like data collection methods in the field of history, where historians are taught to assemble different documents in writing their histories (e.g., Barzun and Graff 1977). A major difference with regard to implementation is that a contemporary event is usually the subject of study. This means that individuals who have participated in the implementation experience are available for interview, and direct observations about the events in question may also be made. These additional sources of information provide a rich and sometimes essential body of knowledge; but this information, with the partial exception of oral history projects, is not generally part of the historian's repertoire. To this extent, the multiple use of evidence in implementation studies is different from the multiple use followed in the field of history.

The second purpose for using multiple sources of evidence was to extend the scope of study to cover more sites (external validity). As mentioned, multiple-site studies can be based on more intensive investigation of a few sites, combined with formal interviewing or other methods to cover (more superficially) a larger number of sites. The intensively investigated sites usually provide that basic information for interpreting and explaining the implementation process; the superficially investigated sites allow the investigator to expand the generalizability of the findings.

In summary, one of the methodological strengths of the exemplary studies of implementation seems to be their use of multiple sources of evidence. The plans for future studies should therefore explicitly call for multiple approaches and involve investigators who have a demonstrated ability to deal with more than one approach. Of the methods described, most future efforts should at least include the use of unstructured discussions, the examination of documents and news reports, and the use of field observations. Whether structured interviews, participant observation, or published reports by the participants can also be used will vary with the individual study. Whatever the combination, however, the collection of evidence is only one major step in the study of implementation. An equally important step is how evidence is analyzed, and to this topic we now turn.

HOW EVIDENCE IS ANALYZED
IN STUDIES OF IMPLEMENTATION

By its loosest but still acceptable definition, "analysis" consists of a sifting, sorting, and combinatorial process. Various pieces of evidence are categorized, compared, and contrasted (e.g., Selltiz, Wrightsman, and Cook 1976, pp. 456-79). Where the evidence takes a quantitative form, analysis can be conducted through mathematical operations. In other situations the analytic procedures are not so formalized, and researchers must follow a course of logical thinking that can be validated only by peer judgments or basic craft rules.[10]

By this definition, the analytic process was conducted in several ways by the exemplary implementation studies. This included a preanalysis step, a piecing together of the "facts" of the implementation experience, a merging of the evidence from various sources, an aggregating of single-site experiences (for the multiple-site studies), and most important, a testing of alternative explanations. Each of these procedures is described in the following subsections.

Preanalysis
Overfamiliarity with experimental research leads one to the simplistic belief that "data collection" and "data analysis" are completely isolatable steps. When one conducts an experiment, for instance, the pertinent variables are identified beforehand, data are collected, and analysis follows. In nonexperimental fields, however, whether a social science or a profession such as law or journalism, these two steps are not so clearly differentiated. In particular, *analysis may occur as part of the process of collecting evidence.* The analysis typically consists

of on-the-spot judgments whereby certain evidence is admitted into the body of a study, while other evidence is ignored.[11] This selection process is essential in studying an organizational process like implementation because the researcher's problem is that there is too much information that is potentially relevant. As Eugene Bardach (1977) has so aptly noted in comparing *implementation* (a complex process that occurs over a long period of time) with *adoption* (a specific decision—not necessarily unitary—that nevertheless occurs within a limited amount of time):

> When one sets out to study the policy-*adoption* process, one has at least a starting point: the authoritative body, like a legislature, that has made [or will make] the ultimate decision on the issue. From there one can trace the various influences that led up to the decision. The nature of phenomenon thus restricts the scope of the relevant data . . . *the nature of the implementation process is exactly the opposite:* instead of becoming concentrated in one place, it gets dispersed at every place. (Bardach 1977, pp. 310-11; emphasis mine)

The selection process, as well as other implicit analytic steps that occur during the data collection phase, is part of what may be called "preanalysis." Among the exemplary studies, the extent of preanalysis varied widely. In several studies (nos. 1, 4, 5, 8, 10) the researchers clearly had access to a vast amount of initial information, only some of which became a formal part of the subsequent study. For most of the single-site studies (or the single-site components of the multiple-site studies), the preanalysis methodology was rarely described or even addressed as an issue. In one exception (study 11, p. 16), the preanalysis step consisted of the development of an explicit *chain of evidence,* in which links between data collection protocols, narrative case studies, and "key events" were deliberately fashioned; the key events then became the data base for the aggregate analysis. In other studies (e.g., nos. 2 and 6) certain quantitative evidence was used and was therefore specified more clearly through the use of an interview instrument or other observational protocols.

Even though the selection process was not well described in most of the exemplary studies, its nature can well be imagined. Whether researchers are working with unstructured discussions or available documents, some notes or records must be created. Ultimately it may be presumed that the notes or records will serve as part of the researcher's information base and thus constitute the "evidence" to be considered part of the study. The first phase of the selection process has already taken place, however, because the researcher has had to decide on the information to be entered into the notes or records. Clearly, not every piece of information will have been entered, and the implicit rules by which certain information is ignored becomes the essence of the selection process.

Other preanalysis activities may include decisions regarding (1) the way that key concepts can be made operational (e.g., data found in the field may suggest a different set of measures than originally planned), (2) the depth and detail for pursuing a line of inquiry, and (3) the evolution of "categories" or classification schemes whereby notes are initially recorded. In experimental research, most of these activities are part of a study's "research design" and are normally specified ahead of time. In the exemplary studies of implementation, as with studies of organizational processes more generally, a formal research design cannot usually be so specific, and the preanalysis activities go largely undescribed. Even so, a more rigid research design would prevent an investigator from fully exploiting field opportunities.

Piecing Together the "Facts" of the Implementation Experience
In dealing with single-site studies (or the single-site reports of multiple-site studies), the most common form of analysis is the piecing together of the major events in the implementation experience. These events have to do with organizational changes, critical meetings, personnel turnover, or other activities that form part of the implementation experience. The piecing-together process is considered an analytic step because some classification scheme, or set of categories, must be used.

The reporting of these events was done in several ways by the exemplary studies. A few of the studies (nos. 1, 3, 4) contained a formal chronology of events, of which a sample is illustrated in table 3.3. The sample shows both the activities and the fact that a temporal sequence is the organizing theme. Other studies (e.g., the individual case studies found in nos. 5, 7, 9) did not construct a formal chronology, but the narrative description of the individual site reports was organized according to a chronological sequence. Finally, a third approach was to organize major portions of the text of the entire study according to a general sequence of phases or stages of events over time (e.g., studies 2, 10, 11).

The use of temporal sequence to piece together the facts of the implementation experience should not be taken for granted. The temporal sequence is a significant analytic step because it allows the researchers to establish the basis for some causal inferences. In general, as with historical analysis, a set of earlier events can be considered candidates for having caused the occurrence of a set of later events (at a minimum, such a sequencing eliminates the possibility of using later events as causal explanations of earlier events). Nevertheless, it should not be assumed that temporal sequencing is the only way of organizing a text; the experimental paradigm, for instance, does not follow such a sequence, and there have been many narratives of organizational processes (though none among the exemplary studies) organized topically rather than temporally.

TABLE 3.3
ILLUSTRATIVE CHRONOLOGY FROM
ONE YEAR OF NELKIN'S 1973 STUDY

1970	
March	Boudreau discusses possibilities of methadone maintenance program with St. Joseph's Hospital and Dr. Pittenger.
April	Boudreau submits application for accreditation of the methadone program to the NACC for $162,000 for fiscal year ending March 31, 1971. Announces plans to seek local and state approval.
June	Negotiations between the county Department of Mental Health and St. Joseph's Hospital.
August 25	Health Committee of Onondaga County Legislature approves proposal and provides a $25,000 loan to initiate a program.
September 10	NACC approves county application and funded $99,523 from September 1, 1970, to March 31, 1971. Accreditation given through August 31, 1972.
	County legislature unanimously approves program.
September 15	Request for FDA forms and approval procedures. Request for approval procedures from Internal Revenue Service. St. Joseph's Hospital is informed of application procedures and FDA forms are sent to the hospital.
September 22	Application for certification and registration is sent to New York State Bureau of Narcotics Control.
September	Negotiations concerning required laboratory support.
October 1	Intended opening date.
October 16	State Department of Health application is sent to St. Joseph's Hospital.
December 24	County Department of Mental Health fills out FDA form when it is realized that hospital had not yet done so.

In addition to temporal sequencing, implementation events were pieced together in other ways. In one of the exemplary studies (no. 1), for instance, the investigators were strongly interested in the apparent complexity of the implementation process. They defined the notion of the complexity as a function of the number of decision points and participants involved in their single-site study. Thus, a key part of the analysis consisted of a tabulation of decision points that occurred during implementation, with the findings that there were 30 such points, involving the necessity for some 70 different agreements among numerous participants (study 1, pp. 103-6). The investigators then went on to make inferences about the effects of the number of decision points on implementation delays and the probability of implementation success.

Merging Evidence from Various Sources
Another analytic step common to all the exemplary studies was the merging of

evidence from various data sources. All the studies, as noted, had employed multiple sources of evidence. This approach to data collection thus necessitated, at the analytic stage, some commingling process.

The commingling process was done by both informal and formal means. An informal approach has been described earlier, when it was noted that documentary information could be combined with evidence from unstructured discussions, to assemble the implementation experience (see section on Documents and News Reports). This was a common step for combining these two kinds of evidence and characterized most of the descriptions of individual site experiences. This approach was usually conducted in such an informal manner, however, that the reader could not always tell when such merging had occurred. It is assumed, for instance, that narrative descriptions containing no formal footnotes or citations (e.g., studies 4, 5, 8) but in which introductory passages indicated the use of several sources of evidence, reflect the merging of evidence from these various sources.

More formal approaches to the commingling process typically occurred where studies had collected more than one kind of quantitative evidence. For instance, tabulations of field observations could be compared with tabulations from interview data (e.g., study 2), with the inferences from each tabulation compared to arrive at a consistent picture of the implementation experience. In this particular exemplary study, this procedure was also followed by merging information from unstructured discussions with that from formal interviews, giving the reader confidence that each finding was based on the entire repertoire of potentially relevant evidence. Similarly, a second study examined separate tabulations, covering identical issues, but where one set of evidence came from an intensively studied set of sites and the other set of evidence came from telephone interviews (study 11, pp. 139-56). However, in both these and other instances, the exemplary studies did not actually merge the evidence through the use of any formal, mathematical operation; what merging occurred really consisted of analytic comparisons of the findings from the various sources of evidence.

In a few cases, mathematical operations were used to create complex measures, based on several variables, but from the same source of evidence. Thus, one study defined its basic measure of implementation from a combination of questions from formal interviews representing "a coding from a variety of questions" (study 6, 7:151-52).

Aggregating Experiences from More Than a Single Site
This analytic step was characteristic only of the multiple-site studies, where there was a need to derive general findings and conclusions on the basis of ob-

servations made at several implementation sites. The exemplary studies coped
differently with the aggregation problem. Most commonly, each multiple-site
study contained a narrative portion that aggregated the lessons from individual
sites by "naming" each site whenever it was relevant. Thus, a typical text from
one multiple-site study, in which all the component sites are named, is the following:

> Four years after the start of the surplus land program, only 120 units of
> housing had been built. At Fort Lincoln, where this housing stood, no
> other construction was under way. In Clinton Township [outside Detroit],
> 160 units were being built. In Atlanta, a developer was ready to start, but
> was being delayed by a citizens' suit. In Louisville, approval had only re-
> cently been received from the board of aldermen. In San Antonio, New
> Bedford, and San Francisco, the projects had been cancelled. This chapter
> analyzes why the program produced so little. (study 5, p. 83)

A slightly more formal version of this narrative approach was to present
simple tabulations of the relevant characteristic at each site so that the reader
could independently discern the validity of the aggregate observation. One
study's main conclusion had to do with the importance of a "bureaucracy-cen-
tered entrepreneur" in the implementation process (study 10, *Analysis and Conclusions* volume, pp. 169-82). The support for this conclusion was provided by
identifying and tabulating the presence or absence of such an entrepreneur for
each of the component sites, and by showing that such an entrepreneur did exist
in a majority of the cases. A similar approach was used in another study, which
conceptualized the implementation and institutionalization process as a function of 10 organizational "passages and cycles" (study 11). The occurrence
of each passage and cycle, as well as their sequence, was formally tabulated
throughout the study as the basic measure of the degree to which implementation or institutionalization occurred. Tabulations, in the form of matrix presen-
tations, were also used in a third study (no. 9) that searched for characteristics
of successful demonstration projects (see table 3.4).[12]
    Other studies coped with the aggregation process in somewhat less con-
vincing fashion. One multiple study (no. 8) did not enumerate the individual
sites at any point in the text, merely discussing the "modal" site throughout the
analysis. This approach may be justifiable with such a program as methadone
maintenance clinics, where the implementation of clinic operations may have
followed a similar course of events at different sites. However, an explicit enumeration of the individual sites would normally have been more preferable. In
two other studies (nos. 6 and 7) there also was little articulated connection—
either through narrative "naming" or through formal tabulations—between aggregate statements and the experiences at individual sites.[13]

TABLE 3.4
ILLUSTRATIVE TABULATION OF
MULTIPLE SITES FROM BAER ET AL. 1976

SHARE OF FEDERAL FUNDING	Little or None	Some	Significant
Less than 50%	Breakthrough	Connecticut Yankee ECG	Yankee
50% to 90%	Minneapolis Corridor Desalination (Freeport)	Resource Recovery Godzilla	RFD Poultry Waste Shipbuilding Chicago Expressway Desalination (Pt. Loma)
90% or more	FPC* Savannah PRT Medicaid*	Marisat Dial-A-Ride (manual)	Hydraulic Knee

DIFFUSION SUCCESS

*100% federal funding.

Testing Alternative Explanations

Overall, no single analytic step was as important as the testing of alternative explanations. In fact, this step may, in itself, capture the essence of studying implementation and other organizational processes. Viewed another way, this step represents the culmination of the other analytic steps; after a preanalysis, a piecing together of the facts, the merging of various kinds of evidence, and the aggregation of single-site experiences, the investigator is left with the task of *explaining why implementation occurred as it did*.

Explanation Construction and Testing

The construction of an adequate explanation is a complex and difficult affair. No formal definitions of an "explanation" exist, and no descriptions of the methodologies whereby explanations should be constructed or tested. The key to an explanation is that it should identify a causal sequence that covers the relevant facts of the implementation experience. Notions of "elegance" and "parsimony," as used in logic and philosophy, are also relevant. Yet one must note that the researcher must determine the scope of the "relevant facts," as well as the reasonable levels of parsimony or elegance.

An analogous example derives from the craft of detective work whereby a detective must construct an explanation for a crime. Presented with the scene of the crime, its description, and possible reports from eyewitnesses, the detective must constantly make decisions regarding the relevance of various factors. Some facts of the case are clearly likely to be misleading or unrelated to the crime; other clues must be recognized as such and pursued vigorously. The adequate explanation for the crime then becomes a plausible rendition of a motive, opportunity, and modus operandi. If the detective is then confronted with another case in which the relevant factors appear to be similar to those of the first case, he or she may try to test the first explanation and establish that both crimes were committed by the same perpetrator. Note that modification may be necessary in the second explanation—and the detective must learn how to ignore irrelevant variations from case to case, even though the same modus operandi is involved. How the detective carries out this work (1) in initially determining what is relevant, (2) in then constructing an adequate explanation of what has occurred, and (3) in knowing the acceptable levels of modification in the original explanation as new cases are encountered may be considered a task analogous to what confronts the researcher who studies implementation.[14]

One of the few descriptions of this research task may be found in one of Donald Campbell's lesser-known articles (1975). In this article Campbell defends the rationale for conducting one-shot case studies, a research design he had previously discredited (Campbell and Stanley 1966). According to Campbell, the search for an explanation is a kind of *pattern-matching* process. The process can be applied even if there is only a single case because the pattern requires a fit based on the multiple implications derived from an explanation or theory about the case. Thus, it is incorrect to judge this situation by the norms of experimental design, which would stipulate that a single-case study (or even a small group of cases) could never provide a compelling rationale for establishing the importance of a single factor (or determinant).[15] An explanation, not a single factor, is what is being tested, and this accounts for the frequent outcome where "even in a single qualitative case study the conscientious social scientist often finds no explanation that seems satisfactory. Such an outcome would be impossible if [single factors were being tested]—there would instead be a surfeit of subjectively compelling explanations" (Campbell 1975, p. 182).

More research needs to be done in defining explanations and the pattern-matching process. Nevertheless, even this preliminary description by Campbell sounds much like the analogy from detective work and like the analytic approaches followed in the exemplary studies.

The exemplary studies dealt with the explanation problem in three different ways. First, two studies (nos. 3 and 4) provided no explanation of the implementation experience, nor did they purport to do so. The studies contain only a description of the experience, but the description is so rich and insightful that the reader is tempted to develop his or her own explanation of why implementation succeeded. (In one study, no. 4, explanations are offered, but on topics other than implementation.)

Second, most of the studies did attempt to construct explanations of the implementation process, whether based on single- or multiple-site experiences. Two studies made it clear, early in the text, that the overarching objective of the study was to arrive at a satisfactory explanation, and the reader is constantly faced with this challenge. In the first study, the goal was to explain implementation failure in spite of a low initial resistance to change (study 2, pp. 7-10);[16] in the second study, the explanation had to cover an initially sensible idea for a federal program that nevertheless failed in its implementation at seven sites (study 5, p. 21). This study provides an excellent example of how a researcher develops an initial explanation and "carries" the full explanation from site to site, modifying the explanation along the way. Three other studies (nos. 6, 10, 11) demonstrated their arrival at an explanation through a prescriptive mode; the texts of these studies conclude with strategies and policy recommendations that therefore imply knowledge of causal process.

Third, two other studies (one a single-site study and the other a multiple-site study) not only constructed an explanation and tested it against the study's own evidence but also compared explanations with those from other studies (no. 1, pp. 90-91, 142; and no. 8, pp. 325-26). One study (no. 1) concludes its comparative discussion by noting that "in both the new towns [a study conducted by a previous investigator] and the Oakland EDA programs [the subject of the present study], we find similar phenomena: federal grandeur, inadequate local support, and a divorce of implementation from policy" (p. 142). Ironically, the other study (no. 8) concludes by modifying the explanations offered by study no. 1, suggesting that the nature of federal-local interactions will differ, depending on whether federal policies have relatively little control over a local phenomenon (as in economic and community development) or in fact assert a monopolistic control (as in supporting the operation of methadone maintenance clinics).

Determinants Approach

At least two studies (nos. 7 and 9) followed a slightly deviant approach to this analytic step. Instead of attempting to construct an explanation of the implementation experience, these studies tried to identify the key determinants associated with implementation success or failure.[17] The determinants approach is different from the explanatory approach in that the identification of key determinants does not in itself provide a causal description of how an organizational process occurs (Mohr 1978). For instance, a determinant might be the observation that " . . . the greater the participation of different interest groups in the overall project, the more likely the success of the implementation" (study 7, p. 4). Such an observation, even if combined with the identification of other key determinants, does not provide an explanation of how and why implementation occurs. One study that followed the determinants approach (study 9) later did try to construct an explanation in terms of policy recommendations regarding the design of future demonstration projects (compare parts 1 and 2 of the summary report). The basic evidence of the study was cast in terms of identifying determinants rather than analyzing processes, however, and thus it is difficult to have confidence in these later policy recommendations.[18]

By its design, the determinants approach falls short of providing a full explanation. Again, to refer to the analogous situation of detective work, one can imagine the dissatisfaction if a detective were to conclude with the observation that the determinants of a series of crimes were a particular kind of household, a certain time of day, and a common weapon. The observation of these determinants would in actuality be the *beginning,* not the *concluding* step, in constructing an explanation of how, why, and by whom the crimes had been committed. In short, the determinants must lead to a fuller theoretical statement that yields the necessary understanding or explanation of the causal process (e.g., Yin 1977*b*).

Interestingly, the worst offenders of the determinants approach have not been the exemplary studies where, as we have seen, only one or two studies erred in this direction. Unfortunately, the worst offenders tend to be those who have attempted to synthesize, through secondary review, the results of numerous empirical studies (e.g., Zaltman et al. 1973, Rothman 1974, Public Affairs Counseling 1976, Fullan and Pomfret 1977). Each of these reviews typically arranges its text by sequentially reviewing the findings on key factors or determinants of organizational change (e.g., factors involving the nature of the innovation, the nature of the innovating agency, the external environment, and so forth). According to one analyst (Mohr 1978), these attempts to identify individual determinants are part of a "variance theory" approach in which the main research result is to account for statistical variation in some dependent variable. The approach is thus not surprisingly bereft of helpful insights; a "process theory" approach—describing the causal steps in some detail—is what is really needed. The variance theory approach, in short, does not provide insights into the way that the innovation or implementation process might work.

In contrast, studies and reviews could set out to compare alternative and competing explanations. One example of such an approach is Richard Elmore's discussion of four models of program implementation: systems management, bureaucratic process, organizational development, and conflict bargaining (Elmore 1978). Each model, based on an existing body of empirical research, is a full narrative description of an alternative explanation of why implementation occurs or fails to occur. The descriptions cover the basic assumptions of each model in terms of how organizations work, the philosophical and value-laden differences among the models, and finally, the alternative (and in some cases, competing) predictions derivable from each model.

To summarize this portion of the discussion, the most important analytic challenge is to construct and test an explanation of the implementation experience. When evidence comes only from a single site, the explanation can nevertheless be "tested" by (1) attending to the pattern of results and (2) determining the degree to which the pattern matches that predicted by the explanation. When evidence has been collected from two or more sites, the same procedure may be augmented by applying the full explanation to each site individually, with the explanation being modified as each site is considered. In contrast, the enumeration of a set of determinants is an insufficient substitute for this explanation-testing process.

REASONS FOR BELIEVING THE CONCLUSIONS OF IMPLEMENTATION STUDIES

The preceding sections have traced the ways in which exemplary studies of implementation have been conducted, focusing on the collection and analysis of evidence. Many specific examples have been cited to guide future researchers in conducting their own studies of implementation or of organizational processes more generally. Another theme has also emerged that the alert reader should have caught and that requires explicit attention: The research craft or methods associated with these implementation studies appear not to be rigidly defined or even very rigorous by standard laboratory or research criteria. Thus, for instance, a preanalysis step seems critical to the amassing of evidence but is rarely described; "unstructured discussions" are a common source of evidence; multiple sources of evidence are commonly used, but the way the varied evidence is later merged is not a formalized procedure; and the culminating step — explanation building and testing — seems to follow few methodological guidelines.

In the light of this state of affairs, why should a reader believe the results of these exemplary studies? Moreover, why are they *exemplary* studies? Could the rest of the lot be that much worse? These and related questions cannot go unanswered if the goal is to advance craft knowledge, and the purpose of the present section is to suggest that good answers may actually be available.

Formal Methodological Discussions
One obvious answer — that each study contained a detailed methodological

statement that justified its choices or indicated an awareness of potential biases and shortcomings—turns out to be an incorrect one. Of the eleven exemplary studies only four (nos. 2, 6, 9, 11) had what could be regarded as comprehensive methodological discussions, covering site selection, data collection procedures, and copies of key protocols or instruments. Moreover, one of these four studies makes a strong reservation in warning the reader about its methods:

> . . . the research aim was not to test hypotheses but to enable the formulation of hypotheses. . . . Our operational measurements of both independent and dependent variables can be challenged . . . the selectivity of our sample raises questions about the generalizability of the findings; and the statistical procedures and the interpretation of the results are open to valid criticism and alternative interpretations. These caveats notwithstanding. . . . (study 6, 7:viii)

A fifth study (no. 10) contained a very brief methodological discussion, mainly covering the issues of site selection. However, the remainder of the studies had virtually no discussion of their methodologies; what few words were said usually appeared in a brief footnote or in the acknowledgments.

The absence of formal methodological discussions may, in retrospect, have been a collectively wise choice. Such discussions would probably have revealed a whole host of shortcomings, by any criteria derived from experimental research, and would also have been difficult to describe because of the varied methods that we have seen were used. For many of these studies, the development of a methodological discussion might even have led, paradoxically, to a decreased sense of confidence in the study and its results.

Clearly the authors, many of whom hold esteemed academic or applied research positions, relied on some other factors to give the reader confidence in the results and conclusions. These factors may be said to fall into two categories—internal and external credibility—concepts that seem useful for judging this kind of research in the future.

Internal Credibility

Internal credibility stems from the information and evidence presented in the body of a study itself. Such credibility was bolstered in several ways by the exemplary studies, the most important of which was the correctness of the basic facts of the implementation experience. Although such facts are always disputable, many of the key implementation events, as noted, tended to be publicly knowable events in that newspaper accounts or other official records could be checked to confirm the researcher's narrative. At the same time, the strength of the researcher's case did not necessarily rest on the absolute correctness of every single fact. The main strength usually lay in the overall pattern of events, where the misconstruing of one or two events would not be enough to call the entire rendition into question. Moreover, the difficulty of constructing this overall pattern should not be overlooked. The authors of the various exemplary studies all seemed to have spent considerable effort in covering different sources of evidence and producing a thorough description of the implementation experiences at individual sites. Thus a first requirement for internal credibility, met by most of the exemplary studies, was the provision of a clear factual account of the implementation experience.

Added to the integrity of the basic facts of the implementation experience was another feature that increased the credibility of a study. This was the researcher's recognition of different points of view by the various participants in the implementation experience.[19] Such recognition constitutes an acknowledgment that most organizational changes, by dint of different role perspectives, are likely to involve conflicting viewpoints. Organizational change, simply put, is not usually a congenial process. Most of the exemplary studies were able to construct explanations that not only accounted for the various events but also appreciated the different viewpoints.

One of the more extreme examples of this phenomenon of appreciating different viewpoints also suggests a high degree of sensitivity on the part of the investigators. In this example, the issue under discussion was that of the value differences between practitioners and analysts in a study of manpower changes in local agencies. The analytic approach had been primarily based on the concept and measurement of *travel time,* or the amount of time required for a fire vehicle to travel to the scene of a fire alarm. The analysis had shown how agencies could make manpower reductions without affecting travel time (or could decrease travel time by rearranging existing resources). However, the analytic results were continually called into question by the firefighters at one of the implementation sites. The firefighters did not seem to disagree with any of the finer points of the analysis. As described in one newspaper account quoted by the study: "The dispute hinges on the firefighters' refusal . . . to accept, for purpose of decision making, the validity of travel time as a performance measure. . . . The firemen argue that *it's the men who put out the fires, not the response time"* (study 7, pp. 64 and 73; emphasis mine).

In a way, the firefighters had a legitimate point of view. As so frequently happens in situations of this sort, disagreements arise over the fundamental assumptions made by one participant or another, not over a particular approach or methodology. Yet this state of affairs has seldom been recognized.

Finally, internal credibility was bolstered by the knowledge that the participants in the implementation experience could and did have an opportunity to voice their opinions about the researcher's findings. In one study, a key participant actually wrote the foreword to the study; in another, the individual site descriptions were given for review, in draft form, to the persons interviewed as part of the study. In the other studies, because the implementation events were relatively recent and highly visible, participants could have been asked to comment, if needed, to corroborate the findings.[20]

External Credibility

External credibility, in contrast to internal credibility, is based on *inferences* about a study, how it was conducted, and the researcher's previous work. For the exemplary studies, credibility in the results and conclusions was especially enhanced by two external criteria: the researcher's reputation for scholarly endeavors and the broad level of effort involved in conducting the study.

Judgments about a researcher's reputation are difficult to make. In all but one of the exemplary studies, however, the researchers had developed multiyear associations with the research topic studied and with the research community at large.[21] In all but one case (study 3), for instance, the researchers had previously published books or articles on organizational topics similar to those of the exemplary studies, either in the form of prior case studies of agency experiences or in the form of publications on related technologies. This extended career interest gives the reader additional confidence that the researcher issues in the exemplary study have been carefully considered over a broad period of time. Although there are occasional injustices in using this criterion to make judgments about researchers (e.g., see Merton 1968), the main point is that these investigators were no "instant experts." Furthermore, most of them did their research within a broad organizational context, whether academically based or not, that reinforced a career interest in the implementation topic.

The second external criterion had to do with the time and effort put into these exemplary studies and their general breadth and depth of coverage. One substantive lesson about implementation is that it is a complex process that can take several years to complete. Thus, as noted by one of the exemplary studies: "The picture that results . . . even for an innovation so straightforward as manpower rescheduling, is one of great complexity. A large number of people, many decisions, and a long period of time were required before a new manpower scheduling system became an operating reality" (study 3, p. 301).

In this case, the implementation process took four years from the initial conception of the idea within city government to full operation within one of its agencies. In other cases, equally long periods of time were involved; for instance, for federally supported implementation projects in education, the typical award period was three to five years (study 6). For innovations in broader fields such as community or economic development, the implementation process can be even longer and involve even more participants and decision points.

If the implementation process is assumed to be such an extensive affair, it is safe to conclude that investigators will be more expert in their judgments if they spend more time and effort in conducting their studies. The exemplary studies, especially when judged against the typically brief time period allowed by sponsored research, were genuinely exemplary in this regard. First, all but one of the multiple-site studies were large-scale team efforts in which several senior investigators contributed to the final effort. Second, in several of the studies the investigators actually spent lengthy periods of time "on-line" with the implementation experience, ranging from a full academic year of field observations (study 2) to three calendar years of participant observation (study 3). Third, most of the studies, where funded by an external agency, involved multiyear awards. One study, for instance, noted that the implementation report represented "the culmination of 5 years of support for the documentation, testing, and evaluation of methods" (study 7, p. v). Another study (no. 6), as judged by a third party (Fullan and Pomfret 1977), was the most comprehensive study of implementation in the field of education and was also conducted over a five-year period. Fourth, the published version of several of the studies was sometimes only the tip of the iceberg, with numerous student papers and lesser efforts also known to have been part of the overall project (e.g., study 1). All these factors serve to raise confidence that the implementation experiences were well analyzed.

To return, then, to the initial set of questions regarding the credibility of these studies, the basic conclusion is that *various factors other than formal methodological discussions* give the reader adequate reason to have trust in the results and conclusions from these studies.

Concluding Comments

This conclusion seems consistent with the notion that craft knowledge in the study of implementation and related organizational processes may be just in its infancy. A mature field, by contrast, is more likely to have formalized methodological procedures.

The findings also suggest several ways in which implementation research may be improved in the future. First, the collection of evidence on implementation was found to consist of the use of multiple sources of information. Most of these data collection methods have been documented in typical methodological textbooks, but the unique flavor in the implementation studies is that the investigator must be facile with the entire variety. *Methodological generalists* rather than specialists may therefore be increasingly needed if implementation research is to thrive. How one trains such generalists, identifies them in research proposals, or judges their qualifications are issues that should be of concern to universities and research-funding agencies.

Second, the analysis of evidence was found to consist of a number of activities (e.g., explanation building, preanalysis, piecing together of the facts) for which there has been little methodological research or documentation. Unlike the situation with data collection methods, existing textbooks rarely address these analytic activities. One suggestion for improving future research is that investigators who currently conduct implementation studies ought to be asked to be introspective about their analytic craft. The introspections should become part of the public record, and a body of methodological knowledge may emerge. Such efforts of course could be enhanced by the initiation of formal methodological research projects.

Third, the absence of formal methodological statements in implementation and related studies should not be considered, at this time, a serious deficiency. The craft is simply not well established, and a formal methodology might become a counterproductive straightjacket. Nevertheless, the ability to make formal methodological statements should be an increasing goal in the future. Without the development of formal methodologies, research on implementation will probably continue to be limited to seasoned investigators; because there is only a limited number of such investigators, substantive breakthroughs on implementation are likely to be intermittent and sparse. In contrast, the development of formal methodologies should be seen as a way of allowing a larger pool of investigators to participate in implementation research—at the same time retaining a high level of research rigor. The formalization of craft knowledge, in brief, permits more investigators to participate in a research field, thereby creating increased competition, more opportunities for corroboratory findings, a greater abundance of ideas, and other conditions through which substantive knowledge can only benefit. The present paper has made a small step toward formalization simply by enumerating and analyzing the methods used in exemplary studies of implementation.

NOTES

1. One study that was seriously considered for inclusion was Bardach (1977). However, the main contributions of this book are to the development of implementation theory, and the book reports on its own empirical study only in a fragmentary manner. Another study that actually could have been included was nevertheless considered redundant with the Mechling (1974) study, which was one of the 11 selected. This was a study of a policy manpower allocation innovation (Moore et al. 1974), taking place at a similar time and with similar actors to those in the Mechling study, and using similar methods.

2. Even though the primary interest may have been cross-site conclusions, this constraint was necessary to facilitate judgments regarding the kind of evidence used by the investigator.

3. One review of an ostensibly larger number of studies, though limited to the field of education, is an article by Fullan and Pomfret (1977). This article identified 15 studies of educational implementation; but a closer examination reveals that most of the studies were conference papers, theses, and other consultant reports that often contain incomplete results and are unreviewed by referees or colleagues. In addition, at least one study was about an implementation experience in the United Kingdom, which would seem to have a dubious relevance to the problems of American governance. Because of the disparate nature of the collected works, the applicability of the aggregate conclusions is unclear.

4. See Yin et al. (1976) for a discussion of the various approaches used in secondary analyses or "evaluations" of evaluation studies.

5. For simplicity's sake, the 11 studies have been numbered in table 3.1 and will be cited in the remainder of this chapter according to the appropriate number.

6. There can be a wealth of documents available about organizations, including memoranda, agendas of meetings, in-house newsletters, records of scheduled activities, manuals, and other issuances. Where externally supported programs are involved, invaluable documents also include project proposals, evaluation studies, and internal reviews.

7. In one other study (no. 7) there is reason to believe that the author was also a participant during certain stages of the site experiences; however, this role is not explicit in the text of the study. In a third study (no. 8, p. 312), the authors refer to their own previously published work in which they were participant observers, but the evidence is not used directly in the exemplary study under review.

8. For other examples of the way that participation observation can be improved as a methodology for conducting urban analysis, see Yin (1972).

9. In the two major exceptions (studies 1 and 5), the studies were about innovations whose major activity had preceded the authors coming on the scene, and hence the studies actually assume a more historical orientation than the other nine.

10. One of the remarkable features of Bernstein and Woodward's *All the President's Men* (1976), for instance, was the attention given to journalistic craft rules, wherein the reporters checked and corroborated various stories in the analytic process of piecing together the Watergate story. Often, participants were given a specific opportunity to deny or comment upon stories that were written about them.

11. Examples would be decisions to interview newly discovered informants or to pursue a line of inquiry in dealing with documents or interviews. Even though there may have been a field protocol at the outset, modifications in data collection should not only be tolerated but may also be desirable.

12. The careful reader will note that the sites in the matrices represent three different cohorts or samples, with the first set of eight sites having served a

"hypothesis generation" and "instrument development" function. To the extent that this was true, it is incorrect to tabulate these sites with the other two samples, as this represents a classic case of mixing the "calibrating" cases with the "test" cases.

13. In study 6, there are numerous tabulations of formal interview data (e.g., see volumes 2 and 7). However, aggregate conclusions from field observations, with explicit references to individual sites, were presented in one volume (3) but not another (6).

14. For some background readings for this analogy, see Sanders (1976).

15. Technically, Campbell claims that the interpretation from the viewpoint of experimental design is based on the incorrect notion that there is only a single degree of freedom (or few, where only a few case studies are involved); in reality, Campbell claims that the population of multiple implications from a single explanation or theory produces multiple degrees of freedom.

16. The design of this study may actually represent a classic use of the one-shot case study. The authors identified "resistance to change" as an explanation that was highly prevalent in the literature at that time. They then chose to test this explanation by deliberately selecting a site predisposed to change (and their initial measures corroborated this predisposition), but which nevertheless encountered implementation problems. This may represent a social science variation of the critical experiment in biology or behavioral research (see Boring 1950, pp. 356-60), in which a critical set of variables is tested within a single experiment. The results should enable the experimenter to draw a conclusive decision between competing theories underlying the choice of variables; the more significant the theories, the more critical the experiment.

17. For a brief review of previous organizational studies following the determinants approach, see Yin (1979, pp. 373-75).

18. What may have happened in this latter study was that the investigators, in the course of conducting their study, developed legitimate knowledge about implementation processes; but this knowledge was not formally presented as part of the study's evidence, thus leaving the reader ignorant about the information base used to support the policy recommendations.

19. This appreciation of different viewpoints has been a main feature in using case studies for teaching purposes. See Stein (1952, pp. xx-xxx).

20. In only one of the exemplary studies (no. 2) was the implementation experience actually reported in anonymous fashion, with neither the location of the site nor the names of the relevant agencies or participants given. Even under these conditions, portions of the text may be shown to participants for their corroboration and correction.

21. Note that this observation does not automatically follow from the operational definition of "exemplary" study that was used to select these 11 studies; if the observation had followed from the prior definition, the argument presented here would be circular.

REFERENCES

ALLISON, GRAHAM. 1971. *Essence of Decision: Explaining the Cuban Missile Crisis.* Boston: Little, Brown.

ATTEWELL, PAUL, and DEAN R. GERSTEIN. 1979. "Government Policy and Local Practice." *American Sociological Review,* 44:311-27, April.

BAER, WALTER S., ET AL. 1976. *Analysis of Federally Funded Demonstration Projects.* Santa Monica, Calif.: Rand Corporation.

———. 1977. "Government-Sponsored Demonstrations of New Technologies." *Science,* 196:950-57, May.

BANFIELD, EDWARD C. 1973. "Making a New Federal Program: Model Cities, 1964-68." In Allan P. Sindler, ed. *Policy and Politics in America.* Boston: Little, Brown, pp. 125-58.

BARDACH, EUGENE. 1977. *The Implementation Game: What Happens After a Bill Becomes Law.* Cambridge, Mass.: MIT Press.

BARNES, LOUIS B. 1971. "Organizational Change and Field Experiment Methods." In James D. Thompson and Victor H. Vroom, eds. *Organizational Design and Research.* Pittsburgh: University of Pittsburgh Press, pp. 57-111.

BARZUN, JACQUES, and HENRY F. GRAFF. 1977. *The Modern Researcher.* 3rd ed. New York: Harcourt Brace Jovanovich.

BERMAN, PAUL. 1978. "The Study of Macro- and Micro-Implementation." *Public Policy,* 26 (2): 157-84, Spring.

———, and MILBREY MCLAUGHLIN. 1976. "Implementation of Educational Innovation." *The Educational Forum,* 40:347-70, March.

———. 1974-78. *Federal Programs Supporting Educational Change.* Santa Monica, Calif.: Rand Corporation, vols. 1-8.

BERNSTEIN, CARL, and BOB WOODWARD. 1976. *All the President's Men.* New York: Warner Books.

BERNSTEIN, ILLENE, and HOWARD FREEMAN. 1975. *Academic and Entrepreneurial Research.* New York: Russell Sage.

BINGHAM, RICHARD. 1976. *The Adoption of Innovation by Local Government.* Lexington, Mass.: Lexington Books.

BORING, EDWIN G. 1950. *A History of Experimental Psychology.* 2nd ed. New York: Appleton-Century-Crofts.

CAMPBELL, DONALD T. 1975. "Degrees of Freedom and the Case Study." *Comparative Political Studies,* 8:173-93, July.

———, and JULIAN C. STANLEY. 1966. *Experimental and Quasi-Experimental Designs for Research.* Chicago: Rand McNally.

CORWIN, RONALD G. 1975. "Innovation in Organizations: The Case of Schools." *Sociology of Education,* 48:1-37, Winter.

DAFT, RICHARD L., and SELWYN W. BECKER. 1978. *The Innovative Organization: Innovation Adoption in School Organizations.* New York: Elsevier.

DERTHICK, MARTHA. 1972. *New Towns In-Town: Why a Federal Program Failed.* Washington, D.C.: Urban Institute.

DOUDS, CHARLES F., and ALBERT H. RUBENSTEIN. 1975. "Review and Assessment of the Methodology Used to Study the Behavioral Aspects of the In-

novation Process." In Patrick Kelly et al., eds. *Technological Innovation.*
Atlanta: Georgia Institute of Technology, February, pp. 185-269.

DOWNS, GEORGE W., JR. 1976. *Bureaucracy, Innovation, and Public Policy.*
Lexington, Mass.: D. C. Heath.

_____, and LAWRENCE B. MOHR. 1976. "Conceptual Issues in the Study of In-
novation." *Administrative Science Quarterly,* 21:700-714, December.

ECKSTEIN, HARRY. 1975. "Case Study and Theory in Political Science." In Fred
I. Greenstein and Nelson W. Polsby, eds. *Strategies of Inquiry.* Reading,
Mass.: Addison-Wesley, pp. 79-137.

ELMORE, RICHARD F. 1975. "Lessons from Follow Through." *Policy Analysis,*
1:459-84, Summer.

_____. 1978. "Organizational Models of Social Program Implementation."
Public Policy, 26:185-228, Spring.

EVELAND, J. D., ET AL. 1977. *The Innovation Process in Public Organizations.*
Ann Arbor, Michigan: Department of Journalism, University of Michigan, March.

FELLER, IRWIN, ET AL. 1974. *Diffusion of Technology in State Mission-Oriented
Agencies.* University Park: Institute for Research on Human Resources,
Pennsylvania State University, October.

_____. 1976. *Diffusion of Innovations in Municipal Governments.* University
Park: Institute for Research on Human Resources, Pennsylvania State University, June.

FULLAN, MICHAEL, and ALAN POMFRET. 1977. "Research on Curriculum and
Instruction Implementation." *Review of Educational Research,* 47:335-97,
Winter.

GREENBERG, GEORGE D., ET AL. 1977. "Developing Public Policy Theory: Perspectives from Empirical Research." *American Political Science Review,*
71:1532-43, December.

GROSS, NEAL, ET AL. 1971. *Implementing Organizational Innovations.* New
York: Basic Books.

HARGROVE, ERWIN C. 1975. *The Missing Link: The Study of Implementation
of Social Policy.* Washington, D.C.: Urban Institute.

IANNACONE, LAWRENCE. 1975. "The Field Study in Educational Policy Research." *Education and Urban Society,* 7:220-38, May.

LAMBRIGHT, W. HENRY. 1977. *Adoption and Utilization of Urban Technology.* Syracuse: Syracuse Research Corporation, September.

_____, and PAUL FLYNN. 1977. "Bureaucratic Politics and Technological
Change in Local Government." *Journal of Urban Analysis,* 4(1):93-118.

LEVITAN, SAR A., and ROBERT TAGGART. 1976. *The Promise of Greatness.*
Cambridge, Mass.: Harvard University Press.

MAZMANIAN, DANIEL A., and JEANNE NIENABER. 1979. *Can Organizations
Change? Environmental Protection, Citizen Participation, and the Corps
of Engineers.* Washington, D.C.: Brookings Institution.

MCLAUGHLIN, MILBREY. 1976. "Implementation as Mutual Adaptation."
Teachers College Record, 77 (3), February.

MECHLING, JERRY E. 1974. "Successful Innovation: Manpower Scheduling."
Urban Analysis, 3:259-313.

MERTON, ROBERT K. 1968. "The Matthew Effect in Science." *Science,* 159:56-63, January.

MOHR, LAWRENCE. 1978. "Process Theory and Variance Theory in Innovation Research." In Michael Radnor et al., eds. *The Diffusion of Innovations: An Assessment.* Evanston, Ill.: CIIST, Northwestern University, July.

MOORE, MARK H. ET AL. 1974. "The Case of the Fourth Platoon." *Urban Analysis,* 3:207-58.

MURPHY, JEROME T. 1971. "Title I of ESEA." *Harvard Educational Review,* 41:35-63, February.

———. 1973. "Title V of ESEA: Impact of Discretionary Funds on State Education Bureaucracies." *Harvard Educational Review,* 43:362-85, August.

MYTINGER, ROBERT. 1968. *Innovation in Local Health Services: A Study of the Adoption of New Programs by Local Health Departments.* Washington, D.C.: U.S. Government Printing Office, February.

NACHMIAS, DAVID. 1978. "Assessing Program Accountability: Research Designs." In Scott Greer et al., eds. *Accountability in Urban Society.* Beverly Hills, Calif.: Sage Publications, pp. 249-72.

NELKIN, DOROTHY. 1975. *Methadone Maintenance: A Technological Fix.* New York: George Braziller.

NELSON, MARGARET, and SAM SIEBER. 1976. "Innovations in Urban Secondary Schools." *School Review,* 30:213-31, February.

NELSON, RICHARD R., and DOUGLAS YATES, eds. 1978. *Innovation and Implementation in Public Organizations.* Lexington, Mass.: Lexington Books.

PRESSMAN, JEFFREY L., and AARON WILDAVSKY. 1973. *Implementation.* Berkeley: University of California Press.

PUBLIC AFFAIRS COUNSELING. 1976. *Factors Involved in the Transfer of Innovations: A Summary and Organization of the Literature.* Washington, D.C.: U.S. Department of Housing and Urban Development.

REISS, ALBERT J., JR. 1971. "Systematic Observation of Natural Social Phenomena." In Herbert Costner, ed. *Sociological Methodology.* San Francisco: Jossey-Bass, pp. 3-33.

ROESSNER, J. DAVID, ET AL. 1979. *Turning Laws into Incentives: The Implementation of State Solar Energy Initiatives.* Golden, Colo.: Solar Energy Research Institute, February.

ROGERS, EVERETT M. 1975. "Innovation in Organizations." Paper presented at the American Political Science Association, San Francisco, September.

———, with J. D. EVELAND. 1975. "Diffusion of Innovation Perspectives on National R & D Assessment: Communication and Innovation in Organizations." In Patrick Kelly et al., eds. *Technological Innovation.* Atlanta: Georgia Institute of Technology, February, pp. 301-68.

———, and REKHA AGARWALA-ROGERS. 1976. *Communications in Organizations.* New York: Free Press.

ROTHMAN, JACK. 1974. *Planning and Organizing for Social Change: Action Principles from Social Science.* New York: Columbia University Press.

SABATIER, PAUL. 1978. "The Acquisition and Utilization of Technical Information by Administrative Agencies." *Administrative Science Quarterly,* 23: 396-417, September.

SANDERS, WILLIAM B., ed. 1976. *The Sociologist as Detective.* 2nd ed. New York: Praeger.

SELLTIZ, CLAIRE; LAWRENCE S. WRIGHTSMAN; and STUART W. COOK. 1976. *Research Methods in Social Relations.* 3rd ed. New York: Holt, Rinehart and Winston.

STAKE, ROBERT E. 1978. "The Case Study Method in Social Inquiry." *Educational Researcher,* 7:5-8, February.

STEIN, HAROLD, ed. 1952. *Public Administration and Policy Development.* New York: Harcourt Brace Jovanovich.

WALKER, WARREN E. 1975. "Applying Systems Analysis to the Fire Service." *Fire Engineering,* 128:38-64, August.

―――. 1978. *Changing Fire Company Locations: Five Implementation Case Studies.* Washington, D.C.: U.S. Department of Housing and Urban Development, January.

WEICK, KARL E. 1968. "Systematic Observational Methods." In Gardner Lindzey and Elliot Aronson, eds. *The Handbook of Social Psychology.* 2nd ed. Reading, Mass.: Addison-Wesley, 2:357-451.

WILLIAMS, WALTER. 1976. "Implementation Analysis and Assessment." In Walter Williams and Richard F. Elmore, eds. *Social Program Implementation.* New York: Academic Press, pp. 267-92.

―――, and RICHARD F. ELMORE, eds. 1976. *Social Program Implementation.* New York: Academic Press.

YIN, ROBERT K. 1972. *Participant-Observation and the Development of Urban Neighborhood Policy.* New York: New York City-Rand Institute, February.

―――. 1977*a.* "Evaluating Community Crime Prevention Programs." Paper presented at the National Conference on Criminal Justice Evaluation, Washington, D.C., February.

―――. 1977*b.* "Production Efficiency vs. Bureaucratic Self-Interest: Two Innovative Processes?" *Policy Sciences,* 8:381-99, December.

―――. 1978. "Are Traditional Research Designs Responsive?" In Scott Greer et al., eds. *Accountability in Urban Society.* Beverly Hills, Calif.: Sage Publications, pp. 293-99.

―――. 1979. *Changing Urban Bureaucracies: How New Practices Become Routinized.* Lexington, Mass.: Lexington Books.

―――, and DOUGLAS YATES. 1975. *Street-Level Governments.* Lexington, Mass.: Lexington Books.

―――, ET AL. 1976. "The Difference That Quality Makes." *Sociological Methods and Research,* 5:139-56, November.

ZALTMAN, GERALD, ET AL. 1973. *Innovations and Organizations.* New York: John Wiley.

4

The Methodology for
Field Network Evaluation Studies

RICHARD P. NATHAN

When the domestic policy of the federal government shifted in the 1970s toward broader and less conditional federal grants-in-aid to state and local governments, there was, as would be expected, interest in policy research studies on the effects of these new intergovernmental fiscal subventions. Beginning in 1972, a group of researchers, initially at the Brookings Institution and later at both Brookings and the Woodrow Wilson School of Princeton University, has conducted "field network evaluation studies" of three major federal grant programs: general revenue sharing, community development block grants (CDBG), and the public service employment component of the Comprehensive Employment and Training Act (CETA). A number of publications are available on the methods and findings of this research (see the list of publications at the end of this chapter).

Once the decision was made to conduct evaluation studies of the New Federalism programs of the Nixon-Ford period, we had to deal with a hard question: How should such studies be designed and conducted? The New Federalism involved more flexible grants than the "categorical" grants of prior periods. It was designed to increase recipient governments' opportunities for discretionary action; this was the decentralization objective of the New Federalism. But other goals entered the picture. The more goals there are, the more difficult it is to say what a given federal grants-in-aid program is supposed to do and then to evaluate whether it actually accomplished its purpose. Was general revenue sharing supposed to enable the recipient governments to cut taxes? Was it supposed to equalize aid among jurisdictions? Was it supposed to spur innovation?

The problem of multiple goals is even more pronounced with block grants. The community development block grant program is an example. Was decentralization its principal or overriding purpose? Was it supposed to aid the poor, the downtowns, the uptowns, the suburbs, the construction industry? Was it, as the law stated, supposed to give especially high priority to achieving "spatial deconcentration"?

The goals of many federal grant programs are not only broad but frequently shifting. Such qualities present both problems and opportunities. The problem is deciding what to evaluate. The opportunity is that in such a setting evaluators can evaluate whatever they want. Hence there is often a subtle opportunity, not recognized as such, for the evaluator to set up the design in a way that biases the research.

This problem of unclear and shifting goals is not the only obstacle to the evaluation of broad-gauged, multipurpose subventions. There is also a problem of "universality." Every jurisdiction that has certain specified statistical characteristics receives a grant under these programs. Researchers cannot select a comparison group of similar jurisdictions to determine the difference a grant made.

The diversity and fragmentation of the American federal system cause further difficulties. So many different jurisdictions receive revenue sharing and block grants that what recipients do with the money is highly varied.

Another barrier to evaluation research on broad-gauged formula grants is that the grants are often relatively small in relation to what state and local governments spend in the aided functional area. We are often looking at a relatively thin margin of federal aid. This, too, complicates our task.

Despite these problems, if social science is to be relevant, researchers need to focus on the hard questions that are most important to policymakers. Does it make a difference that we now have revenue sharing or that the grant system was changed to provide block grants for community development or public employment programs and training services?

It is not easy to define "making a difference." Are we interested in whether Grant A changed the way the recipient governmental jurisdictions do their business or changed the business they do? Or should we focus on whether Grant A made a difference to individuals—the man or woman who got a public-service job, the homeowner who got a housing rehabilitation loan under the community development block grant program, or the taxpayer who felt better because the general-revenue-sharing program helped reduce his property tax bill?

THE TOOLS OF SOCIAL SCIENCE
FOR EVALUATION RESEARCH

Social scientists have three major tools for evaluating universal and broad-gauged grant programs. First are statistical and mathematical techniques. With these we can construct models of how the world would look without Grant A. We can then say something about how the real world — with Grant A — compares to the model. But the statistics are weak and limited. They are collected infrequently. Often they are not available for the units of analysis we want to work with. And the regression techniques applied involve many definitions requiring assumptions that may not be sufficiently clear, or may not be acceptable, to users of the research results.

The second tool is survey instruments. We can go out and ask people: Did Grant A make a difference? But who do we ask and how do we ask them? Suppose we ask officials of the recipient governments. Shouldn't we expect the respondents to give us back chapter and verse of what the law says, or what they think we want to hear, or what they want to tell us (whether true or not)? What if we go out and ask the final recipients, What do you think of CDBG or CETA? No matter how we spell it, the man in the rehabilitated house or the woman in a CETA job is often unlikely to have the foggiest idea of what we are talking about.

The third instrument available is the case-study approach. We can have smart people look closely at specific cases. But no matter how smart a person is, he or she can study only so many cases. And if different people study different cases, they are likely to do so in different ways. So you do not have comparability.

To recap, we have looked at problems in evaluating broad-gauged formula grants-in-aid that distribute funds widely. We have considered three research approaches that can be used to evaluate these grants and the kinds of problems involved in using them. It has also been asserted that the game is worth the candle — that policymakers want, and should seek, answers to questions involving whether a given program has made a difference, and if so, what kind of difference.

FIELD NETWORK EVALUATION RESEARCH

The emphasis of our field network evaluation research at the Brookings Institution and Princeton University has been on the intergovernmental effects of the New Federalism and other broad-gauged grants — that is, their effects on the recipient governmental jurisdictions. Attention has also been devoted to the effects of the grants studied on various groups and individual recipients and, in the case of the community development block grant, on urban neighborhoods. Our orientation is both analytical and descriptive. We are most interested in the effects of large and important grant programs in three main areas: (1) on the finances of the recipient jurisdictions; (2) in terms of the program content and incidence of the benefits provided under the aided activities; (3) on the political processes for determining their allocation to specific program uses.

Our view from the outset has been that formal survey research is not a good instrument for evaluating these effects of federal grants-in-aid programs. Furthermore, the other two approaches mentioned above—econometric and field network evaluation studies—in our opinion work best when they are used together. We have used such a tandem approach in two studies, the general-revenue-sharing study and the study of the CETA public-service-jobs program.

Note that in the last paragraph, the wording was changed from "case studies" to "field network evaluation studies." There is a difference. The way we have adapted the case-study approach is not unique, but it is notable because we have used this methodology both on an extensive scale and for impact analysis.

What we have done is to build networks of indigenous field researchers, along with a central management group to work with the field researchers, so that they use a common approach to answer a common set of analytical questions. The field researchers (called "associates") *do the analysis*. They make their assessments on the effects of a given grant. The central group then compiles these assessments—with the close involvement of the field associates—into a common report that cuts across a representative sample of jurisdictions.

Two points in this description need elaboration. First, we have used the word *effects* in referring to what is studied. This terminology is important. As already stated, the objectives of broad-gauged programs are diverse, frequently shifting, and sometimes inconsistent. Because we cannot at the outset of our research define the goals of a particular program in a precise way, we have concentrated on studying what emerge and are judged to be *the most policy-relevant effects*. The second key point introduced in the description above has to do with the samples used for these studies. We have chosen "representative" samples. These samples, typically including forty to sixty recipient jurisdictions, are much larger than can be used for the more conventional comparative case-study approach. They are not random samples, although we have from time to time considered using a random sample for one of the field network evaluation studies.

The main reasons for using representative samples have to do with cost and logistics. (I elaborate on these reasons later in this chapter.) To have a manageable research group, in many cases we need to ask a field associate to report on more than one site. In addition, in order to make sure that associates are familiar with field sites and have good access to the best sources of data about them, we decided to have some sites organized in clusters. Such a cluster might, for example, include three or four rural jurisdictions close to a university research center, a central city and one or two of its suburban jurisdictions, or a state capital and a nearby small city.

The field network research method is longitudinal. We had three rounds of field observations on revenue sharing. There will be four each for the CDBG and CETA public-service-jobs studies. Although the basic research design has not changed, we have changed the emphasis of our reports on these studies to reflect current issues and the specific stage of a particular program—just starting, changing, or resulting in expenditures. For example, in the CDBG study, our first report concentrated on what was being planned and how it was being planned; the second report concentrated on whether the program had a decentralization effect; the third report focused on whether CDBG funds were being "targeted" on the poor within jurisdictions; the fourth report emphasizes how CDBG money actually has been spent (i.e., program implementation).

Associates in a field network study submit a research report for each round of field research. These reports include extensive and specific data that associates use to reach and justify their analytical findings. The associates review their analytical findings and supporting data with the central staff. However, the central staff does not change a field associate's findings without the associate's involvement and concurrence.

COMPLEMENTARITY OF ECONOMETRIC AND FIELD NETWORK EVALUATION STUDIES

From a methodological point of view, the most interesting issues we have dealt with in the field network evaluation studies are *impact issues*: Did jurisdictions that received revenue-sharing money spend more, or did they substitute these funds for locally raised money they would have spent anyway and cut back their own revenue? Did the CETA jobs program result in the creation of new jobs, or did it result in displacement—that is, the substitution of CETA funds that would have been paid to workers who would have been hired anyway? These are difficult yet very important questions. They have been studied in our research with both the field network and econometric approaches.

Think of it this way: In evaluating a program that is operating everywhere, we must find a way to study the counterfactual state. That is, we need to determine what the world would be like if the program were not operating. Two ways to do this are the econometric approach and the field network evaluation approach. Both require a construct of what would have happened if the program did not exist; they then compare that model to the real world in which the program does exist. The econometric approach does this modeling in a computer with a system of equations. In constructing these equations, the researcher must make judgments about economic conditions, program conditions, administrative structure, and so forth. The field research associate in a field network evaluation study builds a comparative construct (no program versus a program in effect) in his head, also making many assumptions. The field researcher can use more variables and can define and manipulate them in more ways. The human brain is a powerful instrument. But there is a catch. The computer model can be replicated, the process can be specified for other researchers to review. Although I believe that the human calculations can deal more effectively with the tremendous diversity and complexity of American federalism, they cannot be specified in replicable form. So, what should we do? *We should do both.*

We should do field network evaluation studies, for one thing, because they can be conducted while a new program is getting under way. Field researchers can begin when a new program gets started, whereas the data needed for statistical modeling often lag years behind the starting date of a new program. If, as is often the case, the legislative cycle is short and renewal hearings commence one or two years after a new program begins, the establishment of a field research network may be the only way to bring independent analysis to bear in the legislative renewal process.

There is a more important reason for doing both. We should do both because they can *reinforce* each other. Information and insights gained from a field network evaluation study can be used to develop and refine the equations for manipulating the program and Census data that go into an econometric evaluation of the impact (public-sector stimulation or displacement) of a particular grant-in-aid program.

We have used such a tandem approach in one of our studies, the general-revenue-sharing study. The econometric analysis was based on a sample from the Census of Governments of 1,424 local units (see the Adams-Crippen report listed in the publications at the end of this chapter). We are currently in the process of using this same dual approach in another field network study, that of the CETA public-service-jobs program. In the case of the revenue-sharing research, quite close agreement was found between the field and econometric findings on the fiscal effects of general-revenue-sharing funds on the recipient' state and local governments. Several other research projects have been launched recently that blend field and econometric analysis. Such studies, we believe, should be watched closely. The work being done in this area comes to grips with a challenge that evaluation researchers have been wrestling with for a long time—the integration of quantitative and qualitative research techniques.

ORGANIZATION AND CONDUCT OF THE RESEARCH

The field network evaluation studies we have conducted use a stratified representative sample of field sites selected on the basis of such factors as governmental type, population size, region, and economic and fiscal condition. Cell sizes of necessity are limited. Because the sampling procedures have concentrated on larger units, however, the studies encompass a high percentage of the total national funding for the programs evaluated. The share of total program funding received by the jurisdictions studied ranges from 11 percent for the study of the public-service employment program to nearly 25 percent for the study of the community development block grant program; the proportion for the general revenue sharing was 21 percent in the first year of the research.

Each of the studies has included an analysis of the formula system for distributing grant funds, although this effort was not part of the field research. This analysis has been done centrally using national statistical data. In two cases (for revenue sharing and the community development block grant program), this work was described at length in the initial reports issued.

Typically the field network evaluation studies have a central staff of three to five professionals and a group of approximately twenty-five research associates. Associates are chosen for their knowledge of local public finances and institutions and the functional area of the particular grant-in-aid program being studied. None is officially connected with the jurisdictions in the sample. Most are either academic political scientists or economists. All are residents of the area they study. They devote an average of thirty days per year to their participation in each round of the research.

Associates work with the central staff in developing the analytical framework and research design. Members of the central staff maintain continuing contact with associates, review and code the field data, and compile the overall analysis. The critical point about the research process is that the analysis is done by the field associates. As indicated earlier, their findings are not changed unless, on the basis of discussions with the central staff, an associate suggests that a change be made. A uniform analysis format for the research for each round of field observations is developed in draft and is then the subject of a conference attended by members of the central staff and the associates. About forty people attend each research conference. After the meeting the central staff revises the analysis framework and reporting formats to reflect the conference discussion.

Associates are also consulted in the report-writing phase. Before a report is issued, chapter drafts are sent to them for their comments. In a number of instances associates have also been recruited to work on the central staff, either on a full-time or part-time basis, to prepare a portion of the analysis.

Field network evaluation research is different from survey research. There are no fixed questions that associates are instructed to ask of specifically designated respondents. When reporting formats requiring fiscal and program data are used, it is up to the associate to decide what sources he or she should use to obtain the information necessary to fill them out. The information provided by the associates consists of the associate's analysis of program effects. The data on program operations and effects and the narrative discussion submitted by each associate are reviewed by the central staff and combined with those from the other associates. In short, field network evaluation studies involve the compilation of the individual analyses of program effects conducted in the field by an interdisciplinary group of social science researchers.

TYPES OF EFFECTS STUDIED

The next sections deal with the four types of program effects studied: (1) fiscal, (2) employment, (3) programmatic, and (4) political. Information about individual field evaluation studies is used to illustrate points made in the discussion.

The work involved in assessing *fiscal and employment effects* (types (1) and (2) above) raise particularly difficult research questions involving the degree to which federal funds have been used for new purposes as opposed to being substituted for programs and activities that would have been undertaken in the absence of these funds. Fiscal effects have been highlighted in the general-revenue-sharing study because of the widespread interest in the degree and nature of the substitution uses of these funds. In much the same way, employment effects have been highlighted in the study of the CETA public-service-jobs program because of the controversy surrounding the extent to which these funds have been used for job displacement, as opposed to job creation, purposes.

Programmatic effects relate to the effects of federal grants on the programs and the program mix of recipient jurisdictions. In essence, this involves the distribution by functional area and activity of the federal grant funds allocated for new spending purposes. Under the heading of programmatic effects, attention has also been devoted to the income incidence of grants-in-aid effects (i.e., the distribution of services by income group for new programs and activities undertaken with federal grant funds). This subject was found to be particularly important for the CDBG program.

The fourth category of program effects, *political effects,* involves the decision process for the allocation of federal grant funds at the state and local levels. Who decides? How is this decision process different (if it is) from that which occurs under more narrowly targeted categorical forms of federal aid?

Fiscal and Employment Effects

Not surprisingly, the application of field observation techniques to study the fiscal and employment effects of federal grants-in-aid programs has sparked some lively debate between persons involved in the field network research and proponents of the econometric method for studying these effects. The point is often made in these discussions that field network evaluation studies are "judgmental," the implication being that this approach is less reliable than statistical studies that use nationally available program or Census data. This issue needs to be treated carefully.

Our review of the results of econometric studies of grants-in-aid impacts (including our own statistical analytical work on the revenue-sharing program described below) brings an important point to the fore: The construction of models and related kinds of statistical analyses often involves assumptions that are just as judgmental and difficult to make as the interpretations of fiscal and employment effects made by the field research associates involved in our studies. In a review of the literature on fiscal impact studies of federal grant programs, Ray D. Whitman and Robert J. Cline make this point: "Despite their very technical character, trend and econometric analyses always involve human judgments."[1] We conclude that neither the econometric approach nor the field network evaluation approach is necessarily better than the other for getting at the fiscal and employment effects of federal grants; they are complementary. They should be used to reinforce each other.

We can show how the field network method works for studying fiscal and employment effects by considering the way in which this research has been conducted for the two programs where the analyses of these effects have been most important.

General revenue sharing. The $5.3 billion that was distributed in general-revenue-sharing funds for calendar 1972 amounted to about 15 percent of all federal aid to states and localities and 3 percent of the total annual revenue of state and local governments. The attempt to follow the trail of these funds to identify their net fiscal effects is complicated by their "fungibility," that is, the ease with which the recipient government can transfer them from one budgetary account to another.

Besides the obvious incentive under a program such as revenue sharing for public officials to emphasize uses with the most popular appeal, several provisions of the act itself may influence the officials of recipient jurisdictions to announce expenditures of revenue-sharing funds that mask their true effects. The law prohibits the use of shared revenue in programs that discriminate, and requires hearings and the publication of budget data. It also requires that federally defined "prevailing wage rates" be paid on all construction projects for which revenue sharing is used to fund more than 25 percent of the total cost. Some officials can be expected to avoid problems by allocating shared revenue to programs on which they run no risk of being found in violation of such federal requirements.

The following nine net-effect categories were used in classifying the fiscal responses by recipient governments to shared revenue. The range of responses captured by these nine categories is sufficiently wide to reflect virtually any expenditure, revenue, or other financial action that might be taken by recipient governments.

1. *New or expanded operations:* Operating expenditures initiated or expended with revenue-sharing funds (excluding pay-level and benefit increases).
2. *New capital expenditures:* Spending for capital projects or the purchase of equipment that, without shared revenue, either would not have occurred or would have occurred at least one year later.
3. *Increased pay and benefits:* The use of revenue-sharing funds for pay and fringe benefit increases that otherwise would not have been authorized, either at all or at the levels approved.
4. *Program maintenance (budget balancing):* The allocation of revenue-sharing funds to ongoing programs where the course of action without revenue sharing would have been to cut existing programs.
5. *Federal aid restoration:* The use of revenue-sharing funds to offset actual or anticipated reductions in other federal grants-in-aid.
6. *Tax reduction:* The use of revenue sharing to finance ongoing programs where the net result was to free up the jurisdiction's own resources and thereby permit a reduction in tax rates.
7. *Tax stabilization:* The use of revenue-sharing funds to finance ongoing programs where the result was to avoid an increase in tax rates that otherwise would have been approved.
8. *Borrowing avoidance:* Substitution of shared revenue for borrowing that otherwise would have been undertaken.
9. *Increased fund balances:* Allocation of revenue-sharing funds to ongoing programs where the net effect was to increase fund balances.

In deciding which of these categories a particular budget decision fit into, associates relied on budget and program data (both current and historical) and extensive personal interviews.

While many assessments of the fiscal impact of revenue sharing in the field research were difficult to make, some were not. There were cases in the field research on revenue sharing in which associates came to decisions quickly and easily on the use of shared revenue—for example, to pave additional roads, buy new construction equipment, launch a new program of social services, or enable town officials to enact a tax cut. This tended to be the case most frequently for smaller and suburban jurisdictions, but was also found to be true for fiscally distressed large cities. In many of these cities, officials publicly announced that they would use these new and essentially unrestricted funds from the federal government to stabilize taxes.

The timing of the research was also found to make a difference. Determining what happens as a result of injecting a new form of fiscal assistance is easier if the research is begun at the inception of the program being studied rather than later in the program.

Public-service employment (PSE). The field network evaluation study of the CETA public-service-employment program was initiated early in 1977 in response to a Senate amendment by Henry Bellmon of Oklahoma directing the National Commission for Manpower Policy to undertake research focused on the job-displacement issue under the PSE program. Displacement under the PSE program refers to the substitution of federally funded positions for positions that would otherwise have been supported by local funds. To the extent this occurs, the employment effect of a federal job-stimulus program is diminished.

Previous econometric studies of the employment effects of public-service job programs had reported large and growing displacement. This was found to have occurred even though displacement had been prohibited under the laws establishing such programs.

As in the case of the field network evaluation research on the fiscal effects of the general-revenue-sharing program, it was necessary before the first observation date to provide the associates with a framework for identifying job creation and displacement. Eight categories were used:

1. *New programs and services:* Cases in which additional programs or services were provided with PSE funding that otherwise would not have been undertaken.
2. *Special projects:* New, one-time projects with a duration of one year or less undertaken with PSE funds.
3. *Program expansion:* Cases in which the level of services was raised or services were improved under existing programs by using PSE funding.
4. *Program maintenance:* Cases in which PSE employees were used to maintain existing services that would have been curtailed in the absence of PSE funding.

5. *Transfers:* Cases involving the transfer of existing state and local government positions to PSE funding.

6. *Rehires:* Cases in which state or local employees were laid off and then rehired with PSE funding.

7. *Contract reduction:* Cases in which PSE participants were used to provide services or to work on projects that had been, or normally would be, contracted to an outside organization or private firm.

8. *Potential hires:* Cases in which PSE participants were hired to fill positions that otherwise would have been funded with other revenue.

Associates used five kinds of data to classify the employment effects of PSE according to this set of definitions. One obvious form of data was interviews with local officials. However, the maintenance-of-effort requirement (i.e., the requirement that prohibits job displacement) in the CETA law was found in some instances to limit the usefulness of interview data in studying the employment effects of the PSE program. Because of this requirement, some local officials resisted discussing the displacement issue, although others provided important information and insights on the program's net employment effects. The four other kinds of data field researchers used were (1) data on budget and employment conditions and trends; (2) budget and employment data for the specific agencies in which PSE participants were employed; (3) assessment of the demands for the services performed; (4) observations of the actual tasks performed by PSE participants and interviews with supervisors at the job site.

Attention needs to be focused here, for the PSE study especially, on the program-maintenance category of employment effects (item 4 in the framework above). Program maintenance consists of cases in which PSE employees are used to continue services that, according to the analysis of the associate, would have been curtailed in the absence of PSE funding. In the first round of the research the associates classified nearly a third of the positions as program maintenance. These positions were concentrated in distressed jurisdictions; 80 percent were in four large, distressed cities. In effect, what the associates told us is that without PSE funds, these cities would have cut out certain services; with PSE funds, they were able to keep the services going. We do not consider this to be displacement; the positions in question would not have been funded in the absence of the PSE program.

These program-maintenance classifications often reflected fundamentally changed attitudes on the part of the officials of local government. The essential question raised is whether attitudes on the part of public officials and the general public toward local public services had shifted in the mid-1970s such that slower growth or net cuts in services would have occurred for some jurisdictions at the time the PSE program was expanding. To the extent that local government employment would have departed from an historic trend line, an econometric or trend study would tend to overstate the displacement effects of PSE by overpredicting aggregate state and local public employment.

Other researchers have noted a decline in the historic growth rate of local public employment and spending in this period. This decline began before California voters approved Proposition 13 in 1978, although that event reinforced the downward trend. George E. Peterson of the Urban Institute stated in July 1978: "For the quarter century ending in 1975, local public spending rose year in and year out relative to national product, but during the present economic recovery city expenditures have grown at a much slower rate than national output. Cities suffering economic and population declines have taken the lead in restraining expenditures."[2] We observed a similar pattern for the large cities in our sample. The sixteen large cities (over 250,000 population) in the sample were divided into two groups of eight cities—distressed cities and other cities. For the cities not classified as distressed, total municipal employment (including PSE) increased by 13 percent from 1970 to 1976. For the distressed cities, total municipal employment *decreased* by 9 percent from 1970 to 1976. Moreover, distressed large cities as a group tend to be aided disproportionately under the PSE program. Distressed large cities in the sample accounted for 8 percent of all PSE enrollees as of December 1977, but only 1 percent of total state and local employment. This concentration of PSE positions on the governments that appear to be departing most sharply from the trend line of city employment growth adds to the difficulty of using statistical techniques alone to study the program's employment impact.

As discussed for the revenue-sharing program, it would be misleading to give the impression that all the classifications in the field of employment effects of the PSE program are as difficult to make as is often the case with the program-maintenance category. In many cases, the central staff and the associate came into agreement easily on the classification of employment effects. For example, several cities used PSE funds for new social services, special clean-up projects, and innovative programs for recreation and the arts. In many of these cases, the associate concluded that these activities had not previously been undertaken and were not likely to have been adopted in the absence of new and additional funds from Washington for job creation. In fact, associates frequently observed that local officials not only wanted to use PSE funds for job-creation purposes but were anxious to avoid their use for displacement.

This point is worthy of elaboration. Several writers about grants-in-aid impacts assume that the achievement of fiscal substitution and job-displacement effects in the use of federal funds is a (or *the*) prime motivation of the officials of recipient governmental jurisdiction. We need in this connection to look more closely at the CETA program as originally established.

The CETA program originated as a result of the consolidation of several preexisting categorical grants. The objective was to decategorize the funding and decentralize the administration of employment and training services. In such a decentralized program there is always the possibility that local objectives will conflict with federal objectives. Later on, when the PSE program was added to CETA, a principal federal objective was to increase employment. This objective was particularly strong in the stimulus portion of the program. Can we expect local officials to behave in this way, that is, to serve as agents of the federal government for new job creation in periods of economic strain? The fact is that in our research, state and local officials were found to resist the use of PSE funds for fiscal relief and job-displacement purposes. We note several reasons for this:

1. Unlike the case of the general-revenue-sharing program, the laws and regulations administered by the U.S. Department of Labor prohibit the use of PSE funds for fiscal relief.

2. Local officials in many cases were found to be concerned about relying on PSE funds for fiscal relief purposes because of the uncertainty associated with the funding for this program. Since PSE is an operating grant rather than a capital grant, the use of these funds for the provision of services or as a source of continuing fiscal relief creates a future liability against locally generated resources should this federal funding be discontinued or significantly reduced. Clearly the "stop-and-go" history of the PSE program justifies concern on the part of local officials about the continuity of this federal funding.

3. Local officials in some cases were found to be in sympathy with the federal objectives, agreeing on the desirability of reducing unemployment and providing additional jobs for the disadvantaged.

As noted earlier, we were in a position in the case of the PSE research to compare our findings with those obtained from econometric studies. Prior to the publication of the first report on our field network evaluation study of the CETA-PSE program, the most widely discussed econometric studies on the employment effects of public-service-employment programs were conducted by George Johnson and James Tomola. A paper by these authors covering employment under the public-employment (PEP) program (precursor to PSE) and its continuation through the end of 1975 as part of the PSE program estimated displacement at zero after one quarter, 58 percent after one year, and 100 percent after one and a half years.[3] Other and more recent econometric studies of the PSE program have come to less dramatic conclusions on displacement effects and have in some cases taken into account a number of the problems with the earlier findings discussed in the various critiques (including ours) of the studies by Johnson and Tomola.[4]

By contrast, the findings on the three rounds of our field network evaluation (conducted in mid-July 1977, December 1977, and December 1979) show that displacement accounted for approximately one-fifth of all CETA-PSE positions. While the differences can be overstated, these findings present a very different picture from that of the earlier econometric analyses.

The stability of the field network findings on the net employment effects is also worth noting because the literature generally holds that job displacement increases over time under federally aided job-creation programs administered through state and local governmental units. What explains this difference in research outcome? The answer appears to lie in programmatic and institutional elements of the environment of the PSE program. This is an important point. Field network studies can take into account the way institutions behave, whereas econometric techniques are based on a more atomistic view of the labor market. We believe that three factors rooted in institutional behavior outweighed any tendency toward greater displacement over time that may have been operating in the period of our initial three sets of field observations of the PSE programs. Without going into detail here, these factors were (1) the considerable uncertainty continually surrounding the state of the PSE program, (2) the shift in 1977 to a more restrictive special-projects approach, and (3) the increase in allocations by local officials of PSE positions to nonprofit organizations.

This review of what our studies have shown about the fiscal and employment effects of federal grants-in-aid programs indicates both the costs and the benefits of field network evaluation research. Reviews of the field network evaluation studies have pointed out (and rightly so) that this research is expensive.[5] Its cost, we believe, can be justified on several grounds. One such justification relates to the ability of this research approach to provide data on the effects of federal grants faster than statistical or econometric studies. A second attribute is its usefulness in refining and improving the statistical techniques used to study these federal grant programs. Third, the field network method can also be used to disaggregate, to look at the institutional setting and program impacts for different recipient jurisdictions under different conditions. The field network approach in this way enables researchers to study the dynamics of the program effects—how they occur under different institutional, demographic, and economic conditions.

A further point needs to be made here about the cost-effectiveness of the field network evaluation approach. As the next several sections of this chapter demonstrate, this method has also been used to study other effects, namely, the political and programmatic effects of federal grants. In the case of political effects, no statistical sources can be used as an alternative to collecting and analyzing field observations. Moreover, in order to understand and interpret the political effects of a particular grant-in-aid, researchers often must be able to classify and compare the jurisdictions being studied on the basis of their uses of grant-in-aid money, that is, on the basis of the economic and programmatic effects of grant funds.

In other words, if we are going to study the politics of how decisions to use federal grant funds are made, we need to know a great deal about the decisions themselves. Returning to the cost-benefit framework, the economics of the field network approach are such that if one is going into the field anyway, it makes sense, on efficiency grounds, to have a broad-gauged research design.

Programmatic Effects

As part of all three of the field network studies, results have been reported on the functional areas to which federal grant funds were allocated. Such findings about the programmatic effects of federal grants are more straightforward than is true of fiscal and employment effects.

From a methodological point of view, the most important field network evaluation study for the analysis of programmatic effects is the study of the community development block grant program. At the outset of this study, one of the questions raised for the field analysis involved the degree of fiscal substitution in the use of CDBG funds. It turned out, however, that most of the funds had been used for new spending. In the first round of the CDBG evaluation, we found that 94 percent of the funds provided to the sample units had been allocated for new spending. We continued to study the fiscal effects of CDBG spending but did not assign them as high a priority as we did in the revenue-sharing study. One of the most important issues related to the expenditure uses of CDBG funds turned out to be their income-group incidence. This issue—the "who benefits" issue—has roots in the program's legislative history.

When President Nixon first recommended a "special revenue sharing" program for urban community development, emphasis was placed on the decentralization objective. Few conditions were proposed. No requirements were recommended to limit expenditures to lower-income groups, even though the largest categorical grants consolidated into this new program (urban renewal and model cities) had such requirements. Considerable controversy developed over this issue.

In the congressional deliberations on the legislation, the strongest sentiment in favor of requirements to target spending on the poor was in the Senate. The Nixon administration opposed such requirements; the House of Representatives was somewhere in between the Senate and administration positions, though generally closer to the administration's. The upshot was a conventional one for the legislative process. Seven objectives, including social targeting, were adopted and given equal billing. The law then stated that "maximum feasible priority" should be given to low- and moderate-income groups. President Ford signed the bill in this form, and the issue moved into the administrative arena.

Under pressure to get the program under way in five months and in line with the Ford administration's decentralization aims, the Department of Housing and Urban Development at first took a "hands off" position. Local communities, the department said, should determine who benefits from the expenditure of CDBG funds. This changed with the 1976 election and the appointment of a new secretary of HUD committed to the idea of social targeting. One month after Jimmy Carter's inauguration, HUD Secretary Patricia Roberts Harris told a House subcommittee that she expected the uses of CDBG funds to be concentrated on low- and moderate-income citizens. "I do not consider this to be just an objective of the block grant program; it is the highest priority of the program."[6]

In the debate on this issue during the Carter years, there was, as would be expected, great interest in whatever data could be brought to bear on the extent to which cities were spending CDBG funds on projects that benefited low- and moderate-income persons. There were three sources of data, none of them very satisfactory. One source was the field evaluation study being conducted at Brookings, in which an attempt had been made in the first round of data collection to get at the social-targeting issue. The two other sources were a HUD survey and a survey conducted by the National Association of Housing and Redevelopment Officials (NAHRO). Our results and the HUD results were similar. The agency survey found 64 percent of first-year CDBG funds allocated to projects that benefited lower-income groups (which includes both the low-and moderate-income groups). We found 66 percent. The NAHRO figure was lower: 51 percent. (These are allocations, not expenditures, in all three cases.) In the second program year, both HUD and NAHRO noted a decrease in the proportion of CDBG funds allocated for lower-income groups. Our data showed a slight increase.

The most important point to emerge from these studies was that they highlighted serious measurement problems. This raises an important general point. Because the field network methodology involves a flexible research design, it is possible to refine the techniques used in the course of the work. In this case, a new approach was developed for the third round of CDBG field research, which was then used in the larger cities in the sample to go back and reclassify the data from the first two rounds of field research.

Close scrutiny of all three studies of the income-group incidence of CDBG spending produced a number of insights about the ways in which a new methodology should be designed. In general the prior studies used data by Census tract and allocated CDBG projects according to the income characteristics of the Census tracts in which they were to be located. These approaches failed to take into account the extent to which projects in lower-income areas benefit higher-income persons, and vice versa. Likewise, insufficient attention was given to what was being observed (what kinds of benefits?) and to the definitions used for income groupings. At the first and second research conferences for the evaluation study of the CDBG program, other research goals and issues had received more emphasis than the incidence issue, though this subject was included in the discussion.

The two most important initial decisions made in developing a new research approach were (1) to disaggregate the data and (2) to analyze income incidence for each kind of CDBG-funded program separately. New definitions and analysis forms were devised and were the subject of extensive discussion at the research conference for the third round of field observations. Nine program categories were adopted: housing, neighborhood conservation, general development, urban-renewal continuation, economic development, social services, social service facilities, other public services and facilities, and planning and administration.

Because the experience in the first two rounds of field research indicated that for most of the sample jurisdictions the number of major projects was relatively small (a manageable number for observation), it was decided to develop individual hypotheses on the distribution of benefits for each of the main program categories. For example, it was hypothesized that benefits for housing and neighborhood conservation projects are distributed among the four income groups (low, moderate, middle, and high) according to the proportion each group represented of the Census tract in which the project is located; whereas the benefits of social services funded under the CDBG program could be assumed to go exclusively to lower-income groups.

Associates were asked to decide whether for a given project they would accept the hypothesis about its income-incidence impact. If they did not accept it, they were asked to allocate the benefits for this project using 5 percentage-point divisions so as to avoid giving an impression of greater specificity than is attainable in this kind of analysis. The instructions for the new format limited the benefits to be studied to "direct" benefits and identified five direct benefits: services, housing and environmental benefits, jobs, and economic development.

The advantages of the new approach are (1) that it is project specific; (2) that it enables the researchers to consider all projects (not just those located in lower income neighborhoods); (3) that it seeks to have the research group apply uniform concepts about possible incidence patterns; (4) that it enables the researchers to remove from consideration projects where the data are insufficient to make an assessment about income-group effects.

Political Effects

An essential aim of Nixon's New Federalism program was decentralization—to increase the policy discretion of the generalist officials of the recipient governments and, in relative terms, to reduce the policy discretion and opportunities for intervention of administrative officials of the federal government. A major aim of the field network research from the start was to gauge, in the best way possible, the manner in which and the extent to which this decentralization objective was carried out.

In our research, a principal objective was to compare the political effects of these newer programs with the effects that occurred under "categorical" grants. This comparative perspective, of course, is most appropriate for a block grant where preexisting categorical grants were folded into the new program, as was true of the CDBG program. It is also possible to draw general conclusions comparing the behavior of recipient jurisdictions under New Federalism grants with what is known from other studies about the effects of narrower and more specific and conditional grants-in-aid programs.

As would be expected, the political effects of the programs studied were found to vary by program. There are two main subcategories of political effects. One is the effects of a grant on the decision-making process. The other is its effect on the structure of state and local government. Under the first heading, we are interested in how a particular program affects the role of the generalist officials of general-purpose units vis-à-vis the officials of a functional agency or a special district. An illustration of the kind of issue examined under the second heading—structural effects—is whether a broad program, like general revenue sharing, tends, as many observers expected it would, to reinforce the role of small units of general-purpose government with limited functions as compared to governments with a broader geographical scope, like counties and states. Again the best way to explain the method used to study these political effects is to consider the work done under specific studies.

General revenue sharing. Both of the Brookings books reporting on the field research on the general-revenue-sharing program contain chapters on the decision-making and structural effects of the program.

In the analysis of the decision-making effects of revenue sharing, emphasis was placed on the budget process. The most important budgetary distinction was found to be between jurisdictions that in some way treated revenue-sharing funds separately and those that merged them into their regular budget cycle and process in a manner that made these receipts basically indistinguishable from other revenue.

The revenue-sharing act itself contains features that work both for and against separate budget treatment. The principal features working in the direction of separate treatment were the reporting provisions, as well as the various federal requirements for nondiscrimination, public hearings, the payment of prevailing wages, and so forth. To comply with the provisions, a jurisdiction may try to hold shared revenue apart from other funds. Other factors contained in the law or flowing from it were found to encourage the merging of shared revenue into the overall budget. The principal requirement having this effect is that recipient governments spend shared revenue "in accordance with the laws and procedures applicable to the expenditure of its own revenues."

The sixty-five sample jurisdictions for the field network study of the general-revenue-sharing program were grouped into categories using this basic distinction between separate and merged budget procedures. Three categories used in the first round of field research involved varying degrees of separateness in budget treatment. The first category included those jurisdictions that adopted a separate budgetary process for the allocation of revenue-sharing funds. The second involved the use of special budgetary procedures when decisions about the use of shared revenue were made in conjunction with the regular and ongoing budgetary process. The third category involved the use of a revenue-sharing budget supplemental. The fourth category, which applied to the majority of cases, was for jurisdictions that simply merged their shared revenue into their regular budget process.

From the point of view of the research process, a number of points need to be made about this part of the analysis. The framework for the analysis of the treatment of revenue sharing in state and local budgetary processes was not developed in advance of the collection of the field data. The analysis format used for the field research asked general questions about the decision process. It was on the basis of the review of the responses to these general questions that the classification system described above was developed.

This ex post analytical procedure, which was used for a number of major areas of the political-effects analysis, points up an advantage of the field network approach. Because the associates have a continuing relationship with the central staff, it is possible to go back to them to obtain data that are found to be needed but that were not included in the field reports originally submitted. It is also possible to devise a general procedure to obtain supplementary data that turn out to be important but that were not originally requested (although this cannot be done too often).

Such a follow-up procedure was used, for example, in the analysis of the budget processes for the allocation of revenue-sharing funds in the first round of field observations. Once the analysis categories for the budget process as described had been decided on, a supplementary one-page reporting format was developed. Using this form, the central staff indicated to the associate how his or her jurisdiction(s) had been classified in the initial review process with the definitional framework derived from the initial reports. Definitions of the categories used were provided on the form. The associate was then asked whether he or she agreed or disagreed with the indicated treatment of the field data. A similar procedure involving supplemental reporting formats was used in other instances, generally for the political-effects data because there tended to be more uncertainty at the outset about the analytical approach to be used in this area as compared with the other program effects.

Turning now to the impact of the revenue-sharing program on the structure of state and local governments, early predictions (including some of our own) were that the program would have a significant structural impact. Among the kinds of structural effects anticipated were (1) that it would perpetuate the existence of small and limited-function township and muncipal units; (2) that it would discourage the establishment, and perhaps promote the dissolution, of special districts; (3) that it would discourage annexations and mergers; (4) that it would cause user taxes paid to special districts to be reassigned, sometimes along with the pertinent functions, to general-purpose units; (5) that it would discourage intergovernmental cooperation among local units; (6) that it would cause state governments to reduce the level of their support to local units.

While field data can get at some of these issues, for others the field study served to identify and sharpen questions that were explored (using the field network research as a jumping-off point) with Census data on the organization and finances of state and local governments. Such subjects as the impact of revenue sharing on incorporation and annexation actions, on the expenditures of small governments, and on the creation and abolition of special districts were studied with Census data, augmented by questionnaires sent to state and local officials. Field data were used to supplement this analysis and study other structural-effect issues. Field data alone were used to study such effects as the adoption of new programs as a result of the receipt of revenue-sharing funds, their impact on cooperation among local units and on interlocal relations, their impact on the consolidation of governmental units and other "governmental modernization" schemes for restructuring state and local units, and the impact of these funds on state-local relations.

The principal conclusion of this part of the research was that the incentives associated with what were anticipated to be the structural effects of the revenue sharing program were not strong enough or clear enough to affect appreciably the behavior of the recipient governments. Although there are several areas in which policy changes were observed that appeared to be at least partly attributable to revenue-sharing funds, these structural effects were neither strong nor widespread.

The community development block grant program. The research on the political effects of the community development block grant program concentrated on four areas:

> The relationship between the federal government and the recipient local governmental jurisdictions
> The local decision-making process for the allocation of these funds
> Citizen participation
> Program execution

The treatment of the first area (federal-local relations) is discussed in this section as an illustration of the way in which field data were handled in the analysis of political effects under the CDBG program.

The initial question to be asked in respect to federal-local relations under the CDBG program—and it is not an easy question—is: What kind of intergovernmental relations were anticipated under the program? The expected intergovernmental effects of this block grant were described by President Ford when he signed the Housing and Community Act of 1974: ". . . [T]his bill will help to return power from the banks of the Potomac to people in their own communities. Decisions will be made at the local level. Action will come at the local level. And responsibility for results will be placed squarely where it belongs—at the local level."[7]

From the outset, many were skeptical about the extent to which decentralization aims would be, or should be, achieved under the CDBG program. Some predicted that in the first year—in the rush to implement the new program—central controls would be few and limited, but that in the ensuing years they would grow. Observers pointed out that, beginning in the second year, HUD was required to conduct performance monitoring reviews under CDBG. For this reason and others, both defenders and opponents of the decentralization objective of the CDBG program saw a possibility of what was called "creeping recategorization" in subsequent grant years.

Others pointed out—correctly as it turned out—that the election in 1976 could produce a Democratic administration less enamored of the program's decentralization aims than its Republican predecessors. In the first two rounds of field research, considerable attention was devoted to federal-local relations under the CDBG program.

Sample units were classified according to the associate's assessment of the level of HUD influence on the local program. Four classifications were used: no HUD influence, minor HUD influence, major HUD influence, and cases in which HUD's influence was so strong that it can be said that HUD determined the local program. Where HUD's role changed from year 1 to year 2, several factors (including the frequency of HUD involvement, the kind of issues raised by HUD, and the outcome of HUD-jurisdiction disagreements) were assessed to produce a single classification for the two years. It was found that in the majority of the sample communities, HUD's influence was limited. Cases with little or no HUD influence were nearly three times as numerous as those where HUD was a major influence or determined CDBG program content.

To put these findings of limited HUD influence in context, the associates were also asked to compare the CDBG experience with that under the previous categorical programs. Was HUD's role in the first two years of the CDBG program different from its role in categorical grant administration? This analysis, of necessity, was limited to the forty-four sample units that had significant previous experience under HUD programs. These data showed that not only was HUD's role limited but that in the great majority of cases it was judged to be smaller than under the preexisting categorical programs.

The second major section of this analysis of federal-local relations dealt with specific issues. The analysis concentrated on three aspects of federal-local disputes: (1) the kind of issue involved and the grounds for HUD's involvement; (2) the importance of the issue to both parties; (3) the outcome, that is, whether HUD or the local community prevailed. Two basic categories of issues were used—substantive and procedural. This classification scheme was set up on an ex post basis and used in a similar manner to the budget-process categories for the analysis of the political effects of general-revenue-sharing funds.

Overall, it was found that the position of the community tended to prevail on substantive issues, whereas on procedural issues HUD tended to prevail. Central cities were found to be more successful than other jurisdictions. Central cities prevailed in about half the cases involving substantive issues; other jurisdictions prevailed on an average only about one-fourth of the time.

The conclusion reached on the basis of this analysis for the first two program years was that the CDBG program resulted in the decentralization of decision-making authority from the federal to the local level compared with the older-style HUD categorical aid programs. There was, however, evidence for the second year of CDBG that HUD's intervention was increasing.

In the fourth year of the CDBG research, the focus for the political-effects research shifted to program execution. This was a logical development in the design of the research. In the early years, we were in a position only to consider allocations (i.e., planned uses of CDBG funds). By the fourth year, many CDBG projects had been completed and others were well along in their implementation. It was logical to turn the attention of the researchers to questions involving the speed and effectiveness of the execution process. New concepts were developed for this purpose at a special research conference held early in 1979.

SAMPLE SELECTION FOR THE NETWORK STUDIES

In essence, field network evaluation studies involve the compilation of analytical findings on program effects on the recipient governmental jurisdictions. Many steps are taken to bring about uniformity in the analysis and to assure, to the fullest extent we can, that the analytical findings of the field associates are carefully arrived at and well documented. Still, the field data cannot be used to arrive at a measure of statistical significance of the findings made about program impact.[8] We have from time to time considered using a random sample, but have not done so because of our view that this would fail to convey the nature of these studies as compilations of analytical findings by a network of social science field researchers.

Another set of reasons for using representative (rather than random) samples is logistical. To have a manageable research group, it has been necessary to have many associates report on more than one field site. Furthermore, in order to make sure that associates are familiar with, and have frequent access to, the best data sources at each site, it was decided that the sites handled by a single associate should be clustered—for example, three or four rural jurisdictions in an area close to a university research center, a central city and one or two of its suburban jurisdictions, a state capital and a nearby small city, and so on.

If, as a variant of the research methodology described here, the design of one of the field network studies had focused on a dominant governmental type, it might have been possible to use a randomization procedure for sample selection. Our experience suggests that locating competent field researchers on this basis would be possible if such a study were focused on large governmental jurisdictions, as for example, a sample of cities having above 50,000 populations. The tradeoff here is between a design focused on one jurisdictional type and a design that permits researchers to compare groups and jurisdictions—central cities and suburbs, northern cities and southern cities, large cities and small ones, cities and counties, rich and poor communities, and so forth.

Another reason for using representative samples relates to the basic nature of the U.S. governmental system. The diversity and fragmentation of American federalism makes it exceedingly difficult to single out one type of government and have all the units in the universe be reasonably similar. It was suggested above that a random sample might have been constructed for large cities. However, persons familiar with the different functions of municipal and other local governments within states and among states will recognize the kinds of problems that would have been involved in generalizing from such data. If the goal instead was a national sample of all local units to avoid the effects of functional diversity caused by focusing on one local governmental type, we would have needed a sample much larger than our resources would have allowed. The universe of local governments includes 39,000 general-purpose units. Yet even a random sample of local units would fail to take into account differences in the functions and scope of state governments. The sample used in the Adams-Crippen econometric analysis of the impact of the general-revenue-sharing program referred to earlier consisted of 1,424 jurisdictions. The size of the sample was determined by the availability of time-series data from the Bureau of the Census. It is possible that we could have used a smaller sample, but not one small enough to fit the resources available for a field network evaluation study. While I expect that this will be a controversial statement, I believe that the multiplicity and diversity of local governmental units in American federalism are simply too great to warrant the allocation of resources to a field network evaluation study with a random sample on the intergovernmental effects of a major federal grants-in-aid program.

CONCLUDING COMMENTS

As in any set of policy studies, many tradeoffs have been made in the design and execution of these field network evaluation studies. The question must always be asked: How does this approach relate to other approaches? Others will have to answer this question in the final analysis. In the real world of limited costs, limited data, and constant policy change, we believe the field network methodology can expand what is known about the effects of large, multifaceted, and broad-gauged federal aid programs in ways that, in our experience at least, have proven to be useful in public policy decision making. By providing a uniform analytical framework for the field analysts and bringing them together in effective working relationships with each other and the central staff, we have been able to enhance both their knowledge of the program effects to be studied and their ability to treat them objectively.

Field network research is a *group* process. It draws social scientists—both centrally and in the field—into a single system. The programs studied are very large and operate in a complex environment. The need to combine many analysts in ways that keep them honest and interested is essential for federal grant-in-aid evaluation research.

NOTES

1. Ray D. Whitman and Robert J. Cline, "Fiscal Impact of Revenue Sharing in Comparison with Other Federal Aid: An Evaluation of Recent Empirical Findings" (Prepared for the Office of Revenue Sharing, U.S. Department of the Treasury, The Urban Institute, 28 November 1978), p. i.
2. Testimony by George E. Peterson, *Hearings Before the Subcommittee on the City, of the Committee on Banking, Finance and Urban Affairs of the U.S. House of Representatives and the Joint Economic Committee,* 25 July 1978, p. 76.
3. George Johnson and James Tomola, "The Fiscal Substitution Effect of Alternative Approaches to Public Service Employment Policy," *Journal of Human Resources* 12, no. 1 (Winter 1977): 3-26.
4. Laurie Bassi and Alan Fechter, *The Implications for Fiscal Substitution and Occupational Displacement Under an Expanded CETA Title VI,* U.S. Department of Labor, Technical Analysis Paper #64, Washington, D.C., March 1979.
5. I particularly have in mind a review by Sidney L. Carroll in the *Journal of Economic Literature,* in which he suggests that one of the reasons the Brookings researchers chose the methodology they used was that it is "expensive and 'contact-intensive' and is probably only available to a few large institutions such as Brookings." *Journal of Economic Literature* 16 (September 1978): 1054.
6. *Housing and Community Development Act of 1977, Hearings Before the House Subcommittee on Housing and Community Development of the Committee on Banking, Finance, and Urban Affairs,* 93 Cong., 1st sess. 1977, pt. 1, p. 9.
7. Gerald R. Ford, "Statement on the Housing and Community Development Act of 1974," *Public Papers of the President of the United States* (Washington, D.C.: U.S. Government Printing Office, 1975), p. 44.
8. In the fourth round of the field evaluation study of the CETA jobs program, we are experimenting with techniques by which field associates will indicate their level of confidence in the assessments they make of program impact. We will combine these observations on a basis that indicates a range of certainty.

SELECTED PUBLICATIONS RELATING TO
FIELD NETWORK EVALUATION RESEARCH

ADAMS, CHARLES F., JR.; and DAN CRIPPEN. 1978. "The Fiscal Impact of Revenue Sharing on Local Governments." Office of Revenue Sharing. U.S. Department of the Treasury, May.

COOK, ROBERT F., and V. LANE RAWLINS. 1978. "Job Displacement under CETA Public Service Employment." American Statistical Association, *Business and Economic Statistic Section Proceedings,* pp. 86-94.

_____. 1979."Local and National Objectives in Public Service Employment." Industrial Relations Research Association, *Proceedings of the Thirty-Second Annual Meeting,* Atlanta, December.

DOMMEL, PAUL R.; RICHARD P. NATHAN; SARAH F. LIEBSCHUTZ; and MARGARET T. WRIGHTSON. 1978. *Decentralizing Community Development.* Prepared under contract with the Department of Housing and Urban Development, Office of Policy Development and Research. Washington, D.C.: U.S. Government Printing Office, June.

_____, and JACOB M. JAFFE. 1978.*Report on the Allocation of Community Development Funds to Small Cities.* Prepared under contract with the Department of Housing and Urban Development, Office of Policy Development and Research. Washington, D.C.: U.S. Government Printing Office, November.

MANVEL, ALLEN D. 1975."The Fiscal Impact of Revenue Sharing." *The Annals* 419, May.

NATHAN, RICHARD P.; ALLEN D. MANVEL; SUSANNAH E. CALKINS; and ASSOCIATES. 1975. *Monitoring Revenue Sharing.* Washington, D.C.: Brookings Institution.

_____; CHARLES F. ADAMS, JR.; and ASSOCIATES. 1977. *Revenue Sharing: The Second Round.* Washington, D.C.: Brookings Institution.

_____; PAUL R. DOMMEL; SARAH F. LIEBSCHUTZ; and MILTON D. MORRIS. 1977. "Monitoring the Block Grant Program for Community Development." *Political Science Quarterly* 92, no. 2, Summer.

_____. 1977. *Block Grants for Community Development.* Prepared under contract with the Department of Housing and Urban Development, Office of Policy Development and Research. Washington, D.C.: U.S. Government Printing Office.

_____; ROBERT F. COOK; RICHARD LONG; and JANET GALCHICK. 1978. *Job Creation Through Public Employment,* vol. 2. *Monitoring The Public Service Employment Program, An Interim Report to the Congress.* Washington, D.C.: National Commission for Manpower Policy, March .

_____. 1979. *Monitoring the Public Service Employment Program: The Second Round.* Washington, D.C.: National Commission for Manpower Policy, Special Report No. 32, March.

5

Tracking Decisions and Consequences:
The Field Network Evaluation Approach

JOHN STUART HALL AND SUSAN A. MACMANUS

As a branch of inquiry, policy analysis is in a growth stage. Although it has not been easy, and can in no way be judged complete, researchers interested in public policy impacts and implementation have finally begun to be weaned from sole reliance on traditional techniques of survey research and crunching official numbers. Recent textbooks discuss elite interviewing, simulation, small-group experimentation, scenario building, and a host of other techniques as substitutes and/or supplements to traditional techniques.[1]

The field network evaluation research practiced in several recent public policy studies is one such approach. The field network approach is used to study policy formation, implementation, and/or impacts in a large number of geographically dispersed jurisdictions. Examples of these studies are contained in table 5.1. They vary on many dimensions, but in all cases a central research staff selects a field associate in each jurisdiction. The associate is usually an academic who resides in or near the jurisdiction. Each associate conducts the evaluation in his or her jurisdiction. The associate's research is directed by a set of uniformly agreed upon questions that are answered and then forwarded to the central research staff for more in-depth analysis. The central research staff analyzes all field reports and then prepares a final research report, which is submitted to the funding agency (for an outline of the process, see figure 5.1 on page 102).

In effect, field network evaluation is a decentralized, grass-roots approach to policy research based on the assumption that researchers closest to the jurisdiction are the most capable of knowing, tapping, and interpreting relevant local policy developments and impacts. This approach requires that field associates combine techniques of field observation, aggregate data analysis, survey and elite interviewing, and case-study analysis.

TABLE 5.1
MAJOR FIELD EVALUATION RESEARCH
STUDIES OF LOCAL PUBLIC POLICY*

Study	Director	Duration of Field Work	Number of Field Sites
Brookings Institution Study of General Revenue Sharing.	Richard Nathan	4 years, 3 rounds	65
Brookings Institution Study of Community Development Block Grant (CD).	Paul Dommel	6 years, 4 rounds	61
Princeton University Woodrow Wilson School Study of Public Service Employment (PSE) portion of CETA.	Robert Cook	5 years, 4 rounds	42
National Academy of Sciences Study of CETA.	William Mirengoff	6 years	28
Northwestern University Center for Urban Affairs Study of Governmental Response to Crime.	Herbert Jacob and Robert Lineberry	1 year	10

*For citations to reports containing descriptions of methods and findings, see the bibliography at the end of this chapter.

The purpose of this essay is to examine the advantages and disadvantages of this approach to policy analysis and specifically to assess the usefulness of field network evaluation methods for studies of policy implementation. Our view is from the bottom up. We have served as field research associates and/or consultants for each of the studies listed in table 5.1. Our experiential biases are probably compounded by our methodological ones. That is, to date our method for developing generalizations that follow has been limited to informal discussion with other field research associates and nonsystematic observation as participants in the research. Our defense is that by sheer size and scope these are important studies whose methods should be examined closely. Most of the discussion of these methods to this point has come from central staff members[2] or from outsiders committed to an alternative approach.[3] Our perspective is different and biased, but to the degree that they represent the view of other field researchers, our views need to be understood in considering the place of team monitoring research in policy analysis.

Stage	Activity
1	Selection as a Team Monitor (field associate) by Central Investigative Staff
2	Review of Information on the Program to be Monitored (central staff supplies each monitor with publications, legislative mandates, program descriptions, etc.)
3	Review of Proposed Research Report Form (central staff sends each monitor the draft of proposed report forms)
4	Collection of Preliminary Data[b] (by each monitor for central staff)
*5	Conference Discussion of the Proposed Research Report Form (and preliminary data) by All Team Monitors and Central Staff
*6	Data Collection (by each monitor after receipt of final report form as adopted by the central staff)
*7	Data Analysis
8	Writing of the Final Field Report (central staff sets uniform deadline date)
*9	Validity Check/Informational Clarification of Report (by central staff with individual monitor)
*10	Postreport Activity (individual monitor often pressured locally to release or discuss findings)
*11	Selection as a Team Monitor—Next Round

[a] Longitudinally designed research is research for which a minimum of two rounds of monitoring have been authorized and funded.
[b] Stage 4 does not occur in all monitoring research.
*Indicates stages at which problems with the method are most likely to occur.

FIGURE 5.1
STAGES OF LONGITUDINALLY DESIGNED
FIELD NETWORK EVALUATION[a]

Team research itself is, of course, nothing new. The "hard" sciences have provided ample evidence of the utility of team research into questions of all sorts including some of the more important ones in areas like nuclear power and genetics.

Social scientists have been slower to adopt the team research approach, largely because their disciplines are relatively underdeveloped; they lack agreement on important questions for inquiry, much less methods. According to Robert Merton, the difference between twentieth-century physics and twentieth-century sociology (and by extension, between the "hard" and social sciences) is "billions of man-hours of sustained, disciplined, and cumulative research. Perhaps sociology is not yet ready for its Einstein because it has not yet found its Kepler."[4] Nevertheless, the economics of division of labor and specialization coupled with the conceptual benefits of research interactions over preliminary theories and findings have resulted in outcroppings of collaboration over important policy and theoretical topics.

The field network evaluation approach described and evaluated here has similar attributes but goes beyond earlier team research efforts. In the first place, the efforts examined here are larger in scope. They employ a larger number of researchers, cost more, and examine a wider variety of settings.

The Brookings/Princeton Public Service Employment (PSE), Community Development (CD), and the General Revenue Sharing (GRS) studies alone are based on the research of teams of approximately 52 Ph.D.-level field associates examining impacts of these components of federal aid in 40 to 65 sites. Research completed and in progress will cost $6 million for 11 rounds of monitoring from 1972 through 1982.[5]

More importantly, these efforts differ in *depth of attachment* of the field researcher to a policy process and/or particular aspects of public policy. In all the projects described here, field researchers collect and analyze information over a significant time span. For several of these studies, multiple "rounds" of observations span several years, and each round requires many weeks of intensive research.

Indeed, despite the most admirable individual and organizational attempts to remain objective, the field research associate is likely, to some degree, to become part of the policy process being studied. Whether this attachment is in the net, for better or for worse, it is a major part of the evaluation that follows. Whatever our conclusions here or in subsequent research of ours or others, it seems clear that the sheer scope and depth of attachment of these inquiries justifies close evaluation of the approach.

THE STUDIES

Because of our interest and experience, we have chosen to begin a general inquiry into the place of field network evaluation research in public policy analysis by focusing on major studies of public policy at the local level. Table 5.1 provides a list and brief description of these major policy research efforts employing the Team Monitoring approach.

There are many differences in specific technique, expectation, and substantive focus of these studies, but they share certain general characteristics. They all made use of a "network" of researchers—generally Ph.D. social scientists working out of a university—to examine local public policy issues and processes over time. In all studies, local field researchers collaborated with central staff to some degree in study design, although most of the development of uniform formats for data collection and analysis was done by central staff. All studies made heavy use of interviews with local policy participants, local records and data, and local news reports.

Important sources of variation among the studies dictate that the remaining analysis will draw largely from experiences with the Brookings CD and GRS studies and the Princeton PSE research. In the first place, whereas these studies demand uniform analysis—response to critical study questions—they allow substantial field discretion in some data collection. Thus, unlike the Northwestern and National Academy of Sciences examples, they are, by design, some distance from traditional survey research design assumptions. Discretion in some data collection continues throughout the length of the field research. As the field associate interacts with local informants and central staff over the time of the study, information for and answers to key questions may change. In these studies the field research associate is the unit for analysis and is asked to make judgments based on the best available information. Judgments are required of all field researchers, but central staff do not presume to know or dictate the best local data sources for making judgments. Field researchers in these studies must be more than local interviewers.

A second major difference that justifies our focus on the Brookings/Princeton studies is that each study is following the course of a policy from its inception over a significant period of time. By spanning several years of data collection and analysis rounds, these studies are truly longitudinal.

GREAT PROMISES

These particular studies, then are distinctively *continuous, longitudinal, inter-*

active, and *interpretive.* These attributes enhance discovery and understanding of cause and effect by focusing more sharply and for a longer time on the process of policy formation, implementation, and impact. The utility of longitudinal analysis for analyzing cause and effect is well known. Field network evaluation builds on the opportunity to observe policy processes over time by designing for maximum interaction between the field research associate and local data sources. This three-way interaction over time among the central staff, the field research associate, and local officials allows

1. Central staff to redesign, to ask new questions, and to reanalyze data based on initial rounds of research
2. The field research associate to interview different informants, trace data sources, and make informed reliability judgments of these sources

Thus the field network approach allows research design revision stimulated by either the field research associate or central office staff, based on an ongoing appraisal of the meaning of variable local data. As the policy changes, so can the focus of inquiry. Because of this flexibility, the method would seem ideally suited to following policy development through its many stages and tracking the multiple consequences of policy decision.

Like many other social science research approaches, including evaluation research in general, the ideals of field network evaluation are sometimes thwarted because researchers and their subjects are human and therefore fallible. The following discussion treats promises and problems of this method's application at different stages of the monitoring process. Figure 5.1 shows different stages of field network research and identifies points at which problems—particularly from the perspective of the field associate—are most likely to emerge.

THE CONFERENCE: STAGING THE RESEARCH

Several conferences of field research associates and central staff were held over the course of these research projects. Conferences were normally held prior to each round of research and were attended by most associates. Each field researcher was initially chosen because of his or her recognition as a scholar and as a person knowledgeable about local politics and programs. Thus, when these individuals were brought together and met with central staff members, a potentially powerful intellectual force was created. Borrowing from the "hard" science model, team members could be used for elaborate theory-building interaction. The division of labor *within* specialties should lead to efficient use of resources.

Actually, overall study direction, purpose, and theoretical orientation receive relatively little attention at the full conferences of research associates. Individual research associates are sometimes asked for research design help during the drafting of the field research instrument, but that occurs prior to these conferences. A major portion of formal conference time is devoted to central staff presentation to field researchers of the draft field report instrument.

Piloting and Planning

The process of going through the report form clarifies study direction and objectivity and accomplishes several other worthwhile purposes. In the Brookings/Princeton projects, the draft report form lists several questions that associates are expected to answer by the end of their field research. In this sense, the report form is like more traditional survey instruments: it provides a preview of questions that lead the research. Field research associates serve as "pilot" groups in going over these questions and often criticize study design and/or intent during interaction over particular questions. As a whole, the group is well qualified and prone to provide substantive and logistical criticism. Although this process does not result in a wholesale revision of questions or study design, examples of "retreat" on the part of central staff are evident at precisely the right points, that is, where associate disagreement is strong and uniform.

In addition to this valuable piloting function, the conference serves as a useful staging point for data collection efforts to follow. Central staff and field associates exchange information concerning data sources, likely informant types, and so forth, that is invaluable in the field work to follow. Different plausible field research strategies and techniques are available to answer the uniform questions of the report form, and conferences help inform associates of the range of data collection opportunities available to them.

Developing a Comparative Perspective

Perhaps more important than specific data collection tips exchanged at these conferences is the creation of a comparative perspective. After the conference, the field researcher applies a uniform analytical framework that asks many broad judgmental questions to a specific jurisdiction case. Although all field researchers are brought into the project with some demonstrated general prior knowledge of the policy in question, empirical work on the same policy question(s) at other sites may be limited or nonexistent. Stories of policy process at other sites lend much needed perspective to the field researcher's subsequent efforts. These reports help in the sorting process required to identify commonalties, trends, and anomalies needing further investigation and checking. Most importantly, they lend greatly to the authority of the field researcher, which in turn makes him or her effective in interviews with local officials who often use similar specialized networks to keep current. A certain amount of this kind of small-group and informal exchange has been included as a part of formal conference activity. It seems to go best in small groups, perhaps meeting for cocktails or dinner.

Indeed, the informal meeting of associates at several conferences goes a long way toward building a network partially independent of the study. Not surprisingly, researchers who share general academic as well as specific field evaluation experiences tend to collaborate on other research and professional ventures. Papers, articles, and professional meeting panels are planned, executed, and encouraged by central staff as a natural outgrowth of the team research experience.

Problems: "We-They" Splits and Monitor Competition

It will surprise no one with an elementary understanding of social psychology that these conferences can become unbalanced and counterproductive. By definition, these conferences require powerful personalities to compete over intellectual turf in a relatively small space for a relatively short time.

A "we-they" split is sometimes evident in formal and informal conference discussions. Much of this can be explained by the different perspectives each group has regarding the research. As diagrammed in figure 5.2, the central staff approaches the research from a broad, theoretical perspective, whereas the individual associate takes a narrower, more practical approach to the research assignment. Associates often complain among themselves that the central staff simply doesn't understand, or seem concerned with, the difficulties of "real world" data collection. Some associates feel that their more practically based recommendations are not seriously considered by the central staff.

This "we-they" syndrome is an extension of what Carol Weiss calls "status rivalry."[6] In this context, the rivalry is between central staff members and team

Research Participants	Extent of Involvement in project	Approach	Assessment of Ability to Change Opinion of Other Group
Central staff ("They")	broad	theoretical	positive
Team monitors ("We")	narrow	practical	negative

NOTE: As seen by the majority of team associates. (Conclusion of the authors after informal interviews with other team associates over a three-year period.)

FIGURE 5.2
A COMPARISON OF RESEARCH PERSPECTIVES:
CENTRAL STAFF v. TEAM ASSOCIATES

monitors rather than between program evaluators and program administrators. Substituting "field associates" for "practitioners" and "central staff" for "researchers," the problem of status rivalry in the team monitoring approach can be stated as follows:

> (Field associates) slave away and do the day-to-day drudgery, while (central staff members) . . . write a report and collect all the kudos — programmatic, academic, and . . . financial. As the (field associate) sees it, the (central staff) collects all the rewards.

These "we-they" distinctions can become more hardened the longer associates are involved in the research, that is, the more "rounds" of research in which they participate.

Perceived inequity of input. Another problem that emerges at the conference stage is competition among field associates for recognition by the central staff. It is important to keep in mind that each associate was initially chosen because of his or her reputation as a scholar knowledgeable about local government politics and programs. This means that strong personalities are competing for attention. Many of the field associates perceive that their individual input is not valued as highly by the central staff as that of a few select ("favored") associates. This perceived "pecking order" further intensifies the "we-they" demarcation between monitors and central staff.

The status rivalry problem identified in the general evaluation literature as between program evaluators and program administrators can be enhanced at the conference stage when the team monitoring approach is used for program evaluation.

DATA COLLECTION: ESTABLISHING RAPPORT

One of the strongest features of the field network method is that it allows the field researcher to practice many of the suggestions of social scientists on establishing and managing entree to the research setting.[7] That is, it is possible over several rounds of field research to establish rapport with and gain the confidence of key informants. Personal skills help, but this process is probably most enhanced when field researchers' questions relate to immediate policy concerns of local officials; when questions fit the policymaker's "action orientation." Many of the questions that Brookings/Princeton monitors have asked concerning CETA, CD, overall federal aid, and local budgets and personnel matters have this quality. For the most part, the critical questions surrounding these programs were unresolved during the research, which made them as interesting to the respondent as to the field researcher. The simple fact that "big league" research institutions like Brookings and Princeton and their associates were asking for the local point of view and trying to find out what was really going on in the new fiscal federalism enhanced interest in, and response to, this research.

When he or she is implementing the research correctly, the field researcher spends substantial time in multiple sessions with key informants. Some informants seem to think of this interaction as a teaching/learning relationship with the local official assuming the role of teacher. Other informants may view the relationship as a problem-solving one in which the researcher and the local official are on relatively equal footing in pursuit of the best number, data source, or answer. Whatever the precise reason, the adversary relationship often established when a researcher is seen by a local official as distant from his or her policy environment and the public official is seen by the researcher as a narrow-minded bureaucrat is often softened and improved by monitoring.

Once established, rapport pays big dividends in the form of answers to interview questions, provision of high-quality data, and tips on good sources and other informants. Some of the most valuable data for this sort of research exists in the form of correspondence, internal memoranda, and in-house reports. Normally, trust needs to be established before these sources of data are volunteered.

Advantages of Longitudinal Data Collection
In summary, field network evaluation provides time, resources, and a framework for overcoming hostility that can be stimulated by data collection efforts that appear to respondents to be some distance from their frame of reference, interest, or both. As this interaction develops and improves, the associate may find — or be presented with — new information that counters a previous finding. By acknowledging this revisionist posture to key informants, the field researcher may reinforce his or her singleminded quest for the best answer, thereby increasing rapport and entree to new information. Thus the field network method encourages persistence in data collection and allows for probes and follow-ups prohibited by normal survey design. It is our contention that respondents often take this persistence as evidence of deeper interest in and/or understanding of their work on the part of the field research associate than is normally associated with public policy researchers.

Problems: The Data Collection Stage
Despite the method's rapport-building advantages, it is not a panacea. Rapport is not always easily achieved and maintained. Normal data collection problems remain, and some are enhanced by field evaluation.

Difficulty of tapping valuable data sources. In federal programs such as CETA and CDBG, there is a high turnover of personnel, which often makes it difficult for even an "experienced" associate to keep a current list of key informants. Similar problems arise when there are changes in the political environment, such as the election of new city officials, restructuring of departments, changes in the form of government, or increases in publicity regarding the program being monitored. The field associate may even inadvertently be thrust in the middle of local political controversies and thereby lose access to valuable data sources. Despite careful groundwork with individuals, the chances of loss of rapport as a result of situational change increase the longer an individual monitors the same program in the same jurisdiction.

Clearance with local officials. One of the unanticipated problems involves clearance or solicitation of the cooperation of local officials. Central staffs have generally sought formal clearance in the form of a letter from the appropriate federal government funding agency (e.g., HUD, HEW, DOL) to a regional office or the local program director. Because of the structural and political fragmentation of many local governments, such a letter effectively shifts the real responsibility for clearance to the individual field associate. Such clearance takes a lot of *time*—it is probably easier in subsequent rounds of research, but is not typically built into the initial research planning.

Research competition. The field evaluation approach has been used most often in the study of new block-grant federal programs, which are of extreme interest to a large number of researchers, many of whom receive funding from the same governmental agency. The individual team monitor has to bear the brunt of a busy program administrator's annoyance with "having to deal with another researcher studying the same program" and sometimes is placed in the embarrassing position of appearing ignorant about other research on the very program that he or she is monitoring.

Narrowness of data sources. Rossi, in his discussion of monitoring methods, identifies "four data sources that should be [included] in the design of a monitoring evaluation: (1) direct observation by the evaluator; (2) service records; (3) data from program staff who are service providers; and (4) information from program participants."[8] A comprehensive evaluation should include data from all these sources. To date, most of the policy research on federal programs, including studies that have used the team monitoring approach, has failed to collect data from program participants. Because of their familiarity with program evaluation theories and techniques, some associates feel that their efforts in the field are incomplete without inclusion of data from program participants.

DATA ANALYSIS

The field research associate's judgments are central to the monitoring method. Theoretically, these judgments rest on the different kinds and sources of data collected by the associate over a round of monitoring. At the end of any given round of research, these evaluations must be made in response to the set of questions contained in the earlier agreed upon report form.

Advantages of Linking Field Analysis to Data Collection
Length of time in the field, entree, and increasing knowledge of policy impacts and local government processes can give the field evaluation studies researcher a solid base for making judgments. The somewhat artificial distinction between data collection and analysis can hinder progress in inquiry and lead to what one researcher has called the "misplaced concreteness fallacy."[9] Under this rather common condition in social science, a set of numbers or other observations are collected. The analysis and reporting that follows presumes that these data are the best available, which often slips into "most objective." As we have indicated earlier, the field researcher learns rather quickly that official reports and other easily accessible sources may be far from the "best data." In fact, one of the field researcher's central tasks is to press for an explanation of official data, to understand anomalies and inconsistencies, and to piece together, while in the field, bits of evidence that are consistent and corroborative. Thus, to take full advantage of the method, the field researcher probably views data collection and analysis as interactive over the course of the research. In practice, this means that a field researcher begins the search by collecting general information from interviews, official reports, news sources, and so forth. After some *analysis* of that information, the researcher can focus on the holes in the story. Missing or contradictory information requires new and more focused data collection. To achieve the best results in this latter data collection requires some analysis of previous data, perhaps even draft responses to some questions. As one researcher has noted, early drafts can play an important role in field research: "My initial review of the rough draft stimulated many thoughts about what additional observational data should be collected, lines of questioning to be pursued, interviews to be conducted, documents to be collected, and so forth."[10]

Officially, central staff analysis takes over where field research analysis leaves off. That is, analyses from the field—completed reports in response to uniform questions—become the central data source for final analysis and subsequent publication of the central staff. When the three-way interaction among central staff, field researcher, and local informants is working properly, however, central staff guidance in the field data collection process and follow-up questions after initial analysis of field reports work to impose theoretical focus throughout case-based collection and analysis of the field researcher. By pushing for additional information in response to early analysis, this research process has obvious advantages for studying process effects, particularly at a time of major change in policies and programs.

The Problem of Personal Bias

The critical nature of the field researcher's judgments in this research heightens the ever-present problem of researcher bias. As noted earlier, the associate is required to be more than an interviewer. But, as the associate becomes more comfortable in extending the role of interviewer (data collector) to that of informed observer (data collector *and* analyst), he or she becomes more vulnerable to the trap of selective perception. Intensive less-structured interviews always increase the possibility of interviewer bias.[11] When the results of these interviews are summarized and analyzed by the interviewer (associate) with no intervening external analysis, it is extremely difficult to assess the amount of bias that enters into the analysis. Researchers in the analysis stage who have collected data through more traditional survey methods are sometimes forced by response patterns to face up to the embarrassing reality of bad questions and ask, "Did I really ask that?" Field researcher's introspection begins with the question, "Did I really hear that?"

A negative answer to that question requires the researcher to be critical of his or her data collection, which seems, without external pressure, to be asking for an unrealistic degree of objective critical skill. Even if some associates are superhuman in this regard and regularly ask and answer such questions, an important deficiency in field evaluation methods is lack of systematic "data quality control," that is, a process to test regularly "the hypothesis that something is seriously wrong with (research) production methods."[12] This is not to say that central staff are oblivious to or unconcerned about this potential problem. Multiple informal steps are taken by those receiving the research to push for consistent, high-quality information. The potential for problems lies in the lack of emphasis on *systematic* data checks at the individual associate level.

A second and equally critical problem is the related danger of a team associate's becoming either an adversary or an advocate of the program, government, agency, or individual being monitored (see figure 5.3). This possibility increases as one's length of service as an associate increases and seems likely to affect data collection in subsequent rounds of monitoring.

One of the oft-stated advantages of field network evaluation is that it reduces "the possibility that the members of the central staff of a national research project introduce a bias by attaching their own particular analytical interpretations and policy views to national and field data."[13] Another possibility, if the three-way interaction is not working effectively, is that the responsibility for bias is effectively shifted downward to the individual associate but ineffectively eliminated as a problem. Communications between central staff members and field associates after the completion of a field report are designed to guard against this possibility. These informal validity checks catch many problems and provide important clarifications, but they do not eliminate the more basic potential problem of team monitor bias that may accompany longitudinal evaluation studies relying heavily on intensive personal interviews.

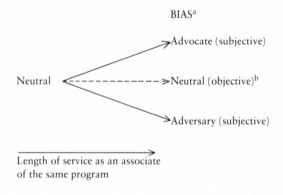

BIAS[a]

Advocate (subjective)

Neutral   Neutral (objective)[b]

Adversary (subjective)

Length of service as an associate
of the same program

---

[a] Bias may extend to overall program or to specific governments, agencies, or individuals being monitored. It is possible for an associate to be an advocate, adversary, and neutral if more than one unit of analysis is being evaluated (program, individual, agency).
[b] The least likely effect.

FIGURE 5.3
THE EFFECTS OF LONGEVITY AS A RESEARCH
ASSOCIATE ON PROGRAM ANALYSIS

POST-FIELD REPORT

Potential Benefits and Costs
Immersion in extensive field research of this sort creates many attachments and commitments. Depending in a large degree on the individual researcher's career

stage and objectives, these attachments take on different meaning and direction. The academic interests that brought researchers into the research in the first place are normally fed and enhanced by the field research experience. Some associates work with the central staff to mine the field report data base and write chapters and sections of final manuscripts. Others continue to work on critical policy issues associated with programs like CETA and CDBG, but merge their monitoring-based observations with other data sources and/or colleagues for papers and articles.

In addition, monitors have learned more about local government process and personalities during the research, and since the research is being conducted at home, they may feel the desire to participate more actively in local politics and government. The knowledge that the field associate will probably be asked to participate in subsequent rounds during the life of the research means that, at a minimum, most monitors will try to keep posted on "off-season" policy developments by informal means such as clipping news articles and keeping in touch with key local informants.

This stimulation to pursue important policy questions and keep abreast of local events builds the credibility of the notion of the associate as "informed local observer." The advantages of the monitoring approach described throughout this paper center on the assumption that the individual associate knows something about *both* policy and process and will continue to learn more about them by observing policy development in a natural setting over time.

Thus individual field researchers often have good reasons to want to remain a part of the network and continue to monitor their jurisdictions for subsequent rounds of the study. In addition, it can be argued that the overall study benefits from the continuity of learning by "informed local observers."

Despite these good reasons for commitment to continued monitoring, several forces may push individual field researchers away from subsequent monitoring research. After the associate's field report is completed, cross-pressures may be placed on him or her, particularly if the program is a new one or a troubled one (see figure 5.4). The associate may be pressured by local elected officials or program administrators to release findings, even though they have been informed in advance (on the directives of the central staff) that such would not be done. Failure to release findings to locals may severely damage future cooperation. According to Weiss, program administrators "are likely to be particularly resentful when the evaluator produces the report, turns it in, and goes away. . . ."[14] The damaging of future cooperation may be even more critical if the monitor is actively engaged in other research in the particular governmental arena, which is often the case in the light of the criteria used in the initial selection of team associates.

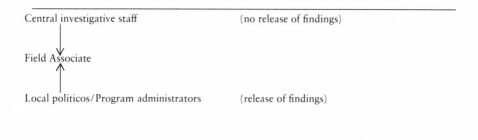

FIGURE 5.4
POSTREPORT CROSS-PRESSURES ON FIELD ASSOCIATES

Another side to the potential problem is that the longer a person serves as an associate, the greater the likelihood of being pressured by local government officials to become part of the program being evaluated by serving as a member of an advisory group, as a consultant, or as a program administrator. Refusal to do any of the above may lead to local accusations of "milking the program"[15] and may damage future access to data and key informants. In practice, this is a less likely outcome than the more subtle danger of unofficial program attachment. It may be that the more knowledgeable and affable the associate, the more likely that he or she will be asked for information and perhaps policy advice. Does one give the advice, thereby affecting the process under study, or does one refuse and run the risk of alienating a key informant? However these questions are answered, the difficulties of remaining neutral and objective in the eyes of the persons being studied increase the longer one serves as an associate.

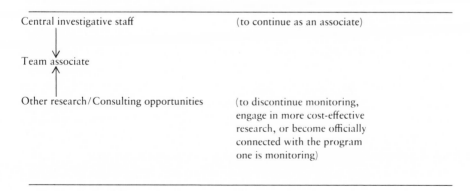

FIGURE 5.5
CROSS-PRESSURES: FUTURE FIELD EVALUATION RESEARCH

Problems in Serving as a Field Associate for Subsequent Rounds
Here, as in the postreport stage, the field associate may experience cross-pressures from the central investigative staff to continue as an associate and from other research or consulting opportunities to leave field evaluation research behind (see figure 5.5 on page 115). At this stage the associate may engage in some personal "cost-benefit" analysis, particularly in view of the time involved in these studies in relationship to the compensation.

Central staff members may underestimate the time that an associate must devote to one round of study. Nathan estimates that a field associate devotes "an average of thirty days per year to [his or her] participation in a monitoring study."[16] This is clearly a conservative figure, but one on which contract fees are calculated. Even should the fee be increased in relation to a longer time served, it would still be significantly below what many associates could make as consultants or researchers on other projects. For these reasons, some associates reach a point at which participation no longer makes economic or academic sense. These cross-pressures may become more intense the longer one serves as a monitor.

SUMMARY AND CONCLUSIONS

This has been an admittedly impressionistic assessment of step-by-step advantages and problems of field network evaluation research as practiced in the Brookings/Princeton large-scale studies of fiscal federalism. Despite its anecdotal character, we feel that the essay demonstrates the need for a more systematic appraisal of the central question that emerges in discussing most stages of the research: What is the net effect of longitudinal design on the research product? On the one hand, we described as critical the need to hire informed local observers and encourage them to push for entree to the policy action arena and new and relatively untapped data sources. This takes time and can pay off with multiple data collection and analysis dividends. On the other hand, we observed that long-term research of this sort can work to increase personal bias and cross-pressures that generally push associates away from the hard-to-maintain ground of researcher neutrality. We need to know more about the full effects of these strains of research maturity on the product and will turn in the future to a much more systematic research approach that at a minimum raises these questions with a larger universe of field researchers and central staff.

For the present, we conclude, however, tentatively, that the flexibility and range of the field evaluation approach makes it ideal for exploratory research, particularly research that focuses on the early stages of new policy development.

Diversity of all sorts is useful at this stage of policy analysis. Differences in associates and the interactive effects of their involvement in the research over time may become more critical, however, as research becomes more theoretical or at least is guided by more specific research questions. If field network evaluation is to remain the method to examine these kinds of questions, it probably needs to change toward more closed-ended and comparable design.

Based on these conclusions, we suggest that field network evaluation research can be an important policy analysis weapon that may be most effective where traditional tools are weakest and when it (1) focuses on the "front end" of the policy process, and (2) focuses more on decisions than on consequences. To the extent that these conclusions are borne out by future research, the utility of the approach for studies of implementation may seem questionable. But if implementation problems associated with new intergovernmental programs and policy changes are the subject for inquiry, the best method may prove to be field network evaluation.

Most importantly, we would argue that, without the benefit of further research, the field network studies described here have already made a major contribution toward the "greening of policy analysis" by providing a new vehicle for decentralizing research and by bringing resources together to promote a group approach to large and complex public policy questions. Refinements that may be needed and eventually adopted in future studies will add shape and precision to the form but probably will not challenge the basic need addressed by this approach for careful fieldwork to complement traditional forms of policy analysis.

NOTES

1. Grover Starling, *The Politics and Economics of Public Policy* (Homewood, Ill.: Dorsey, 1979); William Ascher, *Forecasting: An Appraisal for Policy Makers and Planners* (Baltimore: Johns Hopkins University Press, 1978).
2. Richard P. Nathan, "The Brookings Monitoring Research Methodology for Studying the Effects of Federal Grant-in-Aid Programs." (paper prepared for presentation to the American Political Science Association, Washington, D.C., September 1979).
3. Sidney L. Carroll, review of *Revenue Sharing: The Second Round,* by Richard P. Nathan and Charles F. Adams, Jr. and Associates, assisted by Andre Juneau and James W. Fossett in *Journal of Economic Literature* 16 (September 1978): 1053-54.
4. Robert K. Merton, *Social Theory and Social Structure* (New York: Free Press, 1957), p. 7.
5. Nathan, "The Brookings Monitoring Research Methodology."

6. Carol H. Weiss, *Evaluation Research: Methods of Assessing Program Effectiveness* (Englewood Cliffs, N.J.: Prentice-Hall, 1972), p. 103.
7. John M. Johnson, *Doing Field Research* (New York: Free Press, 1975).
8. Peter H. Rossi, Howard E. Freeman, and Sonia R. Wright, *Evaluation: A Systematic Approach* (Beverly Hills, Calif.: Sage, 1979), p. 144.
9. This phrase was used by David Altheide of the Arizona State University in a conversation with John Stuart Hall on field research. For an excellent treatment of research problems associated with sole reliance on "official" numbers, see David Altheide and John M. Johnson, *Bureaucratic Propaganda* (Boston: Allyn & Bacon, 1980).
10. Johnson, *Doing Field Research,* pp. 199-200.
11. Jerome T. Murphy, *Getting the Facts: A Fieldwork Guide for Evaluators and Policy Analysts* (Santa Monica, Calif.: Goodyear, 1980).
12. Raoul Naroll, *Data Quality Control—A New Research Technique* (New York: Free Press, 1962), p. 10.
13. Nathan, "The Brookings Monitoring Research Methodology," p. 42.
14. Weiss, *Evaluation Research,* p. 103.
15. Ibid.
16. Nathan, "The Brookings Monitoring Research Methodology," p. 3.

BIBLIOGRAPHY OF STUDIES
LISTED IN TABLE 5.1

DOMMEL, PAUL R. and others. 1980. *Targeting Community Development.* Third Report on the Brookings Institution Monitoring Study of the Community Development Block Grant Program. Washington, D.C.: HUD. Reports of the first two rounds of monitoring are also available from HUD.
MIRENGOFF, WILLIAM and others. 1980. *CETA: Assessment of Public Service Employment Programs.* Washington, D.C.: National Academy of Sciences.
NATHAN, RICHARD P.; CHARLES F. ADAMS, JR.; and Associates. 1977. *Revenue Sharing: The Second Round.* Washington, D.C.: Brookings Institution.
_____; ALLAN D. MANVEL; and SUSANNAH H. CALKINS. 1975. *Monitoring Revenue Sharing.* Washington, D.C.: Brookings Institution.
_____, and others. 1978. *Monitoring the Public Service Employment Program,* vol. 2 of *Job Creation Through Public Service Employment,* Washington, D.C.: National Commission for Manpower Policy.

6

The Utility of a Longitudinal Approach in Assessing Implementation: A Thirteen-Year View of Title I, ESEA

MICHAEL KIRST AND RICHARD JUNG

What directions should public policy implementation research take in the 1980s? Certainly the embryonic and interdisciplinary field of implementation research will benefit from experimentation with and evaluation of numerous research approaches. Still largely unexplored are cross-program comparative case studies and statistical prediction models of implementation. There is also much to be learned from macro case-study analyses tracing implementation from policy formation through the measurement of a program's impact on intended recipients at a single point in time. We also are benefiting from an increased number of in-depth descriptions of individual subunits within the implementation scenario.

One largely overlooked direction appears to hold considerable promise in the 1980s. We believe a longitudinal case-study approach (ten years or more) merits serious consideration. An extended time line of ten years or more seems especially necessary in an implementation context where responsibilities and powers are shared among federal, state, and local agencies. We also contend that evidence for a long-run implementation perspective needs to be collected from a confluence of sources. We base our contention on an inspection of previous implementation case studies, "meta-implementation" analyses, political and organizational theory, and primarily our current investigation of federal efforts to implement the largest federal program in elementary and secondary education.

Relying largely on our present implementation research of Title I of the Elementary and Secondary Education Act (ESEA), a program that to date has funneled over $26 billion to state and local educational agencies with high concentrations of low-income families, in this chapter we detail theoretical and empirical arguments for the utility of a longitudinal case-study approach. Moreover, we outline procedural considerations for conducting such investigations, and in the process, make explicit some of the limitations and problems inherent in such an approach.

THEORETICAL RATIONALE FOR A LONGITUDINAL APPROACH

Less than a decade ago, implementation research pioneers such as Pressman and Wildavsky complained that "except for a few pieces mentioned in the body of this book, we have been unable to find any significant analytic work dealing with implementation."[1] That statement was debatable in 1973; it certainly is not the case today.

Within the last ten years, implementation research of federal domestic programs has passed through two distinct, although overlapping, periods. The first period began in the late 1960s and peaked in the mid-1970s. It was characterized by a flurry of case studies describing the initial few years of implementation for a variety of specific Great Society social service and regulatory programs in education, civil rights, urban development, employment opportunity, health services, and environmental protection.[2] In the aggregate these initial, predominantly descriptive case studies represented the first stage of theory development, a stage Eckstein has called "probability probes." These early case studies began identifying variables, mapping relations among variables, and formulating preliminary research assertions before more rigorous theory building and hypotheses testing were initiated.[3]

The most widely cited of these "first generation" of short-run case studies

Were factually dense accounts, usually lacking explicit theory or conceptual frameworks

Found more failure than success during the initial phases of implementation

Underscored the wide scope of political, organizational, and socioeconomic factors that influenced the implementation process

Used multiple sources of evidence

Concentrated primarily on the first one to three years of implementation[4]

Although this kind of case study continued to proliferate in the late 1970s, these earlier analyses along with conceptual models drawn from a variety of disciplines served as fodder for a new kind of implementation analysis in the middle and late 1970s, a meta-implementation literature.[5]

Some of these meta-implementation analyses were primarily concerned with setting out conceptual maps for subsequent case studies,[6] while others gleaned methodological lessons and gaps in the first-generation case studies.[7] These first attempts to conceptualize the implementation process ranged from Bardach's metaphoric concept of a "fixer" who "watch-dogged" the implementation "game" to prototypes of multistaged, recursive causal models.[8] Generally agreeing that at least some generalizable propositions can be formulated about the implementation of legislated public policy, these researchers and theoreticians still differ on fundamental issues such as

> The factors most affecting the implementation of legislated social programs
>
> The linkages among these factors
>
> Procedures and scales for measuring variations within proposed explanatory "variables"
>
> Appropriate sources and uses as well as limitations of existing data sources and research methodologies
>
> How to describe or measure implementation

Certainly the most comprehensive of the implementation perspectives to date is Sabatier and Mazmanian's attempt to integrate several previous conceptualizations[9] into a broad-scoped systems model that emphasizes the legal, political, and socioeconomic variables structuring the implementation process.[10] They postulate that four variables most affect a program's first three to five years of implementation

1. The "strength" of the statutes and ensuing regulations	(a) how precisely and consistently the objectives are specified and ranked, and (b) how clearly authority is delegated to organizational subunits
2. The presence of a "fixer"	a key legislator or administrator ideologically attuned to program requirements who controls resources important to crucial actors and who has the status, desire, and staff to monitor closely the implementation process

| 3. The resources of various constituency groups | the salience of an issue, the solidarity, the access to policy channels and information, and availability of side payments for representatives from implementing agencies and intended target group recipients |
| 4. The commitment and leadership of agency officials | *(a)* the direction and ranking of statutory objectives in officials' preference ordering; *(b)* the skills in realizing these preferences |

Yet they concede implicitly for the first three factors and explicitly for their most important explanatory factor—the commitment and leadership skills of implementing officials—that these variables are essentially "elusive concepts."[11]

The two factors they hypothesize to have the most significant effect in the long run (after five years)—changing socioeconomic conditions and the ability of supportive constituencies to intervene effectively—are equally difficult to quantify.[12] The slippery and global nature of such factors and the inextricably complex dynamics of their interactions lead Yin to conclude that "the research-measure, research-design approach, even in its modified quasi-experimental form, may not readily be applicable to the study of organizational processes."[13]

We are not quite so pessimistic. Instead, we recognize the limitations of the present social science technology expressed in Tukey's research caveat: "Far better an approximate answer to the *right* question, which is often vague, than an *exact* answer to the wrong question, which can always be made precise."[14] One pervasive feature of implementation case studies is that they have concentrated almost exclusively on the first three to five years of implementation. This preoccupation with short-run time lines continues in the face of growing empirical and theoretical evidence that a long-run perspective may reveal different patterns. Although the methodology for longitudinal analyses is not particularly exact, it appears that such an approach will broach at least the right questions. For organizational theorists and researchers have observed that when power is distributed widely among a variety of administrative units, legislative factions, and interest groups, one center of power can rarely impose its policies on others.[15] In such a situation, policies that are the outcomes of bargaining among these actors are likely to reflect only a small degree of change over existing procedures. Incrementalism typically dominates the federal budgetary process,[16] and although perhaps more difficult to measure precisely, regulatory outputs are also likely to change only marginally over the short haul. Cyert and March have noted in their study of various large private and governmental organizations that (1) goals are often vaguely stated initially to attain consensus; (2) incrementally these goals are operationalized in standard operating procedures through bargaining and compromise; (3) over time, "[m]inor changes can lead to more fundamental ones."[17]

Salamon provides additional theoretical justification for a longitudinal approach in asssessing the effects of Title I. Using a review of previous evaluation research and primarily his analysis of New Deal land-reform experiments, he argues that programs which call for the alteration of established social structures are likely to have delayed effects that could be systematically ignored by evaluation designs with short-run time lines.[18]

Our preliminary research findings in studying the implementation of Title I from a thirteen-year perspective reinforce these theoretical arguments for using a longitudinal time line. Specifically we have found:

1. Given the pluralist nature of the groups responsible for policy setting and implementation of Title I within a highly political and bureaucratic setting of decentralized power, changes in established administrative policies and procedures have been dominated by incremental change.

2. When aggregated, these incremental changes have resulted in significant structural and substantive changes in implementation policies and practices.

3. The direction of these changes over the long haul has been toward a more aggressive federal rulesetting, monitoring, and enforcement role in implementing some of the program's crucial categorical requirements, and more congruence with key provisions in the law.

4. The following set of interrelated factors have most affected the pace and directions of these changes:

    a. a shifting interest-group scenario from one initially dominated by professional education lobbies to one with an orientation toward compliance with federal mandates, including categorical program personnel, beneficiaries of Title I services, and lobby groups championing the recipients' causes;

    b. the emergence of a vertical network of administrative, evaluative, and teaching specialists with careers dependent upon the program;

    c. broad-based social movements.

We have traced in depth two pivotal program requirements across time: targeting of funds to disadvantaged pupils and program design regulations that result in interventions for target pupils (discussed in more detail in the appendix). Although in the short run, improvements in the operationalization, monitoring, and enforcement of the requirements have occurred slowly and intermittently, when viewed from a thirteen-year perspective, one observes a dramatic shift in the implementation of these two program regulations. In effect, the standard operating procedures are much closer to federal intent in 1979 than in 1965.

THE PASSAGE OF ESEA, TITLE I

The Elementary and Secondary Education Act was primarily crafted by a handful of top-level assistants from the Johnson administration and by Francis Keppel, then commissioner of education, who oversaw the operation of the U.S. Office of Education (now the Department of Education). They had two primary purposes that were not totally complementary. First, they wanted to find a legislative strategy that would successfully attain what almost every other Congress since World War II had futilely attempted—a strategy that would establish the precedent of federal aid to elementary and secondary schools. Second, they wanted this education legislation to serve as the cornerstone of President Johnson's War on Poverty program. To realize the first objective, the legislative and administrative strategists devised an ESEA "package" to satisfy "perhaps the widest constellation of interest groups ever assembled on a domestic issue."[19] The original legislation contained five titles with multiple and even conflicting goals.[20]

The political viability of the bill was, in fact, enhanced by promising something for most major interest groups and by circumventing, often through obfuscation of statutory language, the issues that had historically contributed to the defeats of previous efforts to increase federal involvement in elementary and secondary education. The three major obstacles revolved around (1) the debate over whether federal aid should support private schools, either directly or indirectly; (2) the politically volatile issue of providing federal dollars to racially segregated schools; (3) a traditional antagonism toward most efforts for federal control over public education.

Title I was and still is by far the largest financial component of the ESEA package with an appropriation for 1979 of over $3 billion. The purpose of the program, as stated in the bill's Declaration of Intent, is "to provide financial assistance to local educational agencies serving areas with concentrations of children from low-income families to expand and improve their educational programs by various means."[21]

Some read this language to mean that the program's top priority was to begin reform of the entire fabric of American education. Reform in this context meant restructuring of state and local educational agencies' allocation priorities, which traditionally spent more per child in those schools with high concentrations of students from *high-income* families.[22] Others saw Title I as a cleverly disguised general aid program. These individuals recognized the political expediency of using the "disadvantaged child" as a symbolic rallying point to get the bill passed and believed that Title I was designed to provide general aid to districts with limited property tax bases. Unlike the reform interpretation, the assumption here is that the present institutions are functioning as well as can be expected, and they just need more money to better address the problem of educating poor children.

These two interpretations called for two very different implementation scenarios. The reformist would accept a strong federal involvement in the development, implementation, and evaluation of state and local projects; whereas the other interpretation would limit federal involvement to determining the size of entitlements and signing checks.[23] The two priorities—the reform agenda of some of the program's original designers and the maintenance of state and local control over federal funds—form the underlying ideological tension for the implementation of Title I over time.

The program had two other objectives as well: accelerating the pace of desegregation in the South and strengthening federal-state relations by increasing the capacities of state departments of education. Hundreds of southern school districts received an increment of 30 percent to their total operating budget. This influx of funds was a "sugar solvent" designed to melt southern resistance to quick desegregation in order not to forfeit the windfall funds. Title I also initially provided 1 percent of its $1.3 billion for state agencies to administer the program.[24] In effect, ESEA represented a deliberate policy of underwriting the growth and reorientation of state departments of education, which had historically been independent of, and in part antagonistic to increases in, federal administrative control.[25]

Compromise and ambiguity were evident in the distribution of administrative responsibilities as well in the program's objectives. The U.S. commissioner of education shared with local and state educational agencies (LEAs and SEAs) responsibilities for administering Title I projects. In summary, the responsibilities were distributed in the following manner:

1. *The U.S. Office of Education*
    a. develops and disseminates regulations, guidelines, and other materials regarding the approval of Title I projects

   b. reviews and assesses the progress under Title I throughout the
   nation

2. *State Education Agencies*
      a. approve proposed local projects in accordance with federal
      regulations and guidelines
      b. assist local educational agencies in the development of projects
      c. submit state evaluation reports to USOE

3. *Local Education Agencies*
      a. identify educationally deprived children in areas with high
      concentrations of low-income families and determine their special
      educational needs
      b. develop and implement approved projects to fulfill the intent of
      Title I[26]

   The inclusion of these multiple objectives and overlapping governance responsibilities facilitated a speedy congressional affirmation of the act. Only during the implementation process did the categorical priorities evolve and the
jockeying for administrative control of the program begin.

   In order to maintain a manageable analytic scope for a longitudinal analysis, we compared across time changes in two of the fourteen major program requirements (or program administrative outputs): targeting and program design
requirements. If a program is to be successful, monies must first reach the intended beneficiaries. *Targeting requirements* detail the criteria for the selection
of eligible schools and children who are to participate in the program within
these schools. Once the monies reach the targeted schools and students, some
reporting mechanisms are necessary for federal officials to determine how the
schools are spending Title I monies. *Program design requirements* set forth that
each Title I school must identify its project's objectives and detail the activities
and services used to realize these stated goals. We have chosen these two requirements for cross-time comparisons as representatives of the two major categories of Title I requirements: funds-allocation requirements and program development requirements. (See table 6.2.)

                     AN EMPIRICAL RATIONALE FOR
                     A LONGITUDINAL PERSPECTIVE

The evaluations of Title I's administration during the first five years splashed
horror stories of weak federal administration and even malfeasance; early im-

pact studies consistently found negligible educational impacts of the program on Title I students.[27] After four years of the program's operation (1965-69), the first comprehensive evaluation of Title I's administration by an external research group concluded that "many of the misuses of Title I funds were so gross that even non-experts can readily spot them."[28] All other early studies of Title I administration by external research agencies or individuals have reinforced this first negative assessment of wide-scale misallocation of Title I funds during the first four years of the program.

The major analysis of Title I administration conducted by a contracted research agency during the middle years of the program, from 1972 to 1973, used extensive interviews with USOE area desk personnel responsible for the monitoring practices of SEAs, site visits to five states, and questionnaire data from a sample of 10 states and 36 LEAs. Their general conclusion was that "the administration of the program in the Division of Compensatory Education is far more effective than the critics would have one believe."[29] Nevertheless, they described the administrative efficiency and effectiveness as "quite depressing." Their major findings were that (1) regulations published by USOE were inadequate for LEAs and basically worthless for SEAs; (2) criteria used by the DHEW Audit Agency to determine noncompliance were drawn directly from the statutes since the regulations were inadequate; (3) USOE did not take into account LEA reporting burdens; (4) evaluations of Title I educational impact were not satisfactory; (5) enforcement of sanctions for noncompliant behavior identified in DHEW audits was virtually nonexistent.

More recent assessments of Title I management by external research organizations depict a strikingly different scenario. Using essentially the same major data source as the first compliance study of Title I (Health, Education, and Welfare Audit Agency audit reports), but covering eleven years rather than just the first four, SRI International noted among its "most important trends" that ". . . most states have developed adequate to good procedures for reviewing LEA [local education agencies] applications for Title I funds. These systems have greatly reduced many of the initial problems. However, more subtle problems remain . . ." and "at the LEA level, blatant misallocation of funds which clearly violated the intent of Title I have been substantially reduced."[30] Based primarily on the findings of three other external analyses of Title I administration using data from 1972 to 1977, a long-time analyst of Title I with the Syracuse University Research Corporation contends:

> The common view of Title I administration may be overly pessimistic and unjustified. A more current "end of the decade" view of the federal-state-local partnership could provide a good deal more confidence in the ability

of the federal government to influence the operation of categorical programs in local school systems.[31]

Over time, for example, our research reveals that federal efforts to *target* more Title I dollars to each participating student have been particularly successful. The ambiguous statutory language requires that Title I projects must be "of sufficient size, scope, and quality" to ensure that monies are not spread too thinly, and thereby threatens to diminish the effectiveness of the projects. In the early years of the program, there was a strong tendency for districts to use Title I as general aid by allowing more students to participate than were actually eligible to receive Title I funds. Table 6.1 indicates, for instance, in 1966 approximately 5.5 million students met Title I's eligibility criteria for poverty. Yet more than an estimated 8.2 million students actually participated in the program, almost one and a half times the number of eligible students. In contrast, in 1978, while about 9 million students were counted for local entitlements, only 5 million students actually participated in the program, or less than 60 percent of the eligible students. This contributed to an increase in per pupil expenditure from $116 in 1966 to $379 in 1978. Discounting for the effects of inflation (row 5), this translates into a 62 percent increase in per pupil expenditure over thirteen years.

TABLE 6.1
TARGETING FIGURES FOR TITLE I FROM 1966 TO 1978[a]

Children (in millions)	1966	1970	1974	1978
1. Counted for LEA entitlements[b]	5,531	6,952	6,247	9,045
2. Participating	8,235	7,526	6,100	5,155
3. Percent participating of counted	1.49	1.08	.98	.57
4. Per pupil expenditure (unadjusted)	$116.46	$161.98	$247.75	$378.52
5. Per pupil expenditure (adjusted for inflation)[c]	$119.81	$139.92	$167.73	$193.71
6. Total Title I appropriation (in millions)	1,193	1,339	1,653	2,247
7. Total Title I appropriation (in millions adjusted for inflation)	1,217	1,151	1,232	1,162

[a] Figures derived from tables provided by the Office (now Department) of Education.
[b] Figures for rows 1 and 2 include only "educationally disadvantaged" children but do not include handicapped, juvenile delinquents, migrants, or children in agencies for the neglected.
[c] All adjusted figures are derived from the Bureau of Labor Statistics "Consumer Price Index for All Urban Consumers U.S. City Average" with 1967 as base year.

It is important to note that during this same time when per pupil expenditures were increasing by 62 percent in real dollars, the total appropriations for Title I in dollars adjusted for inflation actually *declined* by 5 percent (row 7). Therefore, larger per pupil expenditures were due to increased targeting of funds by local districts rather than additional appropriations.

Longitudinal studies aggregating more recent implementation data are also needed to partially abate the tendency by some researchers, even those quite knowledgeable in public policy literature, to cite dated, short-run analyses as if these accounts still applied today.[32] For instance, a prominent economist who has written prolifically on educational equity issues and specifically on Title I, concludes in 1977: "The ostensible inability of Title I Programs to create even a nominal impact on student scores in basic skills seems to be endemic to the program."[33] The studies on which he bases his conclusion, however, contain achievement data collected between 1965 and 1969, the first four years of the program. More than a decade of changes have occurred since then. Substantial changes have been documented in the program's legal framework,[34] federal and state monitoring procedures,[35] and federal enforcement efforts.[36] In fact, the most recent impact study for Title I argues for an extension of Title I programs into the summer months to maintain the increases in reading and math attained during the regular school-year Title I programs.[37] While the evidence on pupil achievement is mixed, we contend the evidence on implementation congruence with federal objectives is more conclusive.[38]

EXPLANATORY FORCES

We have found that an interest-group framework integrated with a social-movement perspective provides a useful model of explanation for longitudinal implementation research. In the context of Title I, an interest-group perspective couches explanations in the political interplay among what has been called the iron triangle, consisting of

> Congress, and more specifically the congressional subcommittees responsible for educational legislation
> Implementing agencies
> Professional education and special-interest lobbies

In the tradition of educational federalism, the symbolic language of the legislation accorded to each level of administration a potential for substantial power. The law gave to the commissioner of education the responsibility to develop "basic criteria" that the states were to use in their review of local applications. The states were reserved the power to approve or disapprove these projects. The local districts had wide latitude in planning, implementing, and evaluating the acutal programs, be they for school construction or remedial programs for a highly selective group of students.

Overall, incremental change in the direction of more federal control has been characterized by an ongoing series of sallies, retreats, and parleys by (1) growing internal and external constituencies who saw ESEA as a vehicle for changing schools and who favored or at least accepted a strict interpretation of the categorical intent of Title I; and (2) traditional education lobbies, most congressmen, and local and state as well as a large number of federal administrators who preferred general aid and minimum federal involvement.

Early in Title I's history the lobby-group scenario was almost exclusively dominated by interest groups representing established *professional* educational constituencies. These lobbies included (1) National Education Association, (2) Council of Chief State School Officers, (3) National School Board Association, (4) American Association of School Administrators, (5) National Association of State Boards of Education, and (6) National Congress of Parents and Teachers. These six major educational lobbying blocks, known in Washington circles as "The Big Six," have rarely joined forces to form a unified lobbying front; however, they in general share an ideological preference for protecting local and state control of education and minimizing federal regulations. Other active lobbies, usually with strong general aid preferences, have been producers of educational materials and supplies. Another general aid educational lobby group more active in the later part of the Title I implementation history is the Council of Great City Schools.

Over the years, the one lobby group promoting categorical restrictions on Title I funds during the initial enactment of Title I, the National Catholic Welfare Board, has been joined by a number of other groups concerned with resisting efforts to turn Title I into a general aid program. These interest groups generally represent special or focused interests of the providers or recipients of Title I funds, and include National Advisory Council for the Education of Disadvantaged Children, the National Welfare Rights Organization, the Legal Standards and Education Project of the NAACP, the Lawyers Committee for Civil Rights Under Law, the National Association of Administrators of State and Federally-Assisted Education Programs, and the Education Commission of the States. Some of the lobbying, technical assistance, and other advocacy processes of the special-focused pressure groups have received financial or consultative support from such organizations as the Ford Foundation and the Harvard Center for Law and Education.

The first round, known by Title I analysts as the "Chicago Affair," favored the traditionalists. In 1965 Commissioner Keppel attempted to withhold all Title I funds from the Chicago schools until a civil rights investigation was completed. Illinois State School Superintendent Page informed Chicago's Mayor Daley of the impending loss of funds, and Daley in turn complained to President Johnson of unlawful federal intrusion into the local domain of providing public education. Under pressure from Johnson, Keppel rescinded the withhold ruling within five days. USOE's first attempt to flex its jurisdictional muscle resulted in a precedent that for a time reduced its autonomy in the implementation of Title I.[39] The battle, however, had just begun.

A handful of new middle-level staff members gave initial impetus to continued attempts from several quarters at translating ambiguous statutory language into a more tightly monitored program. This small band of reformers in effect formed an internal constituency group within the largely traditional USOE bureaucracy. They had two basic strategies.

First, they persisted in pushing for an expansion of the "basic criteria" powers delegated to the commissioner by making more explicit the regulations guiding states' approval of local applications. The criteria they initially developed were to a large degree successfully resisted by more traditional elements within USOE and opposed by state and local administrators. After the widely publicized release of the Martin and McClure report in 1969, other task forces again recommended tougher restrictions on the allocation of Title I funds, increased monitoring, and improvements in the resolutions of complaints by outside groups. As might be expected, the traditional forces were partially successful in watering down these recommendations, but when compared to the initial requirements and monitoring practices, substantial changes had accumulated through year-by-year incremental movement toward a more active federal involvement in the program's administration.

Second, these reformers took several steps to build constituencies at the state and local levels that would advocate or at least accept a stricter categorical interpretation. For instance, they encouraged the use of funds set aside for the state administration of Title I to establish special compensatory education units in each state department in order to circumvent the Chief State School Officers who generally were strong supporters of general aid. They actually invented the title of "State Title I Coordinator" and began bombarding these mythical figures with letters and bulletins and inviting them to regional meetings where Title I regulations and program materials were discussed, modified, and disseminated.[40] The figures are not so mythical today. In 1977 at least forty-five states had categorical units headed by special directors of compensatory education.[41]

The $26 billion spent on Title I has spawned a national-to-local professional hierarchy with careers dependent upon and commitments more aligned with providing special services to disadvantaged children. With state and federal categorical programs assuming a larger percentage of public school expenditures, most urban and large suburban districts have not only local categorical program directors but also special program units operating at the district level. These staffs are versed in the technical skills required to cope with the bureaucratic minutiae seemingly endemic to federal social programs. In California, the special program coordinators from the state's thirty-three largest school districts, to which more than 80 percent of the state's Title I funds are targeted, have formed an informal consortium that holds monthly meetings and provides a vehicle for frequent and rapid exchange of information about technical aspects of implementation. These statewide consortiums are linked in a national network through regular regional meetings, yearly gatherings in Washington, and frequent newsletters and special bulletins under the auspices of the National Association of State and Federally-Assisted Education Programs. These formal and informal organizations foster strong informal norms to watch-dog district decisions so they are consonant with categorical program requirements.[42]

Parents of Title I children and of several state compensatory education programs are also organized from the school to the federal level in district, state, and federal advisory councils. At the federal level, the National Advisory Council for Education of Disadvantaged Children and several civil rights groups have proven to be increasingly effective lobby groups.

Duane and Bridgeland in their study of Michigan's educational politics noted that (1) special and compensatory education lobbies were among the most powerful education lobbies in the state, and (2) directors of special education and compensatory education were among the most influential individuals in the state educational policy process.[43] A Washington-based public-interest law firm, the Lawyers Committee for Civil Rights Under Law, has played a subtantial role in improving enforcement of Title I categorical requirements. Its activities have included the preparation of manuals for bringing suits against districts believed to be in violation of Title I statutes and comprehensive analyses of the program's legal framework.[44] Several of the committee's recommendations for strengthening the program requirements are evident in the 1978 amendments.[45]

The point to be made here is that the character of interest groups participating in implementation decision-making processes has slowly moved from a virtual monopoly of traditional professional interest groups (such as the National Education Association and the National Association of Chief State

School Officers) with a strong general aid preference to a more diverse interest-group situation. Numerous constituencies are now articulating an emphasis on enforcing the categorical goals for the program. Further, from a longitudinal perspective, these incremental changes, when aggregated, have resulted in a substantive shift in the nature of the interest-group agendas toward targeted aid as intended by the Congress and USOE. These enforcement-oriented interest groups found allies in the Congress such as Senator Mondale and Senator Kennedy. They were reinforced by aggressive OE Title I administrators such as DHEW Assistant Secretary Timothy Wirth and USOE Compensatory Education Director Richard Fairley.

Recently, political scientists have recognized that beyond relying on a readily observable, but perhaps somewhat myopic, iron-triangle explanation for public policy formation and implementation, some consideration should be given to the impact of broad-based social movements. Explaining longitudinal changes in Title I's implementation involves more than documenting how one or several ideologically consonant interest groups have coopted other lobbying constituencies serving their own private interests. Increased monitoring and oversight of Title I operations need to be seen in the light of a broader public demand for accountability in government and business during the late 1960s and early 1970s. Malpractice suits, in unprecedented numbers, held physicians accountable for their diagnoses and treatments. Automobile manufacturers were made liable as never before for injuries resulting from improper design of their products. Few government agencies were immune from such accountability reforms as management by objectives, programmed budgeting, and PERT charts. Monitoring was just one remedy in the accountability movement's grand grabbag.

One spinoff effect of the desegregation and antipoverty movements over the last two decades has been to legitimate federal administrative and judicial intervention in the schools. Court-appointed monitors have taken control of entire districts when judges have deemed the response of local school boards to be inadequate to long-standing desegregation mandates. Federally funded legal-aid lawyers prepared a large number of lawsuits charging school districts and states with Title I violations.

Like Cyert and March, we have found vague, consensual goals are eventually more specifically operationalized in organizational routines or standard procedures. And we believe explanations for the direction of these changes, while influenced by numerous other factors, are best understood by integrating an interest-group perspective with attention paid to the long-term effects of how relevant social movements affect policy reformulation and implementation.

THE USES AND ANALYSES OF DATA

Recent meta-implementation studies have generated some useful guidelines for the use and analysis of data for a longitudinal implementation perspective.

In examining the approaches of eleven "exemplary" implementation studies conducted over the last decade, Yin found one salient methodological similarity of these studies was that "evidence is collected from every possible source in every conceivable manner," including

> Unstructured discussions
> Structured interviews
> Documents and news reports
> Participant observations
> Field observations
> Published reports written by one or more of the participants

He concludes that "one of the potential lessons is that two or more of these methods should be used in any given study of implementation."[46]

The use of a confluence of sources can both increase the reliability of the findings and appears necessary in view of the gaps likely to exist and the biases inherent in any one source of information. Reliability is enhanced by the utilization of a confluence of data, since once a proposition is confirmed by two or more sources, even with all their sources of error, the certainty of an interpretation is greatly improved.[47]

For instance, one of the more problematic and yet pivotal considerations in implementation studies is the determination of congressional intent. Most researchers proceed with the implicit assumption that a careful reading of the statutes suffices for arriving at the legislative objectives. Our research has repeatedly demonstrated that a "triangulation" of evidence relying also on Senate and House hearings and their special reports in conjunction with the statutes provides a much more accurate portrayal of congressional intent than the statutes by themselves because the symbolic language of the statutes is often more fully articulated in these other documents.

Primary data sources for a longitudinal implementation study of this type should include:

1. Legal framework documents
   a. relevant statutes and subsequent amendments
   b. original regulations and subsequent modifications
   c. program guides

2. Technical assistance materials
    a. program guides
    b. audit checklists
    c. other technical assistance packages and notices

3. Audits and other compliance reports

4. House and Senate hearings and reports

5. Personal accounts of implementers (for Title I, these usually interweave the personal experiences of these individuals with a rich source of internal documents, conversations, interviews, and public documents which detail key sequences of events)

6. Short-run implementation studies by contracted research firms and internal compliance and enforcement reports

7. Articles in professional journals and other publications

Methodologically, then, longitudinal implementation research primarily involves a secondary and tertiary synthesis and reinterpretation of an extensive source of existing documents. When key pieces of information are missing or existing documentation is in conflict, interviews with appropriate staff members, congressional aides, or researchers involved in previous implementation studies can be helpful. Despite the biases and limitations of documentary evidence, we have found a good deal of truth in the Chinese proverb that "The palest ink is clearer than the best memory."[48]

The substantive reliance on existing documentary evidence does require assessing the validity of the information in these documents since one can expect internal reports especially to contain as much a rhetorical as an informational intent. In weighing the validity of these secondary analyses, we consider three factors:

1. The position and agenda of the person or organization responsible for the writing and publication of the report

2. The motivation for the report

3. The factual accuracy of the information on which the interpretations are based

Unless there is strong evidence to the contrary, we judge information contained in external reports by contracted researchers to be more valid than the agency reports. This does not suggest that analyses by external research organizations are without biases. Their analyses are limited by the data available to them, time constraints, personal and professional assumptions, and other factors. They, for example, generally lean toward a Washington view of the world since their research services are typically contracted by federal agencies. Besides these rather simple decision rules, the method in which the facts of the implementation experience are pieced together and how the evidence is merged from various sources remains largely an informal process that must be entrusted to the discretion of the investigator.[49]

METHODOLOGICAL CONSIDERATIONS

Although empirical and theoretical arguments abound for assuming a longitudinal implementation perspective, little guidance exists for how to actually conduct such research. In our exploratory efforts to analyze the implementation of Title I over a thirteen-year period, three major methodological questions have continued to resurface that have generalizable import:

1. What explanatory and dependent factors should be traced across time? How is variation in these variables described?

2. What kinds of evidence should be used?

3. How is such evidence best analyzed?

Our response to these questions reflects as much the limitations of the present state of the art as it sheds light on partial answers to perplexing methodological issues.

Longitudinal implementation case studies that are most likely to contribute to theory building fit under the rubric of what Alexander George has called "controlled focused case studies." In such studies seemingly idiosyncratic aspects of explanation for each case are formulated in terms of variables that can be compared across cases (i.e., across programs or time periods). In a longitudinal study, a "case" represents a block of years of implementation that can be compared to one or more other blocks of years. Meaningful comparisons are highly dependent on "the sensitivity and judgment of the investigator in choosing and conceptualizing his variables and also in deciding how best to describe the variance in each of his variables."[50] First, an investigator must decide what class of events he will choose to depict "implementation" for cross-time comparisons. That is, what are the dependent variables that will be compared across periods?

We postulate at least three related dimensions describing implementation should be considered across time: (1) policy outputs of implementing agencies,

(2) compliance with policy outputs by lower-level subunits, and (3) actual impacts on intended beneficiaries.

Policy Outputs of Implementing Agencies
A comparison of relevant policy documents both for determining the internal consistency of these documents at a particular point in time and for noting changes across time provides one vehicle for assessing a program's implementation.

Such documentary analysis, of course, should include tracing changes in the initial enabling legislation and affiliated legal documents.[51] However, statutes, sometimes allocating millions of dollars at the stroke of a single subsection, are often plagued with deliberately obfuscated language to broaden political support for the legislation. Winning coalitions are often held together by the adhesive of ambiguous language that successfully masks unresolved differences among competing interest groups and legislators. Statutes are as heavily laced with symbolic rhetoric as they are replete with allocative formulae and regulatory prescriptions.[52] Therefore, in order to detect shifts in objectives and priorities it is also necessary to closely analyze those documents that in essence operationalize the symbolic import characteristic of most statutes. These include regulations, mandatory and explanatory criteria, guidelines, technical assistance packages, audit checklists, application forms, evaluation mechanisms, and complaint resolution processes.

Some scheme for categorizing policy outputs is usually essential for comprehensive and manageable cross-period comparisions, given the typical proliferation of policy documents over time and the regulatory complexity characteristic of most federally sponsored social programs. (See table 6.2 in the appendix for one method of categorizing policy outputs at one point in time for cross-time comparisons.) Such a categorization scheme would identify the major program requirements and block them into some logical groupings. The Title I legal framework, for instance, contains fourteen major program requirements, which roughly can be divided into two categories: funds-allocation requirements and program-development requirements. Funds-allocation requirements are intended to ensure that Title I funds actually reach the intended schools and students and are spent on appropriate categories of expenditures. Program-development requirements encompass a potpourri of qualitative issues such as program evaluation, parent participation, and planning activities.

In order to maintain a manageable analytic scope, we have compared across time changes in two of the major program requirements (or program outputs): targeting and program design requirements. Title I schools are chosen on the basis of economic criteria so that limited Title I funds can be concentrated on those schools within a district with the highest concentration of children from low-income families. Once the schools in a district are identified by these *economic criteria,* children within each eligible school are selected for participation on the basis of lowest test scores or methods for assessing *educational deprivation.* There are, then, two steps embedded in law to help ensure that funds are not spread too thinly: (1) economic criteria for limiting the number of eligible schools, and (2) educational criteria for restricting the number of children participating in Title I projects within these schools.

A focused comparison of the criteria used to operationalize these targeting requirements across time allows the analyst to determine whether auditors had adequate indicators for assessing if Title I funds were actually reaching the intended beneficiaries.

The *program-design* regulation requires that a formal plan be developed by districts receiving Title I funds. This plan must set forth the school's objectives and specify the activities and services to accomplish the desired ends. A cross-time focused comparison of the criteria for these requirements provides partial insights into the detail of information federal officials could obtain from local districts on how they were spending Title I funds. These "snapshots" of policy outputs then can be compared across time along several dimensions:

> Changes in the degree of local discretion
> The legal force of the interpretation (a mandatory regulation vs. an advisory suggestion)
> The frequency and scope of the dissemination of these interpretations
> The specificity of the information required in applications, audits, and evaluation reports.

In addition to tracing any changes in the conceptualization (usually in the regulations, guidelines, and audit checklists), one needs to compare across time the monitoring and enforcement policies and procedures in place, as well as other incentives for compliance with policy standards. Some descriptive scales for comparing variance could include the kinds and frequency of sanctions for misspent funds, the kinds and frequency of monitoring reviews, and the kinds of procedures for adjudicating alleged violations of program regulations and for enforcing appropriate sanctions.

For both requirements we have traced (targeting and program design), each of these dimensions has increased dramatically over the last thirteen years in terms of the procedures intended to enhance the congruence between the categorical intent of the legislation and the actual local implementation activities.[53]

Compliance by Lower-Level Subunits

For Title I there are two major types of compliance documents. Primary compliance reports include comprehensive audits conducted by the Health, Education, and Welfare Audit Agency (HEWAA) and usually less rigorous Program Reviews conducted by USOE officials annually for each state since 1970. In addition several external research agencies and special task forces have produced numerous "snapshot" compliance and enforcement reports covering one to five-year periods.[54] These reports have used a number of approaches including reanalyses of primary compliance documents, structured and unstructured interviews, field observations, and in-depth case studies of selected states, or some combination of these methodologies.

Even with this plethora of compliance documentation, several problematic methodological issues have surfaced in constructing cross-time comparisons of subunit compliance. First, federal efforts to monitor the program have increased substantially over time. USOE did not begin conducting annual on-site visits to state and local districts until 1970, five years after the initiation of the program. In 1967 only three states were audited by HEWAA. Now almost a third of the states are audited each year. Second, the process for selecting states for audits is hardly random. The principal selection factors are the date of the last audit, available manpower, requests or complaints from various sources, and other indications of problems. Third, the lack of mention of problems or noncompliance, especially in the early years, may be due to inadequate criteria for substantiating allegations of noncompliance; to a lack of interest in enforcing a requirement at a particular time; or to benevolent neglect in order to maintain a cooperative working relationship among federal, state, and local officials.[55] Therefore, simple numerical comparisons of violations across time are likely to reveal more about the changes in the rigor of the monitoring efforts than improvements or slippages in state and local agencies' compliance. For instance, during the first five years of the program there were no quantitative criteria for determining whether a district receiving Title I funds were providing comparable services to Title I and non-Title I schools. Only after 1972 were "comparability" criteria integrated into the audit checklists, and it is exactly at this time that such violations began showing up in primary compliance documents.

In 1965, USOE had neither the history, resources, nor mandate from Congress to closely monitor the expenditures of educational funds from federal coffers. Local control of schools, vested in over 16,000 independent school boards, remains a dominant, although increasingly mythlike, value in the United States —a value that, prior to 1965, had run counter to federal employees observing elementary and secondary classroom activities and monitoring district-level operations. Before the passage of ESEA, USOE was known primarily as a check-writing and statistics-collecting operation. The original Title I statutes merely required that states submit broadly worded assurances that they would approve local applications that complied with the ambiguous intent of the legislation. After a well-publicized wrangle with the Senate Education Subcommittee in 1967, USOE finally disseminated the first authorized set of guidelines in March of 1968, a full three years after the passage of the enabling legislation. The violations uncovered in the scattered HEWAA audit reports were not publicized until the publication of the Martin and McClure report in 1969.[56]

Quite a different scenario exists today. Although numerous problems persist, a magnum opus study of Title I's legal framework concluded that the program's requirements are generally necessary, consistent, and flexible.[57] In contrast to even five years earlier, USOE in 1979 recovered nearly $1.5 million in misspent funds and was working to collect at least $2.2 million more as a result of audit findings over the previous four years.[58] Even though the funds actually collected by USOE for disallowable expenditures were a small percent of the dollar expenditure exceptions noted in DHEW Audit Agency reports, there is growing evidence that state and local education agencies feared that they might be next and that a shift to federal aid with "no strings" attached would be highly unlikely in the near future.[59]

Impact Studies

During the first seven years of Title I alone, over $50 million was spent on impact evaluations.[60] Typically these studies have attempted to assess the program's impact by reducing the goals of the program to monthly or yearly growth rates on standardized reading, writing, and math tests. Much more has been learned about how *not* to go about conducting such impact studies and about the resistance of local education agencies to federal efforts at collecting data for such assessments than about the actual impacts along these dimensions on program recipients. In short, these kinds of impact studies have raised more questions than they have answered. And there is little to suggest that they have made much impression on congressional attitudes about the program. Measures of "impact" other than standardized reading scores merit consideration. Some attention should be given to

> The influence of Title I on the design and proliferation of state compensatory education programs[61]
>
> The influence of Title I on the design of other more recent federal education programs[62]
>
> The effects of ESEA and other federal categorical legislation on the involvement of parents in school and district advisory councils

The effects of state "set asides" for Title I and other federal education initiatives on the growth and organization of state departments of education

Our basic argument is that the concept of "impact" is often too narrowly defined and that indirect impacts of legislated social programs should receive further consideration. Our synthesis of the evaluations cited in the notes section demonstrates the value of our approach when a thirteen-year perspective is employed.

CONCLUSION

In his poem "The Rock," T. S. Eliot inquires, "[W]here is the knowledge we have lost in information."[63] Although some deplore the paucity of implementation research and usable information, our claim is that we face an abundance of information on implementation. More original research is no doubt required, but perhaps more importantly, we need to know how to extract knowledge from the information we already have. Implementation and organizational theory, growing empirical evidence, and our own exploratory investigation into the implementation of Title I provide a compelling rationale for using a long-run perspective. Our longitudinal research demonstrates that (1) initial consensual goals, often vaguely stated, are formalized incrementally over time in organizational routines through an ongoing bargaining and compromise process; (2) the directions of these changes are influenced by the strength, agendas, and resources of the constituencies participating in the policy formation and implementation processes as well as broader social movements; (3) the evidence for longitudinal implementation studies needs to be garnered from a confluence of sources.

There is, nonetheless, a need to further develop protocols and methods for a more orderly integration of primary and secondary implementation data sources in order to carry out such longitudinal analyses more systematically during the next generation of implementation research.

APPENDIX
CATEGORIZATION SCHEME FOR TITLE I PROGRAM OUTPUTS

The table that follows illustrates one method for categorizing policy outputs in the Title I context for cross-period comparisons. On the horizontal axis, major categories of regulations are identified. The Title I legal framework, for instance, contains fourteen major categories of requirements that roughly can be divided into two categories: funds-allocation requirements and program-design requirements. Funds-allocation requirements are intended to ensure that Title I funds actually reach the intended schools and students and are spent on appropriate categories of expenditures. Program-design requirements encompass a potpourri of qualitative issues such as program evaluation, parent participation, and planning activities. On the vertical axis, the major rule-setting policy outputs are specified and ranked in order of degree of legal forces, from statutes having "the full force and effect of law" to interpretative suggestions.

A brief definition of each requirement in the table*:

Eligibility provisions delineate which school districts are eligible to receive assistance.

Targeting criteria establish which children will be served.

Maintenance of effort criteria apply to district-level expenditures and require that funding from state and local sources does not decrease.

Comparability criteria apply to the school level and require that the level of services for Title I and non-Title I students be roughly comparable from state and local sources.

Supplement not supplant requirements apply at the child level and are intended to ensure that Title I funds are added to, and not used to replace, state and local funds.

Excess cost provisions clarify the supplanting provisions by stipulating that Title I funds pay only for excess costs of Title I programs.

Equitably provided provisions extend the comparability regulations to the child level.

Needs assessment qualitative requirements are intended to ensure that educationally disadvantaged children are identified and their educational needs assessed.

Program design requires a formal plan establishing objectives for Title I projects and the specification of activities and services to accomplish the desired ends.

Concentration requirements are intended to ensure that Title I funds provide services of sufficient size, scope, and quality.

Coordination provisions are intended to prevent Title I from duplicating benefits provided to target populations by ensuring that Title I services are planned in conjunction with other federal and state agency programs.

Program evaluation requirements provide that the effects of Title I programs be assessed.

Parent involvement provisions prescribe the nature and extent of parental involvement in the development and operation of Title I programs.

*Definitions summarized from NIE, *Administration of Compensatory Education*, pp. 9-12.

TABLE 6.2. POLICY OUTPUT CATEGORIZATION SCHEME FOR CROSS-TIME COMPARISONS

Program Requirements	Eligibility	Targeting	Maintenance of Effort	Comparability	Nonsupplanting	Excess Cost	Equitably Provided	Needs Assessment	Program Design	Concentration	Coordination	Program Evaluation	Parent Involvement
Formal legal framework • statute • regs. • criteria													
Informal legal framework • guides • audit checklists • informal suggestions													

FUNDS-ALLOCATION REQUIREMENTS   PROGRAM-DESIGN REQUIREMENTS

TYPES OF POLICY OUTPUTS

NOTES

1. Jeffrey Pressman and Aaron Wildavsky, *Implementation* (Berkeley: University of California Press, 1973), p. 166.
2. For a summary of the most frequently cited of these first-generation case studies, see Paul Sabatier and David Mazmanian, "The Implementation of Regulatory Policy: A Framework of Analysis," No. 39 of Research Reports of Institute for Governmental Affairs, University of California, Davis, 1979, n. 2-7; and James March, "Footnotes to Organizational Change" (paper prepared for 1980 National Assembly sponsored by the National Center for Higher Education Management Systems, Denver, Colorado, 17 January 1980), n. 1-5.
3. Harry Eckstein, "Case Studies in Political Science," in *Handbook of Political Science,* ed. F. I. Greenstein and N. W. Polsby (Reading, Mass.: Addison-Wesley, 1975), 7:79-138.
4. Robert Yin, "Studying the Implementation of Public Programs" (paper prepared for Solar Energy Research Institute, Golden, Colo., 1979), pp. 2-18.
5. "Meta-Analysis" refers to an analysis of a large collection of results from individual studies for the purpose of integrating these findings. For a more comprehensive treatment of depicting, organizing, and interrelating data from diverse impact studies, see Gene Glass, "Primary, Secondary, and Meta-Analysis Research," *Educational Researcher,* no. 10 (November 1976): 3-8.
6. See, for example, Eugene Bardach, *The Implementation Game: What Happens After a Bill Becomes a Law* (Cambridge, Mass.: MIT Press, 1977); Richard Elmore, "Organizational Models of Social Program Implementation" in *Making Change Happen?,* ed. Dale Mann (New York: Teachers College Press, 1978), pp. 185-223; Sabatier and Mazmanian, "Implementation of Regulatory Policy"; and Carl Van Horn and Donald Van Meter, "The Implementation of Intergovernmental Policy" in *Public Policy Making in a Federal System,* ed. Charles O. Jones and Robert D. Thomas (Beverly Hills, Calif.: Sage, 1976), pp. 39-62.
7. For instance, John Meyer, "The Impact of the Centralization of Educational Funding on State and Local Organizational Governance," draft report No. 79-C5, Institute for Research on Educational Finance and Governance, Stanford University, 1979; Walter Williams, "Implementation Analysis and Assessment" in *Social Program Implementation,* ed. Walter Williams and Richard Elmore (New York: Academic Press, 1976), pp. 267-92; and Yin, "Implementation of Public Programs."
8. Sabatier and Mazmanian, "Implementation of Regulatory Policy."
9. Primarily, Bardach, *Implementation Game;* Theodore Lowi, *The End of Liberalism* (New York: Norton, 1969); and Van Horn and Van Meter, "Implementation of Intergovernmental Policy."
10. Sabatier and Mazmanian, "Implementation of Regulatory Policy."
11. Ibid., pp. 21-22.
12. Ibid., p. i.
13. Yin, "Implementation of Public Programs."

14. John Tukey, "The Future of Data Analysis," *Annals of Mathematical Statistics* 33 (1962): 13-14.
15. Charles Lindblom, "The Science of Muddling Through," *Public Administration Review* 19 (Spring 1959): 79-88; Charles Lindblom and D. Braybrooke, *A Strategy of Decisions* (New York: Free Press, 1963); Ira Sharkansky, *Routines of Politics* (New York: Van Nostrand Reinhold, 1970); Aaron Wildavsky, *Budgeting: A Comparative Theory of the Budgeting Process* (Boston: Little, Brown, 1975).
16. Aaron Wildavsky, *The Politics of the Budgetary Process* (Boston: Little, Brown, 1964), chap. 3.
17. James March, "Footnotes to Organizational Change," p. 23. See also Richard Cyert and James March, *A Behavioral Theory of the Firm* (Englewood Cliffs, N.J.: Prentice-Hall, 1963).
18. Lester Salamon, "The Time Dimension in Policy Evaluation: The Case of New Deal Land-Reform Experiments," *Public Policy* 27, no. 2 (Spring 1979): 178-80.
19. Samuel Halperin, "The Elementary and Secondary Education Act: Five Years Later," *House Congressional Record,* 9 September 1970, H. 8493.
20. The original ESEA legislation had five titles. In addition, to Title I, which receives the largest share of the ESEA appropriation, the other four titles included Title II, which provided funds for local library service expansion; Title III, which funneled financial aid and technical assistance for "innovative programs" and supplementary centers; Title IV, which financed federal educational research and development efforts; and Title V, which invested federal dollars into the strengthening of state departments of education.
21. P.L. 89-10.
22. See, for instance, Allan S. Mundel, *Resource Distribution Inside School Districts* (Lexington, Mass.: Lexington Books, 1975); John Owen, "The Distribution of Educational Resources in Large American Cities," *Journal of Human Resources* 7 (Winter 1972): 171-90; and Stephen Barrow, "The Impact of Intergovernmental Aid on Public School Spending" (Ph.D. dissertation, Stanford University, 1974), pp. 59-66.
23. Floyd Stoner, "The Implementation of Ambiguous Legislative Language: Title I of the Elementary and Secondary Education Act" (Ph.D. dissertation, University of Wisconsin-Madison, 1976), pp. 84-89.
24. Title V complemented the Title I state set-aside with an initial allocation of $30 million to strengthen general administrative capacities of state departments of education.
25. Frederick Wirt and Michael Kirst, *Political and Social Foundations of Education* (Berkeley, Calif.: McCutchen, 1972), p. 155.
26. Ibid., pp. 154-55.
27. Early administration evaluations of Title I include: Ruby Martin and Phyllis McClure, *Title I of ESEA: Is It Helping Poor Children?* a report by the Washington Research Project of the Southern Center for Studies in Public Policy and the NAACP Legal Defense of Education Fund, Inc., 1969; Jerome Murphy, "The Education Bureaucracies Implement Novel Policy: The Politics of Title ESEA, 1965-72" in *Policy and Politics in America,* ed.

Allan P. Sindler (Boston: Little, Brown, 1973), pp. 160-98; and Michael Wargo et al., *ESEA Title I, A Reanalysis and Synthesis of the Evidence* (Palo Alto, Calif.: American Institute for Research, 1972).

Major impact studies of Title I projects between 1965 and 1969 are Gene Glass et al., *Education of the Disadvantaged: An Evaluation Report on Title I, Elementary and Secondary Education Act of Fiscal Year 1969* (Boulder, Colo.: University of Colorado, 1970); David Hawkridge et al., "A Study of Selected Exemplary Programs for the Education of Disadvantaged Children," Parts 1 and 2, Final Report No. 08 9013 for U.S. Office of Education (Palo Alto, Calif.: American Institute for Research, 1968; mimeo.); and Harry Picariello, "Evaluation of Title I," U.S. Office of Education, Division of Program, Planning, and Evaluation, 1969; mimeo.

28. Martin and McClure, *Title I of ESEA,* p. 104.
29. *The Silken Purse: Legislative Recommendations for Title I of the Elementary and Secondary Education Act,* HEW OS-72-224 (Washington, D.C.: Planar Corporation, 1973), pp. 16-18.
30. SRI International, *Trends in Management of ESEA Title I: A Perspective from Compliance Reviews,* vol. 1, *Overview, Findings, and Conclusions,* prepared by Harold Winslow for the Office of the Assistant Secretary for Education (Menlo Park, Calif., 1977), pp. i-iii.
31. Robert Goettel, "Financial Asistance to National Target Groups: The ESEA Tidal (sic) I Experience" in *The Federal Interest in Financing Schooling,* ed. Michael Timpane (Cambridge, Mass.: Ballinger, 1978), p. 156. The results of the findings of Title I administration studies conducted by Booz Allen and Hamilton, Inc., Syracuse Research Corporation, and Policy Research Corporation are summarized in National Institute of Education, *Administration of Compensatory Education* (Washington, D.C.: NIE, 1977), chap. 4.
32. For instance, Paul Berman, "Thinking About Programmed and Adaptive Implementation: Matching Strategies to Situations" (paper presented to Institute for Educational Finance and Governance Seminar, San Francisco, 29 February 1980); and Martin Orland, "The Implementation of Title I of the Elementary and Secondary Education Act: A Comparative Intergovernmental Analysis" (Ph.D. dissertation, Syracuse University, 1978).
33. Henry Levin, "A Decade of Policy Development in Improving Education and Training for Low Income Populations" in *A Decade of Federal Anti-Poverty Policy: Achievements, Failures, and Lessons,* ed. Robert Haveman (New York: Academic Press, 1977), p. 156. And Levin is still citing dated 1969 Title I administration studies with implications that they apply today. See, for instance, Henry Levin, "Education and Earnings of Blacks and the *Brown* Decision," program report No. 79-B13 from the Institute for Research on Educational Finance and Governance, Stanford University, October 1979, p. 90, n. 15.
34. Lawyers Committee for Civil Rights Under Law, *An Analysis of the Legal Framework for State Administration of Title I of the Elementary and Secondary Education Act of 1965* (Washington, D.C.: LCCRUL, 1977), contracted by NIE 400-75-0081; Robert Silverstein and Daniel Schember, "An

Analysis of the Basis for Clarity and Restrictiveness of Program Requirements Applicable to Local Districts Applying for Grants Under Title I of the Elementary and Secondary Education Act of 1965" (Washington, D.C.: LCCRUL, 1976); and Stoner, "Implementation of Ambiguous Legislative Language," pp. 111-12.

35. SRI International, *Trends* . . ., especially pp. i-iii; and Planar Corporation, *The Silken Purse.*

36. Harold Pollen, "Study of the Audit Resolution Process in the U.S. Office of Education" (unpublished internal USOE document, August 1975); Elizabeth Demerest, "The HEW Sanction Study: Enforcement Policy in Title I ESEA: Analysis and Recommendations" (unpublished internal DHEW document, 1977); and "OE Collecting Misspent Title I Funds," *Education Daily,* January, 1980, pp. 4-5.

37. SRI International, *Research on the Effectiveness of Compensatory Education Programs: A Reanalysis of Data,* Final Report (Menlo Park, Calif.: SRI, 1977), pp. 43-52 and 57-61.

38. Martin E. Orland with assistance from Bernard Kaplan and Robert Goettel, *A Study of the Administration of ESEA: Title I at the Federal, State, and Local Levels: A Final Report* (New York: Syracuse Research Corporation, June 1977), draft, chap. 2.

39. John Hughes and Anne Hughes, *Equal Education: A New National Strategy* (Bloomington: Indiana University Press, 1972), pp. 63-66.

40. Ibid., pp. 41-42.

41. As reported in *United State Government Manual, 1979-1980* (Washington, D.C.: U.S. Government Printing Office, 1979).

42. Based on interviews with Charlie Cooke, director of Federal Education Programs for California (30 January 1980) and Lillian Barna, special programs coordinator, San Jose, Calif. (28 January 1979).

43. Edward Duane and William Bridgeland, "Power Differentiation Among Educational Interest Groups" (unpublished paper, Michigan, 1979).

44. Interview with Joel Sherman, researcher for LCCRUL (12 December 1979).

45. Robert Silverstein, *A Policy Maker's Guide to Title I of the Elementary and Secondary Education Act and Its Relationship to State and Local Special Programs* (Denver, Colo.: Education Commission of the States, 1979), pp. 1-2; and interview with Charlie Cooke (20 January 1980).

46. Yin, "Implementation of Public Programs," p. 19.

47. Eugene Webb et al., *Unobtrusive Measures: Non-active Research in the Social Sciences* (Chicago: Rand McNally, 1971), p. 2.

48. We are grateful to Eugene Webb for bringing this aphorism to our attention.

49. This informal merger and analysis of information from a confluence of surveys was found by Yin to be typical of most "exemplary" studies he analyzed.

50. Alexander George, "Case Study and Theory Development: The Method of Structured, Focused Comparison," a chapter to appear in *Diplomatic History: New Approaches,* ed. Paul Lauren (1 July 1978 draft), pp. 14-15.

51. For instance, for Title I to describe changes in federal implementation policy, one needs to consider not only changes in Title I legislation but also

modifications in the General Education Provisions Act which applies to all federally funded programs administered by the U.S. Office of Education.

52. Murray Edelman, *The Symbolic Uses of Politics* (Urbana: University of Illinois Press, 1964), chap. 1.

53. See notes 23, 30, 31, 34, and 38.

54. For example, Martin and McClure, *Title I of ESEA;* Planar Corporation, *The Silken Purse*; and Orland et al., "A Study of the Administration of ESEA."

55. SRI International, *Trends . . .*, pp. 4-5.

56. Stoner, "Implementation of Ambiguous Legislative Language," pp. 118-20.

57. Lawyers Committee for Civil Rights Under Law, pp. 50-63.

58. *Education Daily,* 7 January 1980, p. 3.

59. Lawyers Committee for Civil Rights Under Law, p. 87.

60. Milbrey McLaughlin, *Evaluation and Reform: The Case of ESEA, Title I* (Cambridge, Mass.: Ballinger, 1975), p. 180.

61. When Title I was initiated, only three states had compensatory education programs; today seventeen states have programs that provide additional resources for disadvantaged students.

62. For example, the recently overhauled Vocational Education Act, the All Handicapped Children Act of 1975, and the recent federal bilingual education legislation.

63. A thanks to Glass, who cites this passage in "Primary, Secondary, and Meta-Analysis Research," p. 3.

7

The Consultant/Researcher Role: Implications for Studying Public Management Problems

BETTY JANE NARVER AND WALTER WILLIAMS

Political and bureaucratic factors came together in 1979 to provide the authors with a chance for an implementation study in which they were active participants in efforts by a public agency to correct its organizational problems. As consultant/researchers (and the order of the two terms is important, as will be made clear), we were able to study closely the dynamics of formulating, implementing, and assessing organizational change. The work gave us an opportunity to try out ideas about studying implementation; and we believe we gained important insights into both implementation research methods and administration *and* means of aiding a specific client in such an undertaking.

The pressure of politics and dollars threatened the administration of Washington State's nursing home industry in 1979. The public agency responsible for managing a $250 million biennial budget was in serious trouble. A special committee of the Washington State Senate made daily headlines charging the program was operated according to a "policy by exception" with thinly veiled implications that the money was greasing the system all the way to the governor's office.

The source of the problem was the absence of an acceptable system of reimbursing private providers for the care of state nursing home patients. Traditionally the state had paid nursing homes a flat rate for every day of care provided for publicly supported patients, but in 1974 the state developed a cost-related payment scheme in response to a federal mandate. Several approaches to such a system were tried, but none worked to the satisfaction of all parties—the nursing home industry, the state, and the federal government.

Confrontation was inevitable. Lawsuits were initiated, nursing homes threatened to cancel their Medicaid contracts, and the media became the forum for communication between the industry and the state. The public policy void was filled by the legislature, which developed legislation to address the entire reimbursements system, particularly in the areas of property reimbursement and return on investment. The Department of Social and Health Services (DSHS), the state superagency responsible for health, welfare, and corrections programs, responded to each stage of the crisis by substituting new management teams to try and cope with an array of internal and external problems.

DSHS's Office of Nursing Home Affairs (ONHA) with its continually changing cast of characters was the focus of resentment, distrust, and frustration on the part of the legislature, the industry, and the public. The external pressures would have been substantial ones to cope with in the best-managed organization, but the breakdown of management had reached almost crisis proportions for ONHA. Leadership changes had left both its staff and nursing home operators uncertain about agency direction. The Office was located far down in the DSHS bureaucracy and was extremely vulnerable to political and financial pressures. As a result of institutional instability and the continual attack on the agency by the legislature, the industry, and the press, organizational morale was extremely low. By the fall of 1979, relations with the industry had broken down almost completely. The industry was very successfully carrying its case to the courts instead of trying to work out administrative solutions to disputes. There was a public perception that the Office was incapable of administering this major state program.

In the middle of this controversy, the harried head of ONHA approached the Institute for Public Policy and Management (IPPM) at the University of Washington, asking staff members to provide some help with the general management problems that were crippling the Office's operations.[1] The focus was on management; the institute's staff was not asked to treat directly important technical issues like rate determination and reimbursement.

This essay examines the role the institute played in working with ONHA to develop an agency management strategy based on recent implementation studies.[2] The institute's first effort resulted in a published report that became the basis for important management changes in ONHA. Circumstances allowed us to return after the first effort to assess the implementation of the management changes, many of which were suggested in the institute's original organizational analysis. The IPPM *Organizational Analysis of the Office of Nursing Home Affairs* was started in March 1979 and completed in September. It is referred to here as the "analysis" or "report." The second IPPM study was started in January 1980 and was completed in June; it is referred to here as the "assessment."

THE ONHA STUDY IN RESEARCH TERMS

We saw the first part of this two-stage study as an opportunity to be participants in a dynamic situation developing specific organizational guidelines that could be used in solving the management problems facing the agency. We assumed an active advisory role, working with our client (the head of ONHA) to identify primary management problems and develop a strategy for change. We considered ourselves, and were viewed by others, as consultants rather than researchers. Our main intent was to help the ONHA chief improve the management of the agency.

In the second, originally unanticipated stage, we drew on recent implementation studies as we returned to the agency to assess the kinds of changes that had been initiated and the impact they were having. We wanted to test, to the extent feasible, the guidelines for management recommended in our organizational analysis to see how useful they were proving to be.

The chief of ONHA with whom we had originally negotiated the contract left midway through the study. But a variety of circumstances that we describe later led to the use of our analysis as a management tool by the new chief for reorganizing the office and improving management practices. It was he who asked us to come back to assess the implementation of change in the agency.

When the contract of the original organizational analysis was being discussed, the authors were completing a book based on a study of the implementation of the Comprehensive Employment and Training Act (CETA) and the Community Development Block Grant (CDBG) program and other recent works on implementation.[3] In a paper growing out of some of this work, one of the authors (Williams) pointed to the development of management strategies and also spoke to the need for a new direction in implementation research:

> Beyond lies the challenge of systematically analyzing implementations either of programs or of organizational modifications such as implementing a new decision approach. Here the key is to develop more and more pointed — and hence refutable — recommendations about how organizations work through their implementations. The need is to get deeply enough into actual implementations so as to see which of our notions really hold up in practice. At issue is the extent to which the present general and still abstract concepts about implementation can be forged into viable organizational arrangements in individual cases.
>
> Implementation studies must be pushed to the point of supporting particular organizational arrangements and seeing in the specific cases whether these organizational arrangements can stand the test of the field. The ultimate criterion must be usefulness to specific implementers in helping them decide how to proceed. This means providing quite specific organizational guidance — specific enough to be tried and found wanting.[4]

This new direction called for the student of implementation to operate jointly in the world of practice (not as an observer but as a participant) and in the world of research. It was a broad charge; the details of how to proceed and the implications of such a role were far from clear.

Staff at the institute had been involved in several projects that had led to the development of a particular style of interviewing. This open-ended, rather informal approach to interviewing had proved successful in gathering information about people's perceptions of roles, agency mission, and relationships. However, no one at the institute had any background in the general issues of long-term health care or the more specific problems associated with the administration of a state nursing home program.

The contract with ONHA gave institute staff the opportunity to develop specific management guidelines to help an agency clearly in trouble and then to test those guidelines in a limited manner. In addition, it gave us the chance to step back from our own efforts and examine some of the questions that arise out of this approach to implementation research. More specifically, we can draw upon our initial experience as consultant/researchers in a particular field situation to pose some questions that we believe need to be explored by others considering this role in different situations. These include

> What structural factors do you look for in the initial setting? These factors may include the kind of decision-making or implementation situation (a new program or an organizational change), the broad institutional setting, the degree of stability in the organization, the need that is driving the prospect for involvement, and the key person or persons involved in the contractual relationship.

> What should you "demand" before going into a contractual relationship? How much control, how much cooperation, how much access, how specific a role as adviser, what freedom with documents, what disposition of final products?

> With how much of a theoretical framework should one enter this kind of situation? Is there a danger that dependence on the analytic framework (in this case based on recent implementation work) will block out "dissonance" which cannot be explained by the theory?

> How far do consultant/researchers go in terms of adjusting an initial study framework to fit organizational, bureaucratic, and political needs of the client or to reflect unforeseen changes? How far should they go in pushing their recommendations? How actively should they pursue a role in implementing these recommendations?

Can the same individuals who help develop the management strategy go back into the organization to assess the way changes based on that strategy are being implemented? How objective can researchers be when the assessment they are doing relates to the advice given earlier?

The next section of this essay lays out the context of the study by describing the organizational and programmatic setting of the Office of Nursing Home Affairs. Subsequent sections examine the IPPM study methodology; the organizational analysis including its findings, recommendations, and results; and the implementation assessment with its methodology and impacts.

SETTING FOR THE ANALYSIS

This section provides enough information about the Department of Social and Health Services, the Office of Nursing Home Affairs, and the programmatic aspects of nursing home care to help the reader understand the context in which the organizational analysis took place.

Department of Social and Health Services

The Department of Social and Health Services (DSHS) was formed as an umbrella agency in 1970. Its main responsibilities include health, welfare, and corrections. DSHS has responsibility both for the major transfer payment and health finance programs administered by the state—Aid for Dependent Children, Supplemental Security Income, and Medicaid—and for a number of service or incarceration institutions including prisons and mental health facilities.

After a reorganization shortly before the IPPM study, the secretary and three assistant secretaries responsible for agency administration and operations became the four top officials. The highest operating unit under an assistant secretary is a division. Within divisions are bureaus and within bureaus are offices. The agency operates in a typical top-down chain of command from the secretary down to the office chiefs.

Office of Nursing Home Affairs

The Office of Nursing Home Affairs (ONHA) was formed in 1975 from existing activities being carried on in different offices. In September 1979, ONHA was upgraded to Bureau status, but we will continue to use the term "Office" in this historical section. ONHA's primary mission is to provide for the development, establishment, and enforcement of standards for the maintenance and operation of nursing homes that are intended to ensure safe and adequate care and treatment for patients. An important secondary activity is the improvement of nursing home practices by educational methods so that these practices eventually exceed the minimal requirements of the basic law and its original standards.

The ONHA budget comprises roughly 11 percent of the total DSHS budget with about half the funds coming from Medicaid. It is the third-largest single category of expenditures in DSHS, topped only by transfer payments and medical assistance.

ONHA is headed by a chief and has several sections with section heads having operational responsibilities for headquarters and field units. There is a headquarters office in the state capitol complex of buildings in Olympia and three field offices located in Olympia, Seattle, and Spokane. In addition to the field offices, a number of staff people who cover large geographic areas live and work out of their home communities. These staff members are housed in the DSHS Community Service Offices located throughout Washington State and attached to other operating elements in DSHS.

The main tasks of the field staff are to determine levels of care needed for individual patients and to ensure that facilities meet federal and state standards for patient care. ONHA has a staff of somewhat over one hundred people, the majority of whom are stationed in the field and actually visit nursing homes. Many on the staff are high-level professionals. The great majority are nurses, but there are also a number of sanitarians involved in the inspection of nursing home facilities.

State Responsibility for Nursing Home Care

The state has the responsibility for setting minimum standards through such mechanisms as the licensure of nursing homes. It administers several major reimbursement and insurance programs that cover long-term care. It also has the responsibility of certifying the need for additional facilities for the care of the chronically ill, disabled, and elderly.

In the state of Washington nursing home care is provided almost entirely by private facilities, including both profit and nonprofit operations. Most of the approximately three hundred nursing homes have contracts with the state that allow them to provide and be reimbursed by the state through the Medicaid program for both skilled and intermediate-level nursing care.

State involvement in nursing home care was limited before the introduction of major federal moneys with Medicaid and Medicare. At that time, substantial funds were injected into a system that had not yet evolved a method of determining the costs of care through either rational development or long years of experience.

DESCRIPTION OF STUDY METHODOLOGY

The original intent of the organizational analysis of the Office of Nursing Home Affairs was to look at management issues that appeared to be affecting the ability of the agency to operate in the field. In designing the analysis we felt it was important to ask people both within and outside the system their perspectives of the Office's performance in delivering services.

In beginning the study we tried to maintain as much openness as possible in order to avoid going into interviews with a preconceived notion of what and where the problems were. We did not want to force structure too early and thereby limit our ability to hear and absorb new information.

We scheduled a number of preliminary interviews with key people in the agency to educate ourselves in general programmatic and administrative terms. We read the few documents that were available laying out Office mission, goals, and procedures. Our study started during a legislative session when critical nursing home legislation was being considered so that hearings provided us with another source of important information. During this first phase of the analysis we immersed ourselves in the terminology of long-term health care and the particular ONHA programs directed toward the state's nursing care providers. In a short period of time we tried to become familiar with the problems of the nursing care field that were absorbing a tremendous amount of staff, and particularly management, time.

After these initial self-instructive efforts, we abstracted what appeared to be a number of cross-cutting issues that reflected management, policy, and political concerns. These issues formed the base of the protocol we used through the rest of our interviews and also the framework for developing a series of working memos (which we discuss later). The issues included: communication and flow of information; physical problems in the new ONHA headquarters office; stability factors in ONHA, DSHS, and the nursing home industry; degree of centralization/decentralization in the agency; reporting relationships; clarity of office mission/objectives/functions; uniformity of policy interpretations; capacity building; agency and staff discretion; assessment and policy planning in ONHA. During the course of the study, we came to recognize the impact a variety of external pressures had on the management of the Office and began to build those issues into our interviewing process. Under each of these categories, we developed a series of questions, which we adapted to the particular individuals being interviewed both within and outside the agency.

The Interviews
The interviews were open-ended in nature. Usually two study team members

would take part in each interview. One person was responsible for asking questions while the other took notes and made sure that all pertinent information was gathered. The interviews were structured in the sense that the interviewer had a clear idea of the kind of information to obtain from that particular individual. However, we did not go into an interviewing session with a set of predetermined questions but instead approached each meeting with perceptions about that person's position and knowledge and attempted to determine that individual's views of the agency and his or her stake in agency affairs. We were looking for perceptions of agency operations and relationships and the questions reflected that intent.

One of the major interests in developing the interviewing process was to produce a nonthreatening climate. This approach reflected in part the interviewers' belief that people are generally more forthcoming in a personally relaxed atmosphere. In addition, people within the agency had been working for some time in a tense, insecure situation. The Office of Nursing Home Affairs has been historically a politically volatile setting, and many of its employees appeared almost shellshocked by the strain and uncertainty surrounding them. Another factor that became apparent shortly after the interviews began was that many of these people had been almost completely neglected in terms of their feelings about their work and their ideas about improving performance and finding solutions to some of the serious problems facing the agency. The sense of isolation, even within the central office, was severe.

For many reasons, we found almost everyone we interviewed not only willing but eager to talk. Interviews were generally far longer than we had originally expected. Because we had a fair degree of latitude in our original design, we built on this openness and encouraged people to communicate further with us after the initial interview was over. We received information by mail and phone calls from a number of people that were both within and outside the agency. People seemed to feel secure with us and trusted our promise that we would protect their anonymity. This was particularly important because some staff members were suspected of being leaks, and there were charges that one highly placed person had been fired because he had given politically damaging information to a select committee of the state senate investigating the Office and its method of reimbursing nursing homes.

It was interesting to note that very few of the people who talked so freely fell into the category of "disgruntled employee." The majority of the staff interviewed seemed to have a strong desire to discuss the agency, what it wasn't doing and why, and what it could be doing to improve services. One of the things we stressed most strongly in our organizational analysis was the caliber and commitment of staff despite difficult working conditions. There was a strong sense, which we tried to communicate in our study, that management was wasting a very valuable resource of experienced professional people who understood a number of the problems afflicting the system.

We interviewed 125 people, some of them more than once. This number included a high percentage of the staff of the Office at all levels both in the central and in field offices. We talked with representatives of the nursing home industry associations, nursing home lobbyists, providers of nursing home care, nursing home staff, and other employees of the Department of Social and Health Services whose jobs related to (or in some cases conflicted with) activities of the Office of Nursing Home Affairs. We interviewed representatives of a number of public-interest and nursing home consumer groups, legislators, and legislative staff.[5]

In addition to interviews, the two members of the study team read background material and documents, attended legislative hearings and consumer groups' meetings, and participated in seminars on long-term health care.

The Memos

The information gathered from these sources was analyzed and presented in three working memoranda. We negotiated ground rules with the chief of ONHA, allowing him to go over a draft with us of each memo before it was circulated internally. We saw these working papers as an opportunity to try out ideas within our institute and also with the agency chief. His analytical background was a key factor in this regard, as was his openness in hearing strong criticism of his management style in administering the Office. As noted earlier, the chief resigned after we had submitted the second memo. This brought a period during there was great uncertainty as to whom to direct the third memo and the final report.

The first memo focused on the central office staff and the working relations that existed between the sections within that office. The second memo turned to the field and concentrated primarily on field perceptions of central office management and support and the relationships existing between headquarters and the field. The third memo explored relations between the Office and a variety of outside actors including nursing home operators, the nursing home industry associations, the legislature, consumer and public-interest groups, and the press. We probed particularly to find out what factors impinged upon the efforts of the Office of Nursing Home Affairs to manage its staff and their operations.

The Final Report

The final report presented recommendations to the organization about developing a management strategy. Considering the state of disruption and instability in the system, we recommended *against* any major organizational changes. The recommendations were consistent with the approach actually used in the analysis in that they required an involvement of staff in a joint problem-solving effort.

The final report had several appendixes. These were the three working memos that had not been published previously, a history of ONHA, and a discussion of our interview methods. Finally there was an appendix entitled "The Rationale and Framework of the Organizational Analysis," which discussed the organizational assumptions that guided our approach to the study. It laid out and discussed the following propositions:

1. The individuals who deliver social and health services will operate in settings where there is significant, irreducible discretion beyond the control of higher organizational echelons; such discretionary behavior is a necessary component of reasonable service delivery.
2. The central concerns of management must be the commitment to program objectives of organizational units directly responsible for service delivery and the capacity of those units to provide particular services and to make discretionary judgments.
3. The "regulatory" mentality that focuses on the issues of compliance can increase complexity and confusion in the field and reduce the likelihood of a continuing concern with organizational capacity and performance.
4. One of the most difficult of institutional problems is how to create a strong, stable, capable organization that also is responsive to change.
5. Complex organizations generally exhibit both strong resistance to structural changes and a high susceptibility to prolonged disturbances when experiencing significant organizational change.
6. Structural change is a limited means of organizational improvement and can be particularly dangerous when imposed from above without active involvement of those whose jobs and statuses are directly affected.[6]

Comments on the Approach

An important element of our approach was the actual presentation of the information. We were determined to write both the memos and the final report in clear, understandable English so that they could be helpful to anyone in the system. We wanted to communicate to all staff members where we felt the major management problems were and how they might be addressed. Because most of this information came from staff members, we were intent on presenting it in straightforward, nonjargon terms. Perhaps the most satisfying part of the study was the fact that virtually all staff members read the report and felt it reflected their concerns and recommendations.

We tested out our ideas about problems and issues all along the way with a variety of people both within and outside the Office. This was done in part to make sure that our perceptions were not being skewed or restricted by too narrow a sample of interviews. We wanted to maintain as much openness as possible throughout the course of the study in order to avoid being captured by our own, relatively untutored pet theories. Listening carefully in interviews to what really concerned people was of the utmost importance. Having come in with certain theories, we tried hard not to fall into the trap of looking for the discussion of things that supported the theory and blocking out other things that might appear as "noise" in the researcher's image of the big picture.

THE ORGANIZATIONAL ANALYSIS

In addition to the decision to approach the study in the way described in the last section, a number of external factors had an effect on the direction the study took and on the impact it had. We now describe briefly some of these factors before discussing findings and results.

On the Way to Analysis

One of the key factors influencing the development of our study was the nature and approach of the Office chief with whom we contracted. His background was in economics and analysis, and he brought with him the focus and energy of a trained technical problem solver. Despite criticism, he remained serious in his original request for help. He shared with us some of the bureaucratic and nursing home industry opposition he was facing, giving us a much richer understanding of what was happening in and around ONHA.

The memos prepared by IPPM contained strong criticism of ONHA management. There was speculation both within and outside the Office that our first memo addressing central office management issues precipitated, in part, the chief's resignation. In our minds, the memo did not seem to play a part in his decision to resign. We believe that he was intrigued with the puzzle of finding a technically workable system for reimbursing nursing home operators for their care of patients and preferred this activity to working on management practices for the Office staff.

Midway through the study a variety of factors including bureaucratic intrigue and overt hostility from the industry contributed to his decision to resign. Although his resignation did not take effect for several weeks, vacation time and testimony at state court cases meant that the Office was essentially leaderless for two months.

To complicate matters further for IPPM, there had been little communication with the chief's superiors in the agency about the institute study. At the chief's request, we had not talked to these individuals. We acquiesced in part because the client asked it of us and in part because we did *not* want to inject ourselves in the middle of a rather nasty internal bureaucratic battle within the DSHS division housing ONHA. But one result of the decision was to cut us off from some key sources of information. Of greater consequence for us, when the chief officially left the Office on September 1, less than a month before our report was due, we found that no one now "owned" the study or wanted the report. We no longer had a client, and there literally was no one to whom to deliver the document.

An acting chief took over for a month. Rumors about a new head and other major personnel changes brought work almost to a standstill in the central office. Insecurity and instability grew to near-hysteria proportions, and the study investigators began to assume a somewhat different role. Some ONHA staff members began to see the institute report as "the only hope." However, they feared that poor communication channels and deliberate bureaucratic blockage would bury the report when it was submitted.

We completed the analysis without any clear indication who the audience was aside from the staff (who had received all the working memos) and a growing number of industry spokesmen, legislators (and their staff), and the press. Nursing homes have been and remain today a politically charged issue in the state of Washington, and any potential fuel for the fires is greeted with great anticipation.

The Findings

In developing the report we wrote three internal memos that were circulated by the chief to all staff members. The first dealt with central office management issues; the second with relations between the central office and its field staff and with ONHA and operators in the field; the third examined somewhat cursorily the relations among ONHA and other elements of the agency (DSHS) and ONHA and the rest of the world, including the legislature, the nursing home industry and various public-interest/consumer groups. These three memos formed the major body of the final report.

External factors. Despite the order of our memos, the first conclusion of our final report addressed a variety of external factors. This reordering came as a surprise to us. As a result of the pressures being imposed on the Office of Nursing Home Affairs, there was good reason to believe that the Office could not be managed within the existing bureaucratic structure and political setting. We had assumed that external factors, many of which the Office could not control, would skew the management effort, but we underestimated at the beginning the crippling effect these factors would exert. Among the most critical external issues identified were[7]

1. *Political vulnerability.* Due in part to the high financial stakes in the nursing home program, the Office has historically been besieged by special interests, particularly individual facility operators and representatives of the industry. Because an agreed-upon system for reimbursement of costs has not been developed, the possibility of pressure being exerted for special dispensations is very high and charges of "policy by exception" commonplace. Nursing home interests contribute heavily to legislative campaigns and, during the 1976 election, to the governor's campaign. Pressure by the legislature, individual legislators, industry spokesmen, and individual operators, as well as by executive branch officials, has produced a policy that reacts to specific crises and circumstances. There has been virtually no policy direction or consistency, leading to public views of ONHA activity ranging from "bumbling" to "capricious" to "dishonest."

2. *Organizational location in DSHS.* Despite ONHA's large budget, it has been located far down in the bureaucratic structure. Because so much money is involved, many decisions actually were made in the top layers of the agency, bypassing the ONHA chief. Responsibility and authority could not coincide so far down in the system. Office chiefs were never safe from a reversed decision that came as a result of pressure somewhere else in DSHS or from the governor's office.

3. *Relations with the Industry/Legislature/Public.* ONHA often is treated as the butt of all external actors' frustration and/or anger. This reflects in part the problems mentioned above. Rather than try to solve problems on a joint basis, there has been nothing but conflict and irresolution. The industry has become increasingly unified in its position, stronger and more militant. It has forced the state into the courts to get decisions favorable to the industry with great success. Legislative and public demands for stronger DSHS leadership and competency and for efforts to resolve the present imbalance brought about by aggressive industry action are constant. Public credibility in DSHS leadership has been exacerbated by shifting policy decisions and the release of poor information.

Crosscutting and in fact underlying these three areas were two major concerns. The first was the question of institutional instability within DSHS brought about by continual changes in leadership in the agency. This instability has extended down to ONHA where, since September 1975, *five* chiefs have come and gone with each change creating further disruption and uncertainty of Office direction. In addition, there have been several politically disruptive changes at the secretarial level of the department during the same time period.

The second concern revolves around the lack of a comprehensive, coordinated executive policy dealing with long term care for the elderly. Both of these are reflected in almost every discussion of the problems which afflict the Office of Nursing Home Affairs.

Internal management. Having questioned the possibility of managing ONHA, the report went on to say that even if all external factors were removed, the Office's management problems would not be solved, and better performance would not follow automatically. The central issues we identified were

1. *Lack of leadership.* No one is in charge of the Office and the lack of strong direction leaves the operation vulnerable to whipsawing tactics of both the legislature and the industry.

2. *Lack of clarity.* Because of the leadership vacuum, there is little clarity in terms of Office mission. Confusion of the regulatory and educational functions between sections has created problems that have extended to the roles and functions of various staff members.

3. *Lack of stability.* In addition to the turnover of ONHA chiefs, there has been a high turnover in central office administration with little consistency of direction or focus. Rearrangement of sections and changes of supervisors have created programmatic as well as policy uncertainty.

4. *Lack of field perspective.* Operating from a top-down hierarchical approach, the Office has not recognized the crucial nature of the field activity.

5. *Lack of support.* Staff members, particularly in the field, have felt isolated and with little support from the central office. They are very vulnerable because of their regulatory role in relation to strong nursing home facilities whose administration very often go to the top of the agency if ONHA staff complain about their operations.

6. *External focus.* External crises generated by pressures from the legislature and the industry have meant that the Office chief has paid little at-

tention to programmatic and personnel concerns. Firefighting, rather than policy and program development, is the normal activity.

7. *Waste of staff resources.* ONHA has a highly professional, dedicated staff, many of whom have been with the agency for a number of years. Rather than use their experience and expertise, the Office administration has basically ignored them.

8. *Lack of staff involvement.* Staff has not been used for problem solving, policy, and programmatic development or evaluation. Many staff members have lost any sense of "owning" the program.

9. *Poor communication.* There is a lack of clearly developed, articulated, and written policies throughout the system. Information appears to be blocked to and from the field.

Running through almost every interview was a sense of frustration, apathy, or anger. All the factors mentioned above, in conjunction with the natural strains of a potentially stressful and depressing job, had led to a serious problem of staff morale. A number of people who had been with the agency for years were seriously considering resigning (a number did resign), and many who were staying were doing so primarily because they had few options. Almost all the people we talked to indicated that they liked their work and felt a real commitment to their job, but they also stressed that they had gotten to the point where job satisfaction was outweighed by lack of Office direction and support. The public perception of the state's incompetence and/or shady practices in regard to nursing homes was personally debilitating for the staff.

Recommendations

We had been clear from the beginning of the study on one central point: Our intent was to provide a framework that management and staff could use in jointly developing a management strategy. We rejected explicitly that IPPM should develop either specific structural recommendations or a new organization chart. This would be "more of the same" with direction exclusively from the top.

In focusing on the development of a management strategy, however, we recognized that out of this strategy, structural changes might well evolve. Our one strong recommendation in this area was that a major reorganization at that point should be approached with caution considering the shaky state of the staff. Organizational stability and a sense of consistent direction had to be prime targets of ONHA leadership. We stressed the necessity of involving staff in any changes being considered, particularly because of the high proportion of professional staff and the effects of prolonged instability.

The final report urged that the Office develop an implementation perspective that focused on the point of service delivery and identified staff, particularly in the field, as the key implementers of Office policy. With this beginning point, the IPPM report recommended a number of specific steps needed to develop a management strategy for ONHA:

> Regular staff meetings to encourage the free flow of ideas and information and to break down the current sense of isolation and distrust
>
> Use of an "inside" person to work closely with staff, listening to concerns and providing a focus for staff development and involvement in policy formulation (suggested because of the continual external demands which absorb so much of the Office chief's time)
>
> Clearly articulated, written policies and procedures circulated to all staff
>
> Regular discussion and review of draft regulations by affected staff members
>
> Expanded staff development and inservice training sessions
>
> Development of a system which allows for program review and fair, consistent personnel evaluation
>
> Development of a system for staff involvement in long-range policy formulation
>
> Increased visibility and accessibility of the Office chief both as an individual and as head administrative officer
>
> Clear indications of support for staff, especially field staff, by immediate supervisors and the Office chief
>
> Assertion of strong leadership by the Office chief making clear the Office mission and instituting strong, consistent, predictable management practices

We stressed the need to take advantage of staff experience and dedication and increase the flow of useful information at all levels. These changes, we believed, could go a long way toward improving the morale of individual staff members and the overall performance of the organization.

Results

Earlier in this essay we briefly chronicled the institutional changes involving key actions in the nursing home area that were taking place while the study was in process. Those and the particular approach we had taken in carrying it out led to unanticipated results, including the extent of impact.

Following the resignation of the Office chief, the study team continued its interviews and the preparation of the third and final memo. We did this with little real sense of the audience for our work since we had been commissioned personally by the outgoing chief. As we mentioned, for bureaucratic reasons he had not discussed the study with his supervisors. When the memo was completed, we gave it to the acting Office chief, an individual clearly destined to be an interim appointee.

Through the grapevine we heard that people higher up in the department, when pushed by staff to comment on the report, basically ignored it. At this point, however, three factors intervened to save the published report from the inevitable shelf.[8]

The first centered on an investigative reporter for one of Seattle's daily newspapers who had been covering the nursing home controversies for some time and had found much in the report that agreed with his own perception of the problems surrounding ONHA and within it. He felt his coverage of the report underscored points he had been making in earlier articles. In addition to the news stories, the paper gave strong editorial support to the study, saying it established a sound basis for making needed management corrections.

Also, a key legislator and certain legislative staff members were interested in the analysis and had been awaiting the results. None of the working memos had been officially released and turned over to the Department before the study was completed, but a number of copies of certain memos had been "leaked" by ONHA staff people. A former DSHS employee who had played a critical part in the development of a controversial cost-reimbursement system, which had infuriated the nursing home industry, was protesting his firing from the Office before the Department of Personnel. A copy of one of the memos appeared as part of his evidence in the suit. At one point one member of the study team faced a subpoena to testify in the case but was not called.

The second key factor was the presence of a staff member in the ONHA central office who, among other activities, had been charged with carrying out management analysis. During the six months we were performing the study, he was unable to convince leadership of the need for making certain changes and was primarily concerned with handling legislative matters for the Office and legislators. We had talked to him early in the study and as the memos came out, he contacted us, feeling that they offered some hope as a management tool.

During the interim period before a new Office chief was named, this staff member stayed in close touch with us. After the report had been publicly ignored, he took it directly to the secretary of the Department and persisted in his claim that it should be read and attended to. Ultimately, when the new Office chief (by now, raised to Bureau head status) was selected, this staff member was on the ground floor in terms of orienting the new head and was assigned the role we had from the beginning recommended—that of the "inside" man. He continues to work closely with the new head and has succeeded in initiating a number of important changes.

The final factor was the response of the nursing home industry. Once a series of articles and editorials on the report had appeared, the industry saw this report as a useful tool because it was so critical of the Office and the Department. Two of the three nursing home associations (as well as a number of nursing home chains) ordered many copies of the final report to send out to their members. Also, the association telephone "hotlines" carried information about the study and the findings. This latter result was perhaps the most surprising, and no doubt points to naiveté on the part of the study team. The study had not intended to examine the role of the industry in this picture but instead tried to concentrate on matters over which the Office (or DSHS) had some control. On a personal basis, there was some concern that we had provided ammunition for a group around which, during the course of the project, we had developed some mixed feelings.

These factors were ones that could not necessarily have been foreseen prior to the study. There were driving forces as well as random events, independent of the team effort, that helped catapult the IPPM report into unusual prominence. Certainly the most important factor was the volatile nature of the nursing home controversy in this state. The stakes were high in financial terms for the state and for the industry. They were just as high in political terms for legislators and the (then) governor. An underlying tension during the last two years had been the intent of the state senator who had led the legislative inquiry into the nursing home problem to run for governor in 1980.[9] Tensions were also high for patients and their families. The press played a key role in keeping the controversy in the public eye, particularly when threatened closure of nursing homes would put elderly patients on the street. Crisis and constant pressure have marked the whole question of nursing homes in Washington for several years. The IPPM report was temporarily seen as a convenient weapon in the continuing battle by several groups.

When the new Bureau head was appointed, he relied heavily on the judgment of the key staff member we mentioned earlier. For this reason, he also came to look upon the study as a tool. Ironically at this point, the report was enthusiastically presented by the DSHS secretary as an indication of the Department's desire and willingness to "clean up their act." In response to an editorial, the DSHS secretary wrote: "The Department of Social and Health Services cannot be held blameless for some of the problems surrounding nursing homes. Frequent changes in personnel, philosophy and management direction have led to a lack of consistent administration. *The Department initiated the University of Washington study so that we might benefit from an objective third party anal-*

ysis of our operations. Since receipt of the study, we have aggressively moved to address identified deficiencies."[10]

Based at least in part on the guidance provided by the Institute for Public Policy and Management's final report, the new Bureau head began a process to initiate managerial and procedural changes within the Bureau. In terms of our own research efforts, one point needs to be underscored: *Whatever role the institute report played in terms of the managerial and procedural changes, the institute staff was not involved in the actual implementation that occurred in the first few months after the new Bureau chief assumed his job.*

THE IMPLEMENTATION ASSESSMENT

Roughly three months after becoming director, the new head of the Bureau (now BNHA) approached the institute staff to consider carrying out a preliminary assessment of the changes he was beginning to implement. The critical nature of the IPPM report had provided substance for organizational change as well as ammunition for those who were intent on attacking the agency. Considering its knowledge of office and staff operations, IPPM seemed a reasonable body to carry out the assessment of change.

Institute staff expressed certain reservations to the director, feeling that it was too early to begin looking for change as a result of the steps currently being taken. Our focus in the organizational analysis had been on the field, and we maintained it would take considerable time for any organizational change to work its way through the system and be felt at the point of service delivery. A number of BNHA staff members echoed our fears about premature assessment, which was not surprising considering the agency's history of instability and flux. There was concern on our part that staff perceptions might be skewed. They might be either cynical and distrustful or oblivious because of the level of change already absorbed.

We were also concerned on two counts about the propriety of the same organization that had worked on the management strategy now assessing the implementation of that strategy. Our first concern was one of credibility. How would the Washington State nursing home community view an assessment performed by IPPM following its first report? The second concern was one of validity. Considering our earlier involvement, would other researchers view this assessment as objective? On the first count, both we and BNHA officials believed that the critical nature of the earlier organizational analysis gave IPPM a certain credibility in the state. As to our second concern, we did not have an answer. Moreover, we had our own doubts about how we would handle the new role of being the assessor of changes that at least in part flowed from our own recommendations.

Our concerns were overridden by the opportunity to go into the organization again as "insiders" to assess the management changes being attributed at least in part to the institute's organizational analysis. We agreed to perform a limited preliminary assessment, looking only at internal management changes being implemented as a result of the new leadership of the Bureau. We were not rejecting our earlier assumption that outside factors presented major obstacles to improved management. Because we were going to work in a limited time period, however, with a relatively short span of Bureau implementation efforts, we decided to focus on certain internal measures to determine what kind of changes management had initiated, what process was being used to implement these changes, and finally staff perceptions of changes and their results.

Methodology

We were primarily interested in assessing implementation by looking at the process of change within the agency and concentrating on the complex of organizational and individual adaptations that occur in the building of a new program or reorganizing agency functions. Therefore, we sought information on individuals' perceptions of change—how they saw themselves adapting their behavior to new requirements and how successfully mutual adaptation among various actors appeared to be taking place. We were looking at the behavior *within* the structure as well as changes in the structure of the organization itself.

The information for our report comes from a number of sources. Prime among these were a series of interviews of both long-term staff members and new ones (hired since the new director had taken office), a questionnaire filled out by approximately 80 percent of all staff, a review of documents, and prolonged conversations with the new director and his "inside" man.[11] We specifically did not talk to nursing home operators and staff, as we did during our first report, because of the short time period of the second study and because it seemed decidedly premature to begin assessing measurable impact at the service delivery point.

In the design prepared at the beginning of the assessment, we indicated a number of key issues we would be examining, including

> Staff involvement in identification of problem areas and
> development of strategies for change
> > Information flow up and down the system
> > Articulation and understanding of policies and procedures
> > Bureau-wide understanding of agency mission

Clarification of individual roles and functions

Communication to staff at various levels of the new director's management direction, style, and expectations

General feelings of morale and the sense of the work environment

The actual time of the study was extended unexpectedly, so the assessment covers a number of items not originally included in this design. In the assessment we indicated areas where Bureau actions *seem* to have had an effect on other outside actors including individual providers, the industry, and the legislature. Nevertheless, we avoided drawing any direct conclusions about the stability of the Bureau in relation to its external environment.

Assessment Findings

"Can ONHA be managed?" was the question posed by the organizational analysis carried out by the Institute for Public Policy and Management. Our conclusions at that time were essentially negative, partly on the basis of a number of powerful external factors and partly because of long-standing internal confusion and a lack of strong leadership and direction. The report was completed in September 1979.

By June 1980, after nine months of changed leadership and an improved bureaucratic position for the Bureau, the institute stated in its implementation assessment that not only *can* the Bureau of Nursing Home Affairs be managed, but that indications from initial assessment lead us to believe it has started to be well managed.[12] We concluded there were both tangible and intangible indicators that change had taken place and that the exceptionally low morale that had plagued the organization had been replaced with a growing sense of organizational pride and personal satisfaction.

The assessment was quick to point out that many problems, both internal and external, had not been solved. In addition, two external factors had a major impact on the future administration of the state nursing home program. During the 1980 legislative session, legislation was passed that directed a major overhaul of the state's nursing home reimbursement system. Because of its complexity and its unknown cost implications, the new payment system is not scheduled for implementation until 1982. The approach put forth in the new law, however, particularly in regard to the thorny issues of property reimbursement and return on investment, was acceptable to the nursing home industry as well as the legislature and DSHS.

A second critical factor that lessened the institutional difficulties was the shift from office to bureau status in the DSHS hierarchy. This bureaucratic move appears to have diminished some of the problems associated with the incongruity of responsibility and authority, of circumvention, and of political vulnerability. Further, the shifts within the department structure meant that the head of the nursing home unit no longer reported directly to a bureau director generally perceived as thwarting that office's efforts but rather to a division director, considered to be among the agency's more effective administrators, who was supportive of BNHA.

The most dramatic change in the situation existing in September 1979 and that of June 1980 was the new management of the agency. The director of the Bureau seems to have taken advantage of the competent professional staff he inherited to focus energy on improving ways in which the agency can deliver its services. Organizational goals have been clarified and communicated, performance standards spelled out, and management practices regularized so that staff can operate in a more secure and at the same time professionally more stimulating environment. These factors combined with improved credibility with the legislature and better relations with the nursing home industry (as well as individual operators) have at least prepared the stage to work on a number of substantive problems in providing care in the state's nursing homes.

In the assessment we focused on a number of crucial issues identified in the original IPPM analysis and used those in building the framework of the assessment. It is useful to summarize our findings concerning certain management practices and future directions and problems.

Management practices. Both from interviews and from the staff survey, it seemed clear that improved morale and new pride in the agency reflected the new director's leadership style. In addition to giving a strong sense of direction to staff, the new director reorganized the agency by differentiating enforcement and education activities, thus removing confusion as to functions for various operating units. Different kinds of technical assistance were defined and assigned to appropriate entitites.

A new operating unit was set up to handle the internal administration of the Bureau; it provided support for other program areas and attended to staff concerns and development. Substantial authority for program and decision making was delegated to program managers following development by managers of explicit descriptions of program-area responsibilities. Extensive reorientation was provided to a newly revised and clarified agency mission and to the interrelated functions of each program area.

The new Bureau management has been developing a more field-centered approach to implementation by working directly with field staff and providers and by allocating additional resources to the point of service delivery. Evidence of this reorientation was that top BNHA management had visited all field offices, had talked to staff, and had accompanied them on surveys and patient reviews. All staff, including clerical and support staff, have been brought to headquarters to discuss agency mission and gave their views on agency operations.

Field staff have participated in the revision and development of new regulations and implementing guidelines and, to a certain extent, have been involved in the development of Bureau and program-area policies. The employee orientation and training program has been expanded with additional resources being earmarked for future inservice training for BNHA staff. More resources are being channeled into additional training for provider staffs. Information about policies, interpretation of regulations, and administration of nursing homes is being compiled and prepared for distribution.

The new BNHA management is trying to concentrate agency attention on program and patient-care activities rather than on strictly political concerns. Considerably more time is being spent in contact with the operators of individual nursing homes. Visits to nursing homes by top BNHA management and dialogue with industry spokesmen evidence concern with issues that affect the kind of care patients receive. At the same time, current BNHA management has taken much stronger action than previous administrations against nursing homes that have clear violations of federal or state standards.

Internal management issues deferred during previous administrations began to receive attention, and BNHA staff were given a role in policy and program development. Staff members are also receiving clearer, more specific information than before about management expectations and are going through regular evaluations. Staff meetings at various levels are being held on a regular basis. Information is being communicated throughout the system by means of written policy directives and a newly instituted Bureau newsletter.

One of the main efforts of the new management at BNHA has been to allocate resources toward developing capacity both in the Bureau staff and in the nursing home industry. The agency has been able to generate state and federal funds for training providers. The unit within BNHA responsible for education and training has been enlarged, and more resources are being channeled into the agency's education function.

Perhaps the most critical symptom of management breakdown in the agency at the time IPPM carried out its organizational analysis was the almost complete blockage of information within offices and between headquarters and the field. Our preliminary assessment showed important efforts had been made to improve communication at all levels through regular meetings, the dissemination of written policies, and the development of policy and procedures manuals.

There appears to be the development of new ways of putting information into the system both in terms of communicating management expectations and programmatic innovation.

Management has also worked with people at all levels of the agency who have contact with other agencies, with nursing homes, and with the public to try to develop a consistent, polite approach to questions or comments.

The Office under previous administrations had suffered from a lack of uniform and predictable personnel practices. The new director started almost immediately to build some sound management practices throughout the system, particularly in regard to staff performance and management expectations. Consistent standards for office behavior have been developed. People who are not performing and do not respond to opportunities to improve have been let go. Management has put into practice a regular system of letters of commendation for staff members who perform particularly well.

A final area the institute analysis had identified as one of major concern was in the relations that had existed between BNHA and a variety of outside actors including other DSHS units, the industry, the legislature, and patient-care public-interest groups. Steps have been taken by the new management to move toward improving those relationships, particularly by providing the central actors with clear, useful information, and by clarifying and stating publicly what BNHA policies are. Indications are that the new BNHA leadership is taking a more assertive stance, particularly in relation to the nursing home industry, and is initiating contact with various groups in problem-solving efforts.

Future directions and problems. The IPPM assessment made a number of relatively specific recommendations in terms of internal Bureau operations. Most of these suggestions came from interviews with staff and the questionnaire distributed to all staff members. A number of these recommendations addressed specific points where there was inadequate support for staff, where information about policies was still insufficient, and where additional orientation and training in particular programmatic areas were needed for staff.

In addition, we included a set of broader recommendations speaking to areas of concern that we felt still needed to be addressed both by the Bureau and by other entities involved in the field of long-term health care.

Finally, on the basis of its involvement both in the original analysis of the Office and the later assessment of the Bureau, IPPM concluded that two things could spell disaster at this point for the state's nursing home program. First, another period of change and disruption in Bureau structure or staff would seriously jeopardize the sense of stability and the momentum that have been built during the last nine months. Staff and providers have begun to count on a predictable environment in which to work. The second point involves the danger of continuing intrusions of bureaucratic turf considerations into comprehensive planning and execution of a program designed to fit the needs of patients. In the formation of state policy toward long-term health care for the elderly, the client perspective can get lost among competing programmatic units within state government.

Impact of Assessment

The institute's second study was delivered to the director of the Bureau at a point when public and legislative attention to nursing homes had diminished considerably. The nursing home industry had fared well in the last legislative session both through the newly enacted (though not yet implemented) cost-reimbursement legislation and extra dollars included in the budget. Problems abounded elsewhere. The state's prisons were in great and highly visible turmoil; the state was facing a growing financial squeeze; the governor was considering extensive across the board cuts as well as selective ones in welfare.

The assessment was not published by the institute but instead was given to the director for circulation within the Bureau. It was a far more positive document than the original organizational analysis and provided little base for charges or countercharges by various factions within the nursing home community. There is no question that the director saw this assessment as an outside vindication of the actions he had taken since he assumed leadership of the Bureau. He has used the document over the several months since its completion to help him win staffing and allocation skirmishes within the bureaucracy. It might be added that he has been effective in asserting his own and the agency position in these struggles.

Other groups, including the nursing home industry, have seen IPPM's assessment. There has been little protest about the positive tone of the study. Moreover, to the extent we have been able to determine, the conclusions reached by the institute appear to coincide with the assessment of others. However, it is important to recognize the *limited* scope of IPPM's assessment. We spoke only to internal management issues and made no attempts to address external factors related to the legislature or the industry other than in very general terms of apparent direction of Bureau efforts.

Certainly the initial organizational analysis with its extremely critical comments, not only in regard to ONHA but to DSHS as well, created far more interest and attention. The assessment was lost in the midst of public disinterest in the whole issue of long-term care for the elderly. Nursing homes apparently command public attention only when there is scandal or crisis—dollars greasing the system or patients on the street.

THE CONSULTANT/RESEARCHER ISSUES

Earlier we posed five sets of issues we felt a consultant/researcher should examine before assuming that approach in performing an organizational analysis. We now try to address them in three separate sections, recognizing that we are pushing our answers rather far based on our limited experience.

Structural Factors and Contractual Conditions

The organizational unit we worked with directly was relatively small. It may be that this approach requires the organization to be manageable in terms of size, allowing a relatively intimate relationship to develop between the consultant/researcher and the people working within the organization. The researcher may need to acquire an "insider's" knowledge so that he or she can sift out "noise" and have a grasp of issues that affect the organization. Small size allows coming back and talking to a sufficient number of the same people over time in order to weigh changes in perceptions and attitudes.

The organization to be served needs to operate with a certain degree of flexibility. If the structure is rigidly hierarchical and the leadership is convinced that change does not need to take place, the likelihood of a good research setting evolving is small. This kind of study is more useful if the management is relatively unthreatened by criticism and change so that the researcher can gain access. In the case of the IPPM study, the environment at the top was highly unstructured, almost to the point of chaos. In this case, the balancing element lay in the professional staff, which had long experience and great commitment to the agency. If the Office chief had been in his position for a long time, the possibility of access also might have been greatly curtailed.

The recognition of the need for change either because of internal or external pressure may provide the necessary climate for an outside group to come in and serve in this special consulting role. In the IPPM case, a series of problems that had culminated in near crisis made the agency vulnerable enough to be examined in this dynamic, involved way. The situation may be so bad or the desire on the part of key actors to improve agency performance so strong that they will make the sacrifices necessary for change.

The validation of this need by the organization is its willingness to take action to support the study effort. Such action might include providing the consultant/researcher with all needed documents, making staff time available for interviews and discussion, making clear that management supports the consultant/researcher's efforts both to the unit staff and to other persons in the larger organization, and laying out reasonable ground rules for preparing and disseminating verbal information and written memoranda and reports.

The Theoretical Framework

As indicated, we went into this project with ideas about organizational behavior and structure that guided how we proceeded. Two broad concepts dominated. First, capacity at the point of service delivery was the organizing concept for our inquiry. That is, the fundamental concern was to center on the question of how BNHA could aid nursing homes in increasing their capacity to serve clients. Not only did we concentrate on talking as much as possible to BNHA staff members who dealt *directly* with fund recipients but the work with management was structured in terms of how organizational changes might improve service delivery. Second, the study effort was guided by the strong conviction, based not only on what we had read but on earlier field work, that (1) the search for sensible changes in organizational structure will benefit from the insights of staff and (2) major organizational changes must be negotiated with staff over time if they are to be well implemented.

Our own experience, then, indicates the value of an orienting framework for the consultant/researcher role. But we hasten to point out that we relied on a few important notions and did *not* try to lay out a large set either of organizational propositions held to be true or of testable hypotheses to form a research agenda. Quite frankly, placing too much emphasis on the research element of the overall consultant/researcher approach could be deleterious. It can overwhelm the main task of helping the client, thereby converting the effort into something it was not intended to be. Indeed, we suspect a research dominated approach well may be a rejection of the untidy ambiguity that is the dominating phenomenon in this kind of setting. Consultant/researchers must remain open to hear what the interviewees are actually saying, even if this new information contradicts cherished theories.

There is a further closely related point: We doubt that the consultant/researcher approach is going to be a comfortable one for researchers who see "hard, quantitative" information as the basic ingredient of their efforts. This is not to deny that numbers can be useful in formulating recommendations. But the basic driving force of this kind of a study is the client's need for organizational help, not descriptive statistics and not the testing out of academically oriented, rather narrow organizational hypotheses needing quantitative validation. The consultant/researcher is going to have to trust the value of largely nonquantitative evidence.

Consultant/Researcher Influence and Objectivity

The question that is perhaps the most ambiguous and deserves special attention involves the role and the influence of the consultant/researcher within the organization being studied. There are particular difficulties in discussing this factor because the personality of individuals in an active role and the interacting among key individuals cannot be clearly determined ahead of time.

In our own study some unforeseen developments are worth examining. We had not expected to become so personally involved with the critical policy and program issues that faced agency staff. Our own level of frustration rose with theirs as energy was diverted from problem solving to bureaucratic and political game playing. We also had not expected to find ourselves in the role of staff advocates. This does not mean advocacy for individual staff members so much as identification with the commonly perceived complaints of staff that there was neglect and lack of support from ONHA and DSHS management. This became more pronounced after the chief who had contracted with us left and ONHA was thrown into an even greater state of confusion and uncertainty. It is difficult to distinguish how much this involvement was due to the particular personalities of the consultant/researchers. It is also difficult to determine how much our involvement might have skewed the results presented in the final report. In any case, the study team was seen as filling a vacuum by "paying attention" to staff concerns and listening to them, particularly to those in the field who felt isolated and vulnerable.

One of the interesting results of this staff-support role was that a number of staff members called the team after the report was released and responded strongly to the report's affirmation of staff professionalism and commitment. A number indicated they believed they should assume more responsibility for trying to change the situation in which they were working by developing their own statements of policy concerns. These staff members believed what was at least an implicit message in conversations with the study team and in the final report: People could be empowered to make changes in a system and did not need to feel (and certainly should not be made to feel) powerless.

Following the assessment, there was an even clearer recognition of the personal involvement felt by the IPPM staff in the workings of the Bureau. There is reason to question how objectively consultants can return to assess the results of change within an organization when that change has come in part as a result of guidelines developed by the consultant/researcher. Over time, as our relationship with staff became close, almost collegial, criticism of staff members became more difficult.

The consultant role, whether linked with research or not, is almost by definition that of an activist. The hiring organization wants help in deciding what it should do in treating a problem and how it should go about doing it. The consultant might also be asked to aid in implementation. That the consultant's efforts may not help and can cause harm must be clear. And researchers may *not* be comfortable with such an activist role even though it clearly is a legitimate one. The issue, then, is not the legitimacy or propriety of active involvement where influence is a prime goal but whether that consultant role can be tied to research in the *same* effort. Is the "researcher's" objectivity distorted by the "consultant's" desire to see an organization improve the way in which it implements organizational changes?

There is no sure answer to the objectivity question, but we feel the dangers can be mitigated. In our particular study, Narver was responsible for the interviewing and had almost all the contact with BNHA management and staff and other interviewees. Williams followed the study, attended some important meetings, and occasionally went along for an interview, but was far less involved in the study both in terms of the amount of time spent and the psychic involvement. We also circulated drafts of papers and memos to knowledgeable people to test our perceptions. We feel that these procedures provide a greater check on bias than if one of us alone had done the entire study. Our point is not to argue that this combination of roles in the project eliminates the dangers discussed but rather that carefully sorting out roles and possibly building in additional safeguards such as a review committee lessen some of the dangers.

SOME FINAL OBSERVATIONS

One case example does not make a case. But we think our experience indicates how the consultant/researcher approach *both* can aid the client *and* offer the consultant/researcher an insider role in a dynamic setting that provides valuable evidence about organizational change.

Consultant/researchers may bring with them a broad perspective on organizational behavior that extends beyond the usual focus on "management problems." They may come to a study with knowledge and sensitivity to the relationship between policy and implementation that provide more useful information and advice for their clients. By marrying the skills, experience, and perspectives of the consultant and researcher, the advice and assessment are more likely to be realistic and effective. Under the right circumstances, the consultant/researcher can have an impact on creating the right environment for change and can help to set the direction change will take.

The kind of information derived from this approach may offer a richer understanding of complex organizational behavior than other more traditional methods. These insights may be particularly fruitful when consultant/researchers have their organizational theories confronted by intimate knowledge obtained from their own involvement in a dynamic situation. Thus, in our case, the study indicated the usefulness of considering organizational changes in the light of two guiding propositions: (1) focusing inquiry on capacity at the point where services are delivered and (2) the importance of staff involvement in bringing about effective organizational change.

That last point needs to be qualified and elaborated on. As discussed in the assessment section, BNHA management used delivery capacity as a central guide to organizational change, drew on staff recommendations, and involved staff in the change process. All were concepts the IPPM report stressed as critical and spelled out means by which they could be incorporated by BNHA. What we do *not* know is (1) whether the new BNHA director would have used a similar organizational change strategy had our report not existed; or (2) whether the new BNHA manager, because of his personal experiences and skills, could have used a quite different strategy and still have obtained similar results. But this is almost always the result when working from a single observation. What we do claim is that the results from our first consultant/researcher effort do *not* refute our organizational propositions drawn from recent work on implementation and seem to offer an interesting base for future research on organizational change.

NOTES

1. At the time of the study IPPM had *not* changed its name from Institute of Governmental Research, but we will use the newer name in this essay.
2. For a general discussion of what has been labeled the "implementation perspective," see Walter Williams, *The Implementation Perspective* (Berkeley: University of California Press, 1980), pp. 1-21.
3. Walter Williams, with the assistance of Betty Jane Narver, *Government by Agency: Lessons from the Social Program Grants-in-Aid Experience* (New York: Academic Press, 1980).
4. Walter Williams, "Developing an Implementation Perspective" (paper presented on 23 March 1979 at the annual meetings of the Western Political Science Association), pp. 33-34.
5. For a more extended discussion of interview strategy consonant with ours, see Yin's chapter in this volume and Jerome Murphy, *Getting the Facts* (Santa Monica, Calif.: Goodyear, 1980).
6. Most of these notions are discussed in more detail and a bibliography is presented in Williams, *The Implementation Perspective,* pp. 10-21.
7. For purposes of exposition these external issues and the internal ones discussed subsequently are cast in the present tense without implying that such issues necessarily are still major concerns in DSHS.
8. *Organizational Analysis: A Report on the Office of Nursing Home Affairs* (Seattle: University of Washington, Institute of Governmental Research, October 1979).

9. That state senator, James McDermott, defeated the incumbent governor, Dixy Lee Ray, in the September Democratic primary but was defeated in the November 1980 general election.

10. "DSHS Trying Hard on Nursing Homes," *Seattle Times,* 21 November 1979; italics added.

11. The results from the questionnaire did *not* turn out to be very useful. This was so for two reasons. First, the issues that concerned us the most were *not* amenable to treatment by a single questionnaire. Second, the questionnaire was used early in the study and changes while we were in the field reduced further its value.

12. "Initial Implementation Assessment of Organizational Change: Bureau of Nursing Home Affairs," IPPM, June 1980.

Index

Adams, Charles F., Jr., 78, 97, 99, 117, 118
Agarwala-Rogers, Rekha, 37, 71
Allison, Graham, 22, 34, 38, 69
Altheide, David, 118
American Association of School Administrators, 130
Arrow, Kenneth, 34
Ascher, William, 117
Attewell, Paul, 40, 43, 69

Backward mapping, 2, 18-35
Baer, Walter S., 40, 43, 69
Banfield, Edward C., 27, 35, 41, 69
Bardach, Eugene, 15, 17, 24, 25, 33, 34, 37, 52, 66, 69, 121, 144
Barna, Lillian, 147
Barnes, Louis B., 39, 69
Barrow, Stephen, 145
Barzun, Jacques, 44, 50, 69
Bassi, Laurie, 98
Becker, Selwyn W., 40, 69
Believability of implementation studies, 7-9, 14-15, 61-66
Bellmon, Henry, 83
Berman, Paul, 16, 33, 37, 40, 43, 69, 146
Bernstein, Carl, 67, 69
Bernstein, Illene, 39, 69
Bingham, Richard, 40, 69
Booz Allen and Hamilton, 146
Boring, Edwin G., 68, 69
Braybrooke, D., 145
Bridgeland, William, 132, 147
Brookings Institution, 3, 16, 73, 75, 91, 101, 103, 104, 106, 108, 109, 116, 117

Califano, Joseph, Jr., 11, 12
Calkins, Susannah H., 99, 118
Campbell, Donald T., 58, 68, 69
Carroll, Sidney L., 98, 117
Carter, Jimmy, 89
CDBG. *See* Community Development Block Grants

Central staff, relation to field researchers, 104-17
CETA. *See* Comprehensive Employment and Training Act
Civil Service Reform Act (1978), 12
Cline, Robert J., 81, 98
Community Development Block Grants, 10, 73, 75, 77, 79-80, 88-91, 94-96, 98-99, 110, 114, 151
Comprehensive Employment and Training Act, 10, 29-33, 73, 75-80, 83-88, 98-99, 108, 110, 114, 151
Consultant/researcher, 4-5
   role and participation in nursing home agency study, 149-78
Cook, Robert F., 99, 101
Cook, Stuart W., 51, 72
Cooke, Charlie, 147
Corwin, Ronald G., 40, 69
Council of Chief State School Officers, 130, 131, 132
Council of Great City Schools, 130
Credibility of implementation studies, 62-65
Crippen, Dan, 78, 97, 99
Cyert, Richard, 123, 133, 145

Daft, Richard L., 40, 69
Data analysis, use, and collection, 44-61, 108-16, 134-36
Demerest, Elizabeth, 147
Derthick, Martha, 27, 34, 40, 42, 69
Determinants approach, 59-61
Documents and news reports, use of, 2, 46-47, 51
Dommel, Paul R., 99, 101, 118
Douds, Charles F., 39, 69
Downs, George W., 37, 41, 70
Duane, Edward, 132, 147

Eckstein, Harry, 70, 144
Economic Development Administration (EDA), 47, 59

180